AF556208

UNDERSTANDING APICULTURE

UNDERSTANDING APICULTURE

By

Dr. Ashok Kumar

Deptt. of Zoology
Bundelkhand University
Campus Department
Jhansi

DISCOVERY PUBLISHING HOUSE PVT. LTD.
NEW DELHI-110 002

Published by:
Tilak Wasan

DISCOVERY PUBLISHING HOUSE PVT. LTD.
4831/24, Ansari Road, Prahlad Street
Darya Ganj, New Delhi-110002 (India)
Phone: +91-11-23279245, 43764432
Fax: +91-11-23253475
E-mail: parul.wasan@gmail.com
info@discoverypublishinggroup.com
discoverypublishinghouse@gmail.com
web: www.discoverypublishinggroup.com

First Edition: **2011**
ISBN: 978-81-8356-854-8

Printed at:
Shree Balaji Art Press
Delhi

PREFACE

The present title *"Understanding Apiculture"* provides a structured approach to learning by covering all the important topics in a uniform, systematic format. The book has been comprehensively designed incorporating recent advances in this fast moving field. It is written to provide accessible information on apiculture in compact form for undergraduate students in biology and related life sciences. It will be useful for both beginning students and those who are more advanced. In addition, busy lecturers who require a quick reference compendium will find it useful, particularly for tutional planning. Simple, yet hopefully clear figures and tables are provided throughout the book.

The over-riding goal of this book, and indeed of the whole *Understanding series,* is to present the essential information concering microbiology in a compact, readily accessible form which leads itself to student learning and revision. The convergence of various approaches has generated a rich panorama of detail, the significance of which we are still attempting to unraval. The present text has been written as an introduction to this rapidly growing field.

To make the work more comprehensive and informative, the author has consulted many authoritative books, research journals, abstracts, monographs etc., so there can be no claim to originality except in the manner of treatment.

The author expresses his thanks to his friends and colleagues whose continue inspirations have initiated him to bring out this book.

The author expresses his gratitude to Mr. Wasan and staff of M/s Discovery Publishing House Pvt. Ltd. for their whole hearted co-operation in the publication of this book.

In the mean time, the author will remain sincerely responsible for any shortcomings of the book and be grateful to the readers for their suggestions and constructive criticism for the continuous betterment of the book. He takes this opportunity to appeal to the readers to send their suggestions straightaway to his Publisher.

Author

CONTENTS

BEEKEEPING DOWN THE AGES

Botanists have classified more than 200 000 species of higher plants and 120 000 species of lower ones. Ornithologists know 10 000 species of birds and zoologists 6000 species of mammals. But entomologists have named more than a million different species of insects. Thus nature is exceptionally rich in variety of insect life.

Most insects, however, are harmful to man. Aphids, which are hardly visible, and locusts, which are quite big, beetles of all kinds, the caterpillars of butterflies and moths, and other pests do tremendous damage to agriculture (if they are not controlled by timely counter-measures). Many insects. are vectors or carriers of infectious diseases and do considerable harm to man.

The *Anopheles* mosquito, for example, which is a vector of malaria, infects millions of people in tropical and subtropical lands with this severe illness. The autumn stable fly (*Stomoxys calcitrans*) spreads the pathogens of anthrax. The tsetse *fly* (*Glossina palpalis*) of tropical Africa is a vector of sleeping sickness. Ordinary houseflies (*Musca domestica*) spread typhoid fever, dysentery, etc.

But there are also insects that do great good-above all bees and the silkworm. Everyone knows that bees are true friends of man and wonderful helpers in the production of material wealth, particularly in increasing crop yields.

Bees appeared on the Earth in the Tertiary period, that is to say approximately 56 million years before primitive man 'evolved. The monuments of ancient culture that have survived indicate that primitive man was extremely active in his search for tasty, nutritious honey. .The oldest memorial, found at Cuevas de la Arana, is a rock-painting in red representing gatherers of wild honey.

Figure 1.1: Rock-painting at the Cuevas de la Arana, Bicorp, representing a gatherer of wild honey.

'Two men are climbing up long ropes, probably woven of sedge grass, to a small natural hole in a cliff, which the artist evidently intended for the dwelling of a swarm of wild bees. In fact, we see one of the persons occupied in taking the honeycomb out of the hole and putting it into a bag or basket to bring down. Some of the disturbed bees are buzzing around the intruder, and are represented on a much larger scale than that of the human figure."

Compared with other insects and animals bees enjoyed exceptional respect among all ancient peoples and gave rise to many myths, legends, stories, superstitions, and fairy tales. Around 5000 years ago, in Ancient Egypt, a bee with lowered head and slightly raised wings was the symbol of Lower Egypt.

It and the sedge of Upper Egypt were joined in the titles of the Pharaohs after the two kingdoms had been united by Menes, the founder of the First Dynasty. The title translated 'King of Upper and King of Lower Egypt', Henri Franklin writes in his *Kingship and the Gods*, was literally 'He of the Sedge and the Bee'.

The bee is beautifully depicted in the two titles of the Pharaoh on a limestone slab from Hurbeit and on a sculptor's trial piece for the palace of Kha'ef-Re.

To express their submission to the Pharaoh Egyptians drew a bee on their petitions as an emblem of loyalty. They considered the

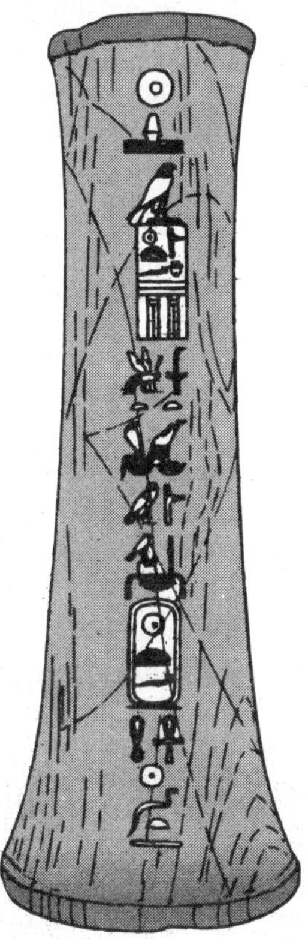

Figure 1.2: Egyptian stele inscribed with the titles of the Pharaoh.

bee their faithful helper in the struggle against the evil god of darkness, Huh, who brought harm to people.

And they saw in bees a symbol of selflessness, fearlessness, and contempt for danger and death, and the custodian of ideal cleanliness and order. The ancient Egyptians already practised nomadic bee keeping widely and with success. They used to take bees up the Nile by boat from Lower Egypt to Upper Egypt where plants flowered six weeks earlier, and then take them back again with a large harvest of honey.

The bees were transported in portable hives made of burnt clay pots, with the hole of the bee-entrance closed by a stone; but they also, in those distant times, built hives of wattle and mud, leaving a hole in the side for the bee-entrance.

From extant monuments of material culture we know that the state arose in Mesopotamia at the end of the fourth and the beginning of the third millenium B.C. As the writings of the ancient scribes testify, beekeeping was vigorously cultivated in Babylonia.

In the first millenium B.C. Assyria was known as a land of honey and olives. In the reign of Sargon I (in the ninth century B.C.), and after his death, the bodies of the dead were coated with wax and immersed in honey. The Assyrians were exceptionally skilful in the way they handled bees.

They knew a 'secret sound' that gave them power over swarms and by which they could drive a swarm out of the hive and then send it back in again. (The Roman poet Virgil, a beekeeper himself, wrote that a swarm of bees could be brought back to the hive by the sound of cymbals. And in-fact, it has been noted in beekeeping literature 'in recent years that a frequency of 600 hertz from a vibrator or loudspeaker placed 60 to 120 centimetres from a hive causes bees to 'freeze' on the honeycomb; the beekeeper himself, however, finds this sound extremely hard to bear.)

In ancient India bees were considered sacred companions of the gods, and occupied a place of honour in mythology. The god Vishnu, who was the embodiment of the sun and gave life to the Universe, was sometimes depicted as a little bee resting in the cup of a lotus flower, or with a blue bee hovering above his head.

The god of love, Kama, was portrayed holding a bow with a bow-string made of a chain of bees, which symbolized that his arrows brought suffering as well as love. Folk poetry, too, contains examples of the remarkable activities of bees.

In the early stages of the development of ancient Greece and Rome the importance of using the gifts of nature properly and sensibly was already understood. The ancient Greeks were extremely successful at nomadic beekeeping, transporting hives in boats to places where nectariferous plants were in flower.

In Ephesus there was a famous temple of Artemis in which her statue was decorated with wreaths made of boughs of various fruit trees on which bees rested. The priestesses of the temple were called Melissi (meaning 'bees'). And bees were depicted on the arms of the rich city itself. (When sacrifices were made in Greece and Rome, incidentally, especially to Aesculapius and Bacchus, honey was poured over the animals and fruits.)

Philosophers, writers, and scholars have been interested in bees for centuries. Archaeological excavations, legends, and the yellowed pages of centuries-old chronicles tell us that among the peoples inhabiting Europe, and especially the territory of the USSR, beekeeping was widely developed, even in antiquity.

Herodotus, the father of history (circa fifth century B.C.), mentioned that the Scythians traded extensively in honey and wax. In Urartu, over two thousand years ago, the people (ancestors of the modern Armenians) kept bees in wattle-and-daub hives. The first Russian chronicler, Nestor (A.D. 1056-1114), described in detail how widely beekeeping was developed in Rus, and how honey and beeswax were important exports to Greece, via Pereyaslavl.

A thousand years or so ago, in A.D. 911, the Russian Prince Oleg and the Byzantine Emperor concluded a trade agreement in which major products for exchange were honey and wax. In A.D. 945 Prince Igor Ryurikovich concluded. a similar treaty with Byzantium. And records have been preserved that in A.D. 946 the Drevlyane (one of the peoples of old Rus) brought a large payment in honey, wax, and furs to Igor's widow Olga, as a fine to expiate his murder.

At the beginning of the tenth century A.D. the famous Arabian writer and traveller, Abu-Ali Ahmed ben Omar Ibn-Dast, wrote in his manuscript *Information* about the Khazars, Buryats, Bulgars, Magyars, Slavs and Russakh:

'The land of the Slavs is a wooded plain and they live in the forest. They make a kind of jug from wood in which bees live and their honey is stored'.

In the old Russian law code *Russkaya Pravda* (Russian Right), published by Yaroslav the Wise in A.D. 1016, we find points protecting the rights of beekeepers and gatherers of wild honey, and imposing heavy fines on anyone damaging trees where wild bees lived or destroying them in order to obtain the honey.

In the *Lithuanian Statute* the death penalty was imposed for this crime. In those days honey was a commodity of exceptional importance. It was possible to lend it at interest; credit operations in honey were called 'putting out in honey'.

In old Novgorod, the historian N.I.Kostomarov said, 'bread and honey served as expressions of value. It was decreed that for such and such causes so much bread and honey should be paid.'

V. M. Vitvitsky, who wrote DD practical beekeeping in the last century, pointed out that the traveller Hall, who visited certain areas in the west and south of Rus (in what is now the Ukrainian SSR) early in the eleventh century, wrote in his *Chronicle:* 'In this land we have seen a surprisingly large number of bees, beekeepers, and bee-gardens in the steppes, and wild bees' nests in the forests. Here we noticed an extraordinary abundance of honey and beeswax.'

Writing about the Mongols' 'Golden Horde', the historians B. Grekov and A. Yakubovsky listed the wares that, according to the Arab geographer Maqsidi, of the latter half of the tenth century, were sent down the Volga 'from Bulgaria to Khoresm'. Honey occupied an important place among them.

In his written reports to Pope Clement VII in Rome *About Affairs in Muscovy* in 1523-4, Alberto Campenze informed the Pope of the considerable harvest of honey and wax in Russia, and said that the population kept 'house' bees close to their dwellings, which were passed down from one generation to the next.

In 1525 the Italian historian Paulus Jovius (or Paolo Giovo) (1483-1552) wrote in his *Book about the Muscovite Embassy* that in the land of Muscovy '... the most reliable harvest is that of honey and beeswax. For the whole country is full of very fecund bees that give excellent honey... .

In the forests and the thickest groves, you can see everywhere excellent swarms of bees hanging from the boughs of trees, and there is no need to attract them by sounding copper.

Vast quantities of honeycomb are often found hidden in the trees, and old honey that has been abandoned by the bees, as the few inhabitants there cannot look into every tree in the broad groves; in such manner they sometimes find fabulous lakes of honey in incredibly thick tree stumps."

Adam Olearius (Olschager) (1643) noted that 'honey and beeswax are found everywhere in the forests and in such abundance that the Russians, besides using the first to make mead and the second for candles for domestic use and divine service (consumption for the latter is very considerable), sell the surplus in vast amounts to other lands.'

In feudal Rus the prince or grand duke would set out every year in the autumn on a progress, visiting his vassals to collect dues (honey, wax, and furs). In feudal Russia peasants had to pay a fee in kind to their lord in the most valuable product, honey.

Primitive beekeeping (or *bortnichestvo*, the exploitation of wild bees in the forest and gathering of their honey) reached its zenith in Russia "at the turn of the sixteenth and seventeenth centuries, when the gatherers of wild honey collected very large quantities. On one of the Lebedinsky's wooded estates in the Kiev Marshes alone, 24 000 poods (around 72 000 gallons) of wild honey were gathered. As such estates numbered around a thousand in those days, the total of honey gathered must have been around 72 million gallons.

Vitvitsky estimated in 1861 that '.. wild honey gathering alone yielded our grandfathers and fathers honey and beeswax worth a thousand million roubles in assignats (eighteenth century Russian paper money), to say nothing of the profits obtained from domesticated bees.' So it is not surprising that Russia used to be famed for its honey and was called 'mellifluous' or 'flowing with honey'.

In Old Russia there were many villages and hamlets whose populations were solely engaged in gathering wild honey; but the role and significance of this occupation gradually began to decline. One reason was that it was a skilled and complicated business to prepare hollows in the trees for the bees and to protect them against that gourmand of the forest, the bear.

But the decline in the economic importance of wild beekeeping was mainly due to the beginning of intensive felling of the forests in European Russia, which deprived the bees of their rich food base. The development of distilling and then of the sugar industry also contributed significantly to the decline of wild beekeeping.

Beekeeping also began to decline in importance in Western Europe. The discovery of the New World and of new sea routes to the East Indies opened up new trade routes. Europe began to import honey from other parts of the world. America alone annually exported 50 million kilograms, and the huge quantities of sugar imported strongly competed with honey.

Peasants began to go in for other crops (potatoes and beetroot) and the fields where they were grown were enlarged at the expense of pastures where nectariferous plants grew.

The talented Ukrainian beekeeper, P. I. Prokopovich (1775-1850), played a major role in developing Russian beekeeping in the new circumstances. He devised the first collapsible frame hive, an invention that rationalized the technique of beekeeping and considerably increased its productivity and profitability.

Prokopovich's hive freed apiculture from the 'swarm-killing' system whereby the strongest families of bees, which collected the most honey, were 'smoked out' of the hive. Despite great advances in beekeeping, the capitalist system did not contribute to the development of this branch of agriculture in Russia. In 1910 there were 5 715 000 bee colonies in the country (of which only one-fifth were kept in frame hives) and about five million gallons of honey were exported. During World War I and the Civil War beekeeping suffered greatly.

But the Soviet Government took measures in the very first months of its existence to foster the development of apiculture. In early April 1919, when the young Soviet Republic was waging a bitter struggle against internal enemies, Lenin signed a decree on the protection of beekeeping that was the first Soviet law on the legal position of apiculture and protecting the interests of beekeepers.

It has a special place in the history of beekeeping in the USSR. By 1940 the Soviet Union had ten million bee colonies and occupied first place in the world for production of honey.. During the war against fascism (1941-5), however, the industry suffered badly.

Thousands of bee-farms belonging to collective and state farms were ravaged and more than two million bee colonies destroyed. In the post-war period apiculture was revived and restored and continues to make its contribution to agriculture.

2 Chapter THE BIOLOGY OF BEES

In 1758 the great Swedish botanist and doctor, Carl Linne, named the honeybee *Apis mellifera* (honey-bearing); three years later he suggested that it should be named *Apis millifica* (honey-making); his first name has been broadly retained to this day.

Honeybees are social insects that live in large families or colonies in hives, each hive being inhabited by one family. The families are characterized by a feature known as polymorphism, and comprise three forms or castes: queens (fertile females), drones (males), 'and worker bees (infertile females).

Thus a bee colony consists of one queen, several hundred drones, and tens of thousands of worker bees (up to 100 000 or more). Leo Tolstoy was well acquainted with the life of bees and skilfully reflected the poetry of beekeeping in his novels. In *Anna Karenina,* for example, we find the following description of a bee-garden, which is both artistically and scientifically accurate.

'In front of the openings of the hives, it made (Levin's) eye giddy to watch the bees and drones whirling round and round about the same spot, while among them the working bees flew in and out with spoils or in search of them, always in the same direction into the wood to the flowering limetrees and back to the hives.

'His ears were filled with the incessant bum in various notes, now the busy hum of the working bee flying quickly off, then the blaring of the lazy drone, and the excited buzz of the bees on guard protecting their property from the enemy and preparing to sting.' The queen bee is nearly 2.5 times as long and 2.8 times as heavy as a worker bee. Her function is reproduction; every day she lays 1000 to 2000 or more fertilized gigs in the cells of the hive.

Depending on the type of food gven to the larvae and the size of the wax cell, the eggs will develop into worker bees or queens. The queen also lays unfertilized eggs, 'from which only drones develop. Thus parthenogenesis, or reproduction without fertilization, has been preserved among bees.

In particular circumstances, as When the queen dies and there are no larvae from which the bees can raise a new queen, or there are plenty of nurses and too few larvae, worker bees may lay eggs (from which only drones hatch)

in the empty cells of the hive. Such bees are called 'dronelaying'. A worker bee is capable of laying 28 eggs in her lifetime. A.bee colony that has no queen is doomed, however, to perish, as only the number of, drones will increase, and they are incapable of gathering food or of any of the other work of the hive.

The Greek historian Xenophon described the role o f the queen as to dwell in the hive and not allow the bees to be lazy. She sent them out to obtain nectar and pollen, and checked what they brought in, put it away, and stored it.

When the time came she doled out the store of things accumulated in the hive fairly among the bees. She also made sure that the honeycomb was firmly and beautifully made and that the offspring were brought up properly.

The seventeenth Dutch naturalist Swammerdam fully determined the female character of the queen and the male character of drones. His observations were subsequently borne out by those of other researchers. The queen, as has been remarked, is the mother of the entire colony; she has no organs for collecting food, as the worker bees have, but the importance of her role is indisputable.

Johann Dzierzon considered her the centre of the bee family and the mother of all the young bees born from the eggs she laid. A. M. Butlerov also drew attention to the fact that the queen is literally the mother of her colony.

. P. I. Prokopovich, who did so much for Russian beekeeping, noted that '. . . the queen has a most beautiful and pleasant appearance, much more so than drones or workers. She looks so imposing and magnificent that we feel a sense of curiosity at first sight; she is the elder of her brood. Her well-proportioned body, the colour of her legs, her length, the fact that she is neither too fat nor very thin, her shortish wings-in brief, her whole appearance seems to us to be particularly beautiful, pleasant, and splendid.

You need to see 'her for yourself in order to appreciate her whole magnificence, excellence, and pleasantness....'

When a bee colony loses its queen, the behaviour of the bees catches the attention of the beekeeper, for they hum and run round the hive in alarm.

As bees cannot live long without a queen, they choose one or more three-day-old eggs and hatch a new queen from them. From the pearly white cylindrical egg a larva emerges which is reared in a roomy wax cell; and because it is fed with royal jelly it develops into a queen. It takes the bees sixteen days to rear a new queen.

When she has matured the queen leaves the hive and goes on her nuptial flight, and mates with a drone. After the nuptial flight she never leaves the hive again. In the hive she is looked after with great care by workers known as her retinue.

These bees not only attend to her personal cleanliness (washing her, combing her, removing her excrement from the hive, and so on), but also feed her with highly nutritious royal jelly. Prof. Remy Chauvin has described in detail how the retinue continue to concern themselves with the queen even after she is dead.

The queen lives five or six to eight years on average, but her fertility decreases with age (so that it is advisable to change the queen in a hive after two or three summers). The queen has a sting which serves both as ovipositor for laying eggs and as an organ of defence.

A queen never stings humans, even when they hurt her badly, but if she meets a rival queen she ejects her sting in fury while in flight. Prof. R. Chauvin and his colleagues have carried out interesting experiments and observations on queen bees that indicate that a live queen in a hive secretes some kind of chemical substance that inhibits the development of the ovaries of worker bees.

They were able to establish that a powder made by finely grinding the body of a queen continues to inhibit the development of workers' ovaries, and that an alcohol extract. of the body of a queen possesses the same property.

The British researcher, Dr. C.G.Butler, determined that this inhibiting substance was oxy-decanoic acid, a sub stance with hormonal properties that control the activities of all the bees in the hive.

It has also been ascertained that the queen affects worker bees in a variety of other ways: she can draw them to her like a magnet; she can prevent them from building queen cells; she stimulates them strongly to build wax cells for worker bees and drones.

The bees in the retinue occasionally, for some reason or other, become 'dissatisfied' with the queen and sud denly surround her, formin a kind of ball, and angrily try to sting her or tear off tier wings or legs. At first only individual bees begin to attack her, then dozens more join in, and occasionally hundreds.

It sometimes happens that they instantly sting the queen to death, as has been described by A.I.Root, who probed more than one such ball and found a sting in the dead queen. More often than not, however, the bees of the retinue close in around the queen in such number that they are unable to turn up their abdomens to thrust out their stings and release their poison, but the queen dies of asphyxiation under their sheer pressure without once being stung.

This closing in upon the queen apparently happens because the bees 'consider' that she is guilty of some misdemeanour in their waxen palace, and they pass over to the attack in order to destroy the culprit.

It has been noted that when a hive is opened the bees sometimes, for no apparent reason, close in a ball around the queen, despite the fact that she has been carrying out her duties for six or twelve months in an excellent manner.

When bees surround a strange queen, it is obviously because she is from a strange colony, but why they destroy their own queen is incomprehensible. The biological function of drones is to fertilize queens. Like a queen, a drone cannot obtain food for himself and is completely dependent on the worker bees.

The drone has no 'baskets' on its legs for collecting pollen and its mouth parts are not adapted to gathering nectar from flowers. In spring and summer drones feed on the honey prepared by the diligent worker bees; but they only survive the summer months, and are driven from the hive in the autumn to die of cold and hunger.

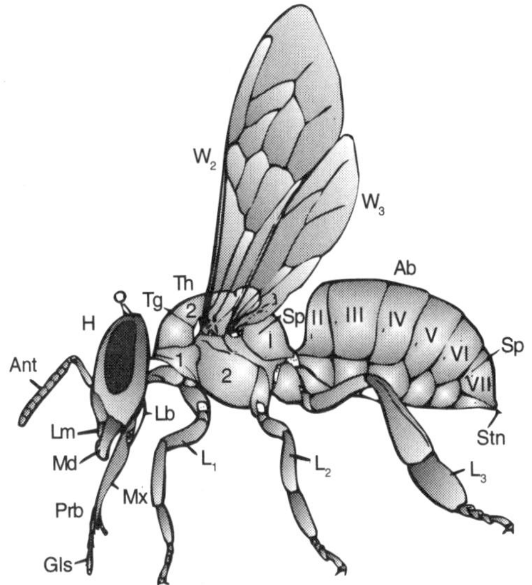

Figure 2.1: Diagram of the anatomy of a worker bee with the body hairs removed, showing the appendages of the left side (after Snodgrass)
1, 2, 3-thoracic segments; 1, 11, III, IV, V, VI, VII—abdominal segments; Gls-glossa; Prb—prohoscis; Mx—maxilla; Aid—mandible; Lm-labrum; Lb-labium Ant-antenna; E-compound eye; 11-head; G-ocelli; Tg-tegula; Th-thorax; W-wing; .\b—abdomen; Sp-spiracle; Stn-sting; L—leg.

Drones do not work at all, A.M.Butlerov wrote, but just play around, flying out at the best time in the middle of the day, chasing young queens and mating with them in flight. At the 1901 International Congress of Apiarists in Paris, however, some delegates spoke in their defence.

In this connection, A.F.Zubarev communicated, the speakers maintained on the basis of observations that drones helped to maintain the warmth of the hive necessary for the hatching of offspring and that their timely destruction should be left to the, bees themselves. Articles in defence of drone bees have als appeared more recently.

Drones take 24 days to develop from the egg. Their sexual organs (two testes, with a vas deferens leading from each to a sperm sac, two accessory glands, an ejaculatory duct, and a copulatory organ) are well developed. The drone's spermatozoa mature eight to fourteen days after its emergence from its cell. It is estimated that 200 million spermatozoa are formed in the drone's testes.

Drones have extremely good vision, which is most important during the nuptial flight, when they have to follow the rapidly flying queen. Worker bees spend the whole of their short lives in tireless toil (which is of great benefit to man).

One can say, quite categorically, that they have no childhood since from the third day of their life they must already maintain the wax cells in a sanitary state, cleaning their walls and floors after the young bees have left them.

From the fourth day onward, as house bees, they feed the older larvae with a mixture of honey and pollen and begin to make flights around the hive, getting the lay of the land. From the seventh day their maxillary glands, which secrete the royal jelly. with which they feed the queen and the larvae that will be future queens, begin to function.

From the twelfth to the eighteenth days house bees develop wax glands and work on the building of honeycomb. During this period they guard the hive, examine the nectar, and help keep the brood warm, acting as a kind of living blanket.

House bees ensure that the future generations develop normally and that the hive is well ventilated. At 15 to 18 days old worker bees take on the most responsible job, that of field bees, exploring or foraging for and collecting nectar and pollen.

To illustrate the energetic way they work at all stages suffice it to say that, during the six days they feed their future sisters, they visit each larva between 8000 and 10 000 times.

Field bees go out in search of abundant sources of nectar, pollen, and water. They collect large quantities of pollen, moisten it with saliva, mix it with nectar, and then place it in special hollows or 'baskets' in their hind legs.

Two pollen pellets (i.e. the load of the 'baskets') contain around four millions grains of pollen. The pellets brought back to the hive are stored in cells in the honeycomb, later to be moistened with honey and turned into beebread.

Only worker bees have special wax glands, located on the last four segments of the abdomen. Flakes or scales of wax are released through eight openings above the wax plates or mirrors. In 1684 John Martin removed the wax plates from the abdomen of a comb-building bee with the point of a needle, and is rightly considered the first to have noticed that wax is a product of the biological activity of worker bees.

But it was only 108 years later that John Hunter showed that wax was produced by their wax glands. One hundred scales of beeswax weigh only 25 milligrams, so there are around four millions of them in a kilogram of wax. From these minute scales or bricks, the worker beyes, real architects, working in the dark, build wax bins of amazing beauty for the storage of honey and pollen, and firm, cosy cells for the developing offspring.

They use 13 milligrams or 50 wax scales -build a cell for a worker bee, and 30 milligrams or 120 flakes for a drone cell. Each cell is hexagonal in shape, and each of its sides is shared with the cells next to it. Honeycomb consists of two layers of these hexagonal cells, with a special partition between them that serves as the floor of the cell.

A comb weighing a mere 150 grams has 9100 storerooms in which four kilograms of honey can be kept. When wax-making bees are three to five days old they already secrete a thin layer of wax on their mirrors; but their wax glands are only fully developed by the twelfth to eighteenth day, depending on the amount of honey and pollen in the hive.

Worker bees are not only skilled wax-founders but also splendid architects. The construction of honeycomb is the most surprising thing about the life of bees. Darwin, who studied them for many years, came to the conclusion that only a narrow-minded person could fail to be amazed by a structure so beautifully adapted to its purpose.

Mathematicians say that bees have in fact solved the difficult exercise of building a cell that will hold the maximum amount of honey with the minimum amount of valuable wax.

The hive is always kept spotlessly clean. The worker bees skilfully fill in cracks and polish the walls of their home with propolis (bee glue). If a mouse should get into the hive, desiring to partake of the honey, the bees kill it instantly with a sharp sting and an extremely effective poison.

Then, in order to avoid fatal consequences from decomposition of the victim, they rapidly immure it in air-tight glue. The air in a hive is always clean and fresh, for the bees ventilate their dwelling as well as keeping it at the optimum temperature.

On a hot summer day you can see orderly rows of bees standing at the bee entrance, with their heads to one side, energetically vibrating their wings. These are the ventilating bees, who send a strong current of cooled air into the hive.

Inside the hive others do the same. When the outside temperature drops the bees gather together more tightly on the frames, thereby reducing the surface of heat loss, increasing metabolism, and consequently raising body temperature.

Some bees have the duty of guarding the entrance to the hive; at the first sign of danger, they go into battle with the unbidden visitor.

The Russian revolutionary democrat, writer and critic, D. 1. Pisarev, noted that they do not have a permanent guard, but, if some incautious or audacious 'member of another tribe' happens to fly into a hive, it will come to a sticky end; hundreds of worker bees

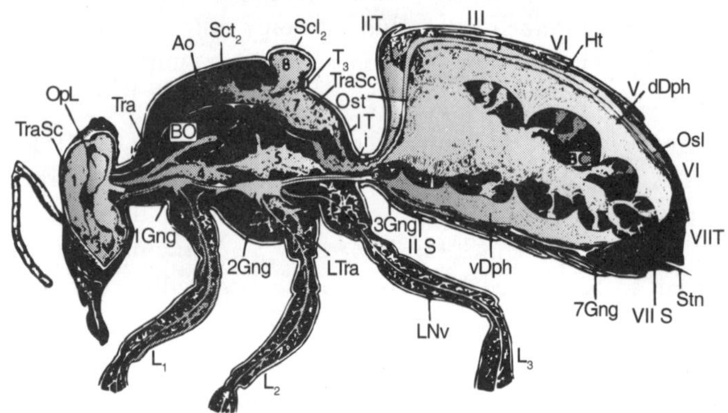

Figure 2.2: Diagram of the body of a worker bee cut longitudinally, with the muscles and alimentary canal removed to expose the dorsal blood vessel, diaphragms, tracheae, air sacs, and ventral nerve cord.
I, II, III, IV, V, VI, VII-abdominal segments; i-convoluted part of the aorta; TraSc-tracheal air sac; Opl-optic lobe, T-tergum; Tra-trachea; Ao-aorta; Sct-scutum; Scl-scutellum; IT-tergum of propedeum; Ost-ostium of heart; Ht-heart; dDph, vDph-dorsal and ventral diaphragms; Stn-sting; S-sternum; Gng-ganglia; LNv-leg nerve; LTra-leg trachea; BC-body cavity.

will fall upon him, thrusting out their mandibles and stings as they do so.

The intruder will most certainly perish and its body will be pushed out of the hive to serve as a warning to others. If we open a hive and take a look at the honeycomb, swarming with thousands of bees, we get the impression that they never rest and are always busy with their many duties. But we would also notice bees resting and sleeping.

In his lectures on beekeeping A. I. Root often used to remark that bees slept more heavily at night than during the day. Prof. Karl von Frisch, who decoded the 'language' of bees, says that when you become acquainted with what goes on inside a hive you soon become aware of how much time bees spend doing nothing at each stage of their life.

The harmonious functioning of worker bees' organs (and those of queens and drones) is governed and regulated by nervous systems (central, peripheral, and sympathetic). The central nervous system consists of a brain and a ventral nerve cord or chain.

The brain of a bee can, to some extent, be compared in significance with that of higher animals, while the ventral chain plays a role similar to that of the spinal cord. The weights of the brains of various insects have been determined quite precisely. It has been found that a worker bee's brain is considerably larger that that of a queen or drone.

It is made up of a layer of cells forming two special mushroom-shaped bodies (the corpora pedunculata) which are considered the centre of higher nervous activity. Researchers have ascertained that the corpora pedunculata are most highly developed in worker bees.

Prof. V. F. Natal, Honorary Member of the USSR Academy of Pedagogical Sciences, maintains that the extremely complicated behaviour characteristic of worker bees accounts for the greater development of their brains, particularly of the corpora pedunculata, compared with queens and drones.

In his book *Studies in Optimism* Ilya Mechnikov wrote in this connection: 'Although worker bees do a great deal for the ood of their own society, they possess one incompletely developed feature. Blessed with a developed brain and equipped with extremely well formed organs for the production of wax and gathering of food, they possess only rudimentary sexual organs incapable of normal functioning.'

The lower part of the brain consists of two antennae or olfactory lobes from which nerves run to the antennae or organs of smell. The optic lobes and the compound eyes are located at the sides of the brain. The ventral nerve cord is a continuation of the brain and consists of two inosculated nerve ganglia (i.e. joined end to end).

From the ganglia nerves reach out, penetrating the whole of the abdominal part of the bee's body. Because of the presence of ganglia in all parts of the body, co-ordination of the work of the organs and muscles is not concentrated solely in the brain. If a bee is beheaded, for example, it will continue to move and react to irritation, and the sting and stinging apparatus will still function.

The sympathetic nervous system begins in the frontal ganglion which is situated near the brain and consists of a few smaller ganglia. From it nerves go out to the organs of digestion, circulation, and respiration.

Norbert Wiener, the father of cybernetics, considered that the nerve tissue of a hive of bees was merely the nerve tissue of each individual bee. How, then, he asked, could a hive function in a co-ordinated manner, and adapt itself to constantly changing conditions? The answer obviously lay in the mutual ties between the inmates of the hive.

Bees do not have a special closed system of blood circulation, and their blood (known as haemolymph) fulfils the function both of blood and of lymph. The main organ of circulation, directing the blood from the abdomen to the head, is a five-chambered dorsal vessel, the heart. In the side walls of each chamber there is a slit-like opening, or ostium, through which blood is sucked into the heart when the chambers expand. When the chambers contract blood is driven from the heart into the aorta and issues from the latter through an open outlet into the cranial cavity, where it washes the brain, and the sense organs located in the head, and then the muscles of the thorax.

As it washes the mid-gut the blood is enriched with nourishing substances which seem to filter through the wall of the gut. It also

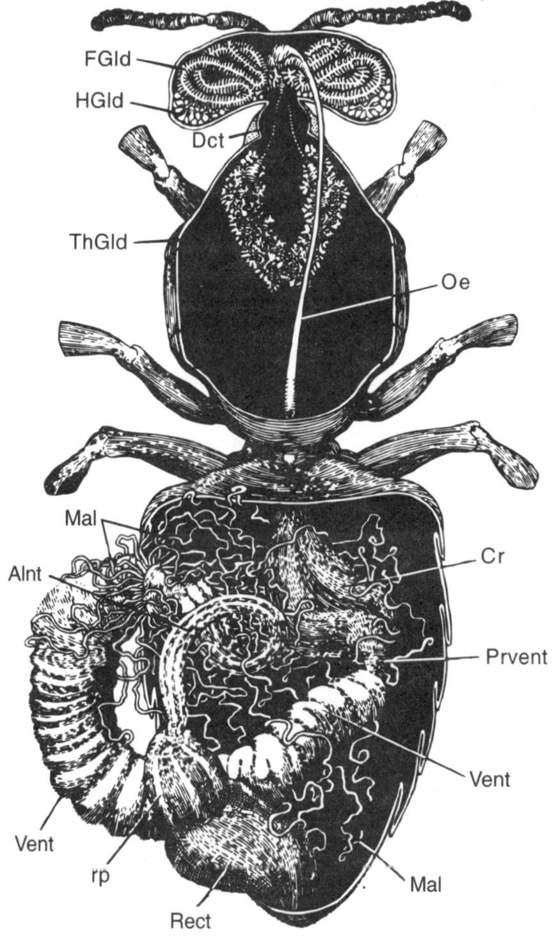

Figure 2.3: Diagram of the alimentary canal and glands of the head and thorax of a worker bee.

FGld-food gland; HGld-head salivary gland; ThGld-thoracic salivary gland; Oe-oesophagus; bct-duct MaI-Malpighian tubules; AInt-anterior intestine; Cr-crop ('honey stomach'); prvent-proventriculus; Vent-ventriculus; rp-rectal pad; Rect-rectum.

rids the bee's organism of metabolic products, which are filtered out by the organs of secretion (the Malpighian tubules) and excreted.

The Malpighian tubules are the organs of excretion in the bee; their function corresponds to that of the kidneys in vertebrates. The heart beat of an adult bee depends on its vital activity, the temperature of the environment, and many other factors. When a bee is sitting quietly on honeycomb or on a flower its heart beats 65 to 70 times a minute. When it is moving the rate is 100 times a minute (in flight 150 times a minute).

Such a rapid pulse is necessary to keep the blood in constant movement and in order to supply the body cells with nourishing substances and, in part, with oxygen.

The blood of bees consists of plasma (the liquid part) and cells or haemocytes, among which the leucocytes and , phagocytes that ensure phagocytosis (that is freeing of the organism from microbes) are extremely important.

The respiratory (or tracheal) system of the bee is well developed. It consists of air sacs, tracheal trunks, branches, and microscopic tracheal capillaries or tracheoles. The tracheoles are narrow tubes a micron in diameter. The body of a bee is supplied with air through special openings or spiracles, of which bees have three pairs on the thorax and six on the abdomen (except drones, which have seven).

The spiracles have a blocking apparatus that prevents dust from entering with the air and protects against loss of moisture. When a bee is not moving the spiracles are closed, but when it is working

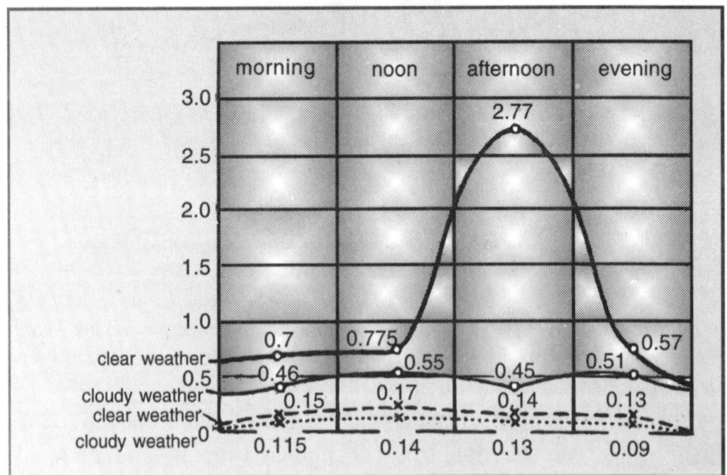

Figure 2.4: Curve of the gathering of nectar from Phacelia according to the time of day.

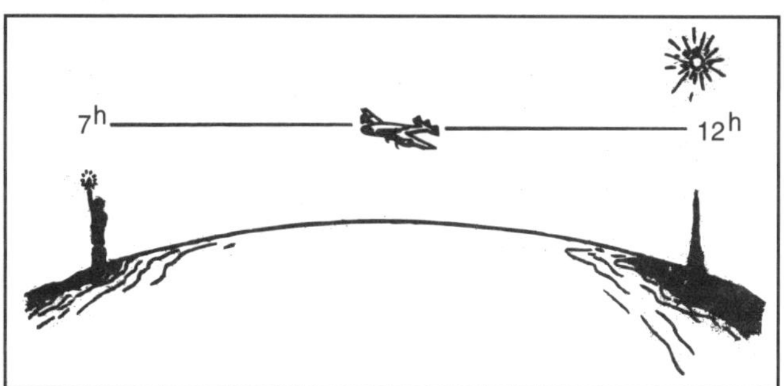

Figure 2.5: Transatlantic flight to test beds' time sense.

and the organism needs a great deal of oxygen they open wide. Respiration is controlled by a respiratory centre; and spiracles open and close according to whether there is a lack of oxygen or an excess of carbon dioxide.

Bees have five eyes, two compound ones and three simple ones. It is thought that they use their simple eyes to distinguish objects close to them (one or two centimetres away) and for orientation during work in the hive and on flowers.

They use the compound eyes to pick out objects at a distance. It is also thought that the simple eyes are organs that facilitate better functioning of the compound ones. The surface of the compound eye of a worker bee or a queen consists of nearly five thousand (in drones more than eight thousand) hexagonal facets or elements from which tapering tubes go down into the depths of the eye, ending in branching nerves. Each facet does not form an image of an object as a whole but only a separate part of it. The several thousand separate parts of the image merge in the brain of the bee and become the image of the object as a whole, a kind of vision known as mosaic vision.

It has been established that bees can distinguish blue, yellow and white colours; they do not perceive red at all and confuse green with yellow and blue. In worker bees the compound eye is located at the side of the head and the simple eyes on the parietal lobe of the head.

Von Frisch, Leconte, and other researchers think that worker bees apparently have ways of orienting themselves when the sun is hidden by clouds. When the sky is clear, bees are possibly guided by certain natural factors relative to the position of the sun, for instance,

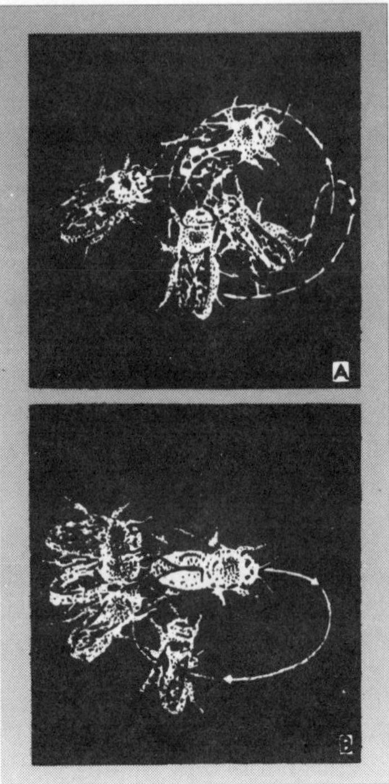

Figure 2.6: The 'language' ('dances') of bees (after von Frisch) A-'round dance' of nectar foragers; B-successive stages of the 'shuffle' of bees foraging nectar and pollen.

the partial polarization of light from the blue sky. When the sky is full of clouds, von Frisch thinks, they find their way by means of the ultraviolet rays that penetrate the cloud. Thus bees are sensitive to ultraviolet light, which is quite invisible to the human eye.

The olfactory organs of the bee are located on tendrils or antennae. According to A. L. Guselnikov each antenna has 500 000 olfactory pores, each with its own nerve endings. There are also tactile hairs between the pores so that the antennae are organs both of smell and touch.

It has been established that bees can distinguish an odour even when it is diluted to one part in five hundred (which is too faint for detection by human beings). The guard bees at the entrance to a hive use their antennae to 'take a sniff' at each bee as it flies in, and are quite able to distinguish strangers from members of their own colony.

The organs of taste are found around the mouth in the form of chitinous taste rods supplied with nerves.

Due to the arrangement of these organs (which are particularly well developed in worker bees) bees have an extremely fine sense of taste. A 4 per cent sugar syrup, for instance, does not seem sweet to them and they will refuse to eat it, preferring to go hungry.

They likewise will refuse an oversweet solution of saccharine with its metallic taste. But they will readily make honey from a syrup with quinine. Worker bees have a well developed sense of time.

They fly out to flowers only at a time of day when they can obtain nectar or pollen from them. The observations of many researchers have shown that bees regulate their activity according to

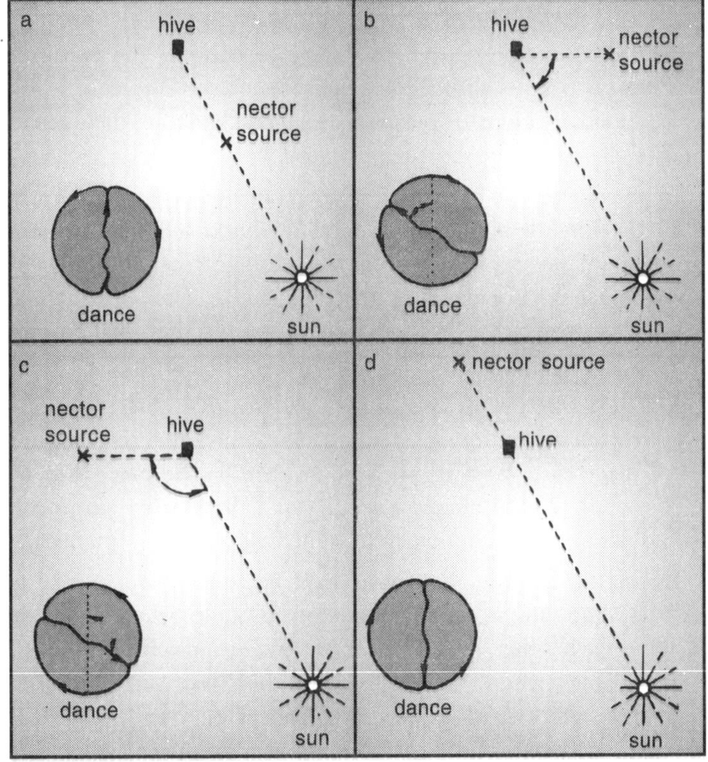

Figure 2.7: How the foraging bee's dance conveys information on the direction to plants according to the position of the sun.

the movement of the sun, atmospheric conditions, and their locality. It has been found from test bees that every day, with clock-like precision, they will set out at the same time of day for sweetened water from feeding cups.

To test whether their accuracy depended on the sun, hives of test bees were put into darkened premises with artificial lighting. The fact that they did not have natural light made not the slightest difference to their behaviour.

They set out for the sweetened water absolutely on the dot, just as in sunlight. It was then decided to make the following experiment. Bees that had-become accustomed to taking the sweetened water in artificially lit premises in Paris, were flown to New York.

There (in similar premises, artificially lit) they set out from the hive in search of sweetened water at exactly the same time as in Paris, despite the five-hour time difference between the two cities. It has not yet been established whether bees possess organs of hearing but, as the observations of practical beekeepers indicate, they perceive sounds well, especially the ring of metal.

In this context it is interesting to recall the experiments carried out by the English biologist, Sir John Lubbock, F.R.S., who wrote: 'The result of my experiments on the hearing of bees has surprised me very much. It is generally considered that to a certain extent the emotions of bees are expressed by the sounds they make, which seems to imply that they possess the power of hearing.

I do'not by any means intend to deny that this is the case. Nevertheless I never found them to take any notice of any noise which I made even when it was close to them. I tried one of my bees with a violin. I made all the noise I could, but to my surprise she took no notice; I could not even see a twitch of the antennae.")

Down the centuries naturalists have been interested to find out how bees communicated with one another. Some believed that they 'talked' to each other by means of various sounds. In 1788 Ernest Spytzner drew attention to the fact that they went through definite movements (which used to be called 'dances').

In his book *From the Life of Bees,* Prof. Karl von Frisch, who has spent many years studying their behaviour, describes his observations and experiments. He established that exploring or reconnaissance bees in formed their sisters in the hive by specific dances that they had found an abundant supply of nectar or pollen.

A 'round dance' told of a rich source of nectar and a 'shuffle' of a pollen find. In a special article in 1946, on the significance of bee dances von Frisch gave details of what he had discovered. By means of new and extremely inte resting experiments, he had managed to ascertain that exploring bees informed the hive through their dances not of the quality of a find (nectar or pollen), as he had thought earlier, but about its distance from the hive.

According to his new observations, when they performed a 'round dance', they were telling their sisters that the source was close to the hive, but when they did a 'shuffle' on returning to the hive, the foraging bees prepared for a long flight.

At the XXII International Congress of Apiarists, in Munich, in 1969, Prof. von Frisch said: 'Thus, it should not be thought that, although over their long history bees have acquired a means of informing their friends in the hive about the distance and direction of the source of food, the other bees do not understand them.

We do not feel that we have gone back to 1823, when Unhoch who described the dances of bees did not understand their significance and thought that the bee family amused itself with dances.'

The life of a bee colony is extremely interesting, and the behaviour of honey bees and the variety of their work arise amazement and make people think that bees have feelings peculiar to human beings, joy, sorrow, love, a sense of self-sacrifice, and so forth; but this idea is incorrect since thought and labour, i. e. rational activity, are peculiar to man alone.

As Karl Marx wrote, the bee, in building its wax cells, puts some human architects to shame; but what differentiates the worst architect from the best bee is that before building his wax cell, the architect already has an idea in his head of what he is going to make.

In his foreword to B. N. Schwanwich's book on the mutual relations between insects and flowers, the famous physiologist I. P. Pavlov wrote: 'The author describes in great detail some of the interesting experiments on insects of Frisch, Knolle, and Minnich, experiments concerned not only with stereotyped, innate, so-called instinctive activity, but also with activity based on individual experience. Thus there are two kinds of behaviour in these animalshigher and lower, individual and specific. The mechanism of the former naturally poses a great problem to the human brain; extension of research into various aspects of the animal world is essential for solving it."

CLEANLINESS AND HYGIENE IN THE APIARY

A beekeeper must be a paragon of cleanliness. Even in ancient times it was known that slovenliness was out of place in a4 apiary, for bees themselves like to live in ideal cleanliness. In Turgenev's *A Sportsman's Sketches,* the storyteller remarked: 'How clean it is in Kalinych's beehouse. "The bees would not live there else, your honour," (Kalinych) said with a sigh.' Bees also have a very delicate sense of smell and soon become irritated by unpleasant odours (sweat, tobacco, alcohol, etc.).

In his novel *Without Titles,* D.N.Mamin-Sibiryak skilfully depicted the apiary of the feldsher (or doctor's assistant) Potapov, which in a short time had become quite large, with some three hundred hives.

Potapov rightly considered 'that one should not approach bees with a guilty conscience' or with dirty hands. 'Now then,' he said, 'don't go near a bee without washing your hands. She makes enough noise as it is. If she could tell you, she would sayy you'd gone mad, my dear fellow, and didn't know the rules.'

When the beekeeper forgets about cleanliness and to keep a washbasin, with water, soap, and a clean towel at the bee-farm, the bees become dissatisfied and also work badly.

The colonies of such a beekeeper usually become weak and the apiary ceases to be profitable, and instead of selling honey, he is forced to buy sugar to supplement their feed. And the beekeeper who works with dirty hands today will become familiar tomorrow with the ills that bees suffer from.

Charles Dadant, speaking of the importance in beekeeping of keeping one's hands clean, remarked that it reminded him of something that happened in his youth, before he left his father, a former doctor. Once a labourer came to—his father and asked him for an ointment for scabies, which he had contracted in the fields around while harvesting.

Dadant's father gave him instructions how to use the ointment and bade him to tell his wife to use it too, so that she would not catch scabies as well. But the wife was quite healthy and refused to use the ointment. Two weeks later the labourer came back for more ointment, for, although he himself was now quite better, his wife had caught the infection.

Dadant Senior gave him the ointment and told him that both he and his wife should use it so that he would not get re-infected. But the man did not listen to this advice and two weeks later he visited the doctor again. 'Well now,' said the old doctor, 'I thought you'd have learnt from these two lessons that you both have to be treated at the same time in order to recover from an illness that is so easily communicated by direct contact.' 'It is just the same with foul brood', Dadant concluded.

Thus a basic and elementary requirement in beekeeping is to keep the hands and body clean, for one's own sake as much as anything, as it is possible to catch a number of diseases, especially gastric and intestinal complaints.

The hands should be washed with soap and water both before and after examining bees. When a colony is infected with either European or American foul brood the hands should be scrubbed three times with soap and a brush and then rinsed with warm or hot water. The water should be poured into a hole in the ground, and the hole filled in with soil.

The beekeeper's main enemy is the larva of the wax moth, which does immense damage. Two consecutive geverations of larvae from one pair of wax moths can destroy up to 100 kilograms of dried wax leaves (equal to 60 kilograms of pure wax). The wax moth finds refuge in apiaries where hygienic conditions do not prevail.

Altman-Reichenber, Cowan, Kulikov, Zander, and others have described instances of helminthic worms getting into hives and the organisms of bees, drones, and larvae Worms do great damage and can bring about the death of a hive by neutralizing queens.

They are mainly passed on by water containing eggs of nematodes (the round worms that infest the organism of the bee). 'The best way to guard bees against them is to provide a good drinking bowl at the bee-farm with fresh water, and to keep the hives clean' (Kulikov).

THE IMPORTANCE OF WATER FOR BEES

Bees need water in order to live normally. Without it they cannot rear a new generation, for water is needed to prepare the food, to dissolve crystallized honey, and to prepare royal jelly from pollen. (Bees have been known to perish on combs of crystallized honey.)

Nowhere in Russian beekeeping literature, N.I.Nevsky wrote in 1912 with regard to drink for bees, 'will you find a single, even remotely significant article devoted to this problem.

Even the best classics on beekeeping do not find it necessary to pay the slightest attention to drink and give limited advice on the need in the apiary for a trough, tub, barrel, or drinking bowl of salted water. But our foreign beekeeping friends long ago realized how important drinking is.'

A.I.Root quoted Park and Lendy to the effect that bees fly out seven to fifteen times a day for nectar, somewhat less for pollen, and up to a hundred times for water. In their search for water water-carrier bees will leave the hive when the temperature is low (6 to 8° C) and so die. It has been known for a bee colony to lose almost all its summer bees in one or two days.

Bees fetch water to the brood every day; if the young are forced to go for several days without water they die. Cases have been noted when, because of lack of water, the bees have pulled larvae out of their cells.

In the spring a colony needs about two glasses of water a day and the bees have to leave the hive some 30 000 times in order to obtain that quantity. Thus a litre of water in drinking bowls in the bee-garden saves 60 000 bees from searching for water and enables them to collect nectar and pollen instead.

It should be added that during the spring and on hot summer days not only are the water-carrier bees involved in supplying the hive, but also the 'reservoir' bees. It has been ascertained that when the water-carriers return to the hive, they do not release the water into cells of the comb, but pass it to other bees which act as reservoirs or cisterns.

An experiment carried out at the Goloseev Experimental Bee-farm in Kiev indicated that when pure and salt water were provided in drinking bowls 47.3 per cent of the bees took the pure water and 52.7 per cent the salt water. The bees readily took water containing 0.5 per cent salt, but refused a 1 per cent solution.

In 1958 Dr. L. Seifer carried out interesting experiments that showed that bees do not simply need pure water, but also need water containing salt, ammonia, etc. In the test, drinking bowls were filled respectively with pure water, and water containing 0.25 per cent ammonium, 0.05 per cent vinegar, and 0.80 per cent common salt.

Over a measured period the bowl containing salt water was visited by 2546 bees, that with pure water by 1510, that with ammonia water by 1442, and that with vinegar water by 1186 bees. It can thus be concluded that bees need salt.

Beekeepers who tend their little winged friends with love and care supply them with salt water (50 grams of common salt to a bucket of water).

If we consider the observation of Serbinov (1913), Zander (1927), and others, that the illnesses affecting bees (foul brood) are in mostly passed on through water, we can see ,that a good, convenient drinking bowl is an extremely important and necessary item in any modern and wellequipped apiary.

HONEY AND ITS PROPERTIES

We have all seen bees on a bright summer's day hovering above the flowers from which they collect sweet drops of nectar. To produce a hundred grams of honey, a foraging bee must visit nearly a million flowers, sucking up nectar with its proboscis and filling its 'honey stomach' (although it isn't really a stomach). Then it flies back to the hive.

To produce a kilogram of honey a foraging bee must bring in 120 000 to 150 000 loads of nectar. If the flowers it works are 1500 metres from the hive, it will have to fly three kilometres for each load and a total distance of 360 000 to 450 000 kilometres for a kilogram (or eight to eleven times the distance round the earth).

A bee colony collects as much as 150 kilograms of honey in a single season. Back in the hive (having passed the 'sentinels' who guard the bee entrance), the forager is met by other workers, the house bees, who relieve it of its load, which they store for some time in their honey stomachs.

There it undergoes complex processing, which had already begun in the honey stomach of the forager. House bees process nectar as follows. The bee opens its mouth parts or mandibles sideways and stretches its proboscis forward and downward a little.

This makes a droplet of nectar appear at the end of its proboscis, which it puts into its honey stomach, at the same time drawing in its proboscis. This regurgitation and swallowing of the nectar is repeated 120 to 240 times; only then does the house bee find an empty cell in the honeycomb and deposit its nectar there.

It is still not honey, however; other worker bees will continue the complex work of turning the nectar into honey. If the house bees are too busy, the foragers themselves attach their loads (drops of nectar) to the upper walls of cells. This is a very interesting and most practical procedure, as the suspended drops thus have a larger surface area, which facilitates evaporation of their moisture.

Nectar contains 40 to 80 per cent water and up to three-quarters of this must sometimes be removed in order to make honey. Ripe honey contains only 18 to 20 per cent water. To help evaporation along worker bees carry every drop of nectar several times from one cell to another until the unripe or green honey becomes viscous.

This business of evaporating excess moisture from nectar also involves many bees fanning their wings (26 400 times a minute) to set up an additional circulation of air in the hive. Apart from this purely mechanical concentration of nectar, it is also concentrated while in the bees' honey stomachs. Prof. I.A.Kablukov held that water was absorbed from it by the cells of the honey stomach, entered the haemolymph, and was then passed to the Malpighian tubules that serve as kidneys, and excreted.

In that way the drop of nectar diminished in volume in the body of the worker bee, and in addition was enriched there with enzymes, organic acid, disinfectants, and other substances. From the honey stomach the drop was transferred to a cell, and the process repeated until the nectar became honey. When the cells of the honeycomb are filled with honey the bees seal them with wax.

The honey thus stored will keep for years. Honey in the comb has the best flavour (and usually costs more), because it comes in natural packaging made by the bees themselves.

VARIETIES OF HONEY

When bees are given the possibility of gathering nectar from flowers of one variety, they will do so, and the honey they produce is more or less homogeneous. Beekeepers then name it after the plant from which it has been collected (e.g. linden, buckwheat, etc.). Honeys differ from one another in a number of ways.

The main types are as follows: floral honey derived from flowers; regional honey, pertaining to the area from which it comes; and technological honey. Depending on the source from which bees obtain the material for honey, it is classed either as floral or as honeydew honey.

Floral honey may be monofloral, produced from the nectar of one main species of nectariferous plant (buckwheat, linden or lime, white acacia, willowherb, sunflower, sairfoin, etc.) or polyfloral (or multifloral), made from the nectar of various plants.

Absolutely monofloral honey is seldom found; it is sufficient, however, for the nectar of one particular plant to predominate to give a honey its character, e.g. in linden honey the nectar of lindens or lime trees.

Insignificant amounts of nectar from other plants have no effect on the specific aroma, colour, and taste of a given kind of honey.

The following honeys are classed as multifloral: meadow, steppe or prairie, forest, fruit or orchard., mountain-taiga, etc. The quality of a honey is often judged from its appearance, smell, and taste; its type can also be determined from its aroma, colour, and flavour.

Three kinds of honey are distinguished by colour: light, medium, and dark. Many sorts differ not merely in colour but also in shade, of which there are many.

And there are some kinds that are quite colourless, as light and transparent as water. When you look at a comb of this honey (e.g. white acacia), it appears empty; a jar of the honey is translucent. Light-coloured honeys are the best.

A. I. Root said that the best honey was usually 'clear as water', and though that expression is not very precise, it is sufficiently accurate for all practical purposes.

It should be noted, however, that there are reports in, the literature that dark honey contains more minerals, mainly iron, copper, and manganese, and should therefore be considered more valuable for the organism.

The type of a honey can also be determined from its aroma. Certain kinds have an exceptionally delicate, pleasant smell. As Gogol's Rudy Panko said: '... and you will find no better honey in any village, I will take my oath on that.

Just fancy, when you bring in the comb the scent in the room is something you can't imagine; it is clear as a tear or a costly crystal such as you see in ear-ring". Apart from sorts with a splendid aroma (citrus, acacia, linden, etc.), there are honeys that have' an unpleasant odour (tobacco, and others).

TRAINING BEES IN ORDER TO OBTAIN HONEYS OF UNIFORM COMPOSITION

In 1948 the bees in the apiary of the Lenin Collective Farm in the Radishchev District of Ulyanovsk Region were fed sugar because honey flow in the locality was poor. The sugar used had been spoiled and smelled of kerosene.

The first day the bees were fed the syrup, swarms of them were seen around the repair shops of the farm; for two days they were stimulated by the smell of kerosene and sought a source of nectar with the same odour. The bees were then given syrup smelling of lilac. The next day there were many more of them on the lilac bushes than on other plants.

The point is that very little time is needed to accustom bees to a certain smell. Another thing that came to light was that bees eating a scented syrup not only collected nectar with that scent themselves but also got their sisters to fly in search of it.

Beekeepers take advantage of this in order to train their bees. The importance of 'training' is that greater numbers of bees are induced to forage for the nectar of particular plants, which can appreciably intensify cross-pollination.

It enables the beekeeper, moreover, to control their activity and send his bees at will to plants that require intensive pollination. The method of training consists in giving the bees 100 grams of a 50 per cent sugar syrup smelling of the flowers that are to be worked, either the evening before, or early in the morning.

The scented syrup is simple to prepare. To make 100 grams 50 grams of sugar are dissolved in 100 cubic centimetres of boiling water. When the syrup has cooled, 25 grams of flowers of the desired type are steeped in it for at least two hours.

A clean glass or enamel vessel should be used, with a tight-fitting lid to prevent the smell from dispersing. The flowers must be freed of their green calyxes, as the smell of the latter differs considerably from that of the flowers themselves.

It should be borne in mind that bees have a very discriminating sense of smell so that the success of training largely depends on the purity of the syrup. It should have no foreign odour either in the fragrance of the flowers used or in the syrup itself. The best procedure is to prepare the syrup during the day, infuse it overnight, and introduce it into the hive early in the morning before the bees are ready to go foraging. The feeder with the syrup is placed on the frames.

Results are best when a syrup is fed throughout the period the plant concerned is in bloom. The foragers taste the fragrant syrup at daybreak and then immediately start off for plants with that smell, the fragrance of the blossoming plants serving as a kind of beacon for them. Then as they return to the hive from the plants and fly back again, they leave scent trails along their airways.

THE CHEMICAL COMPOSITION AND FOOD VALUE OF HONEY

Honey contains some eighty different substances of importance to the human organism, but consists mainly of sugars (glucose and laevulose or fructose). Glucose and fructose are monosaccharides that are very easily assimilated by the organism.

Disaccharides like cane or beet sugar have to be broken down by hydrolysis in the small intestine under the action of saccharase or invertase, before entering the blood. The glucose and laevulose resulting from their breakdown are absorbed through the portal vein, from which the glucose enters the liver and is stored, being returned to the blood when the sugar level of the latter falls.

Monosaccharides pass directly into the blood from the intestine without transformation; and glucose can be injected directly into the blood, as is commonly done in certain illnesses.

More than half the energy required by the organism is provided by sugary substances in our food. Sugar considerably reduces fatigue; honey is particularly important in this connection since it consists almost entirely of pure glucose and fructose.

Many athletes eat honey before meetings and games, and between events, in order to restore the energy they have-used up swiftly. And doctors prescribe honey for old people and children who need to build up their strength quickly.

In addition to its simple sugars, honey contains a number of enzymes and other substances needed by the cells, tissues, and organs.

The enzymes at the command of the living organism are more subtle than the common reagents available to chemists.

Hydrolysis of starch, for example, can be induced by heating it with water to 170° C in sealed tubes or in an autoclave; the same result can be obtained at a lower temperature if hydrochloric acid is added to the starch, and an even better result is obtained if ptyalin, an enzyme in saliva, is added.

Fat can be converted into soap by boiling it with an alkali at 100° C; in the body saponification is effected by lipase at body temperature. 'Without enzymes the organism would die of exhaustion, even if it had an abundant supply of food,' Prof. V.N.Bukin wrote, 'for this food could not be assimilated. Without enzymes the organism would suffocate in an atmosphere of pure oxygen, just as if it were in an airless space.

To illustrate the efficiency of minute doses of enzymes let us recall peroxidase, an enzyme obtained by Academician A.Bach from horseradish, which is active in concentrations as low as one in two hundred million.

Honey has been found to contain the following enzymes: diastase, invertase, saccharase, catalase, peroxidase, and lipase. Its enzymatic content is one of the highest of all foods. Diastase (or amylase) converts starch and dextrin into sugar; saccharase converts beet and

Table 3.1.

Elements	*Human blood (after Palladin)*	*Honey (after sherman)*
Magnesium	0.018	0.018
Sulphur	0.004	0.001
Phosphorus	0.005	0.019
Iron	Traces	0.0007
Calcium	0.011	0.004
Chlorine	0.360	0.029
Potassium	0.030	0.386
Iodine	Traces	Traces
Sodium	0.320	0.001

cane sugar into glucose and fructose; and catalase decomposes peroxides.

Some authors, among others the German writer Enoch Zander, attribute the excellent properties of honey to the enzymes it contains. Enzymes, gander said, turned the lifeless matter brought into the hive by the summer bees into a .living substance that then went on working, maturing, and dying outside the body of the bee.

Dr. Anna Maurizio, working in the apiculture department of a Swiss experimental station, also believed that the enzymatic processes did not cease after the bees had sealed honey in the comb but continued during its storage.

Honey that had been collected by bees in 1895 was found in an old house in Switzerland. It was approximately sixty years old when it was analysed. The chromatogram gave the results expected: obvious spots of fructose and glucose and traces of unhydrolysed sugar and typical spots of the maltose and oligosaccharide groups.

Other constituents of honey are salts of calcium, sodium, potassium, magnesium, iron, chlorine, phosphorus, sulphur, and iodine. Some varieties even contain radium. The percentage of certain salts is about that in human blood serum.

Spectrum analysis of buckwheat honey and polyfloral honey in E.S.Przhevalsky's laboratory at Moscow University showed that they contained salts of aluminium, boron, chromium, copper, lead, lithium, manganese, nickel, osmium, silicon, tin, titanium, and zinc.

The importance of mineral salts for the human organism is very great. Experiments have shown that test animals die when they are systematically given food lacking in mineral salts, even though it is rich in proteins, carbohydrates, fats, and vitamins.

It has been remarked that microelements and mineral substances found in infinitesimal concentrations in the organism have a most important biological role, since their interaction with a number of enzymes, vitamins, and hormones affects the irritability of the nervous system, tissue respiration, circulation, and so on.

As metabolism changes with age, the amounts of such biologically important micro-elements as cobalt, copper, manganese, nickel, zinc, etc., in the blood and organs vary. Their intake in food, particularly in honey, is therefore specially important.

In addition, honey contains certain organic acids. As Enoch Zander wrote, much nonsense used to be talked about the nature of the acids in honey. It was commonly held that its acid content depended on the presence of formic acid, which the bees in jetted into it in order to preserve it, before sealing the comb.

Honey primarily contains organic acids, above all malic, citric, tartaric, and oxalic acids. It also contains vitamins, proteins, acetyl-choline, hormones, antibiotics, phytoncides, and other nutritious substances.

Prof. V.P.Filatov, the eye specialist, thought that honey contained biogenic stimulators, i.e. substances that heighten the activity of the organism. Experiments at the Botanical Gardens of Lvov University have established that honey contains substances, bioses, affecting growth. Cuttings from trees planted after treatment in an aqueous solution of honey rooted quickly and grew well.

The nutritive properties of honey have been extolled for centuries purely from an empirical point of view, but in the last twenty or thirty years they have been confirmed by science.

Honey has a high calorific value, one kilogram containing 3150-3350 calories (depending on its water content). By way of comparison a litre of whole cow's milk yields 620 calories, a litre of skimmed milk 310 calories; a kilogram of rye bread 2040 calories, a kilogram of fresh edible mushrooms 270 calories, a kilogram of White Sea navaga fish 620 calories, a kilogram of lean veal 740 calories, a kilogram of dried Caspian roach 850 calories, a kilogram of apples 400 calories, a kilogram of oranges 230 calories, a kilogram of cucumbers 140 calories.

But we do not only need food as a source of energy; when vitamins, enzymes, and other substances, for instance, are burnt up in the organism, they produce no calories at all, but they are nevertheless basic elements in the diet, without which the organism cannot survive.

Honey used to be compared to sugar. Sugar consists solely of carbohydrates that provide the organism with 'empty' calories, while honey contains more than eighty different substances needed for normal development and functioning.

Vitamins are not only essential food elements in the diet; many of them are used as medicaments. Vitamins have conquered such terrible diseases as beriberi, hemeralopia, pellagra, rickets, and scurvy.

The famous biochemist Prof. A.Bach, Member of the USSR Academy of Sciences, wrote that 'vitamins, which were only recently considered dietetic factors of secondary importance, producing a very limited specific effect, have acquired tremendous biological significance.

It would be hard to find a department of physiology or biochemistry that does not deal with the science of vitamins. Metabolism in living organisms, the activity of the sense organs, the functioning of the nervous system, enzymatic processes, the phenomena of growth and reproduction-all these different and basic domains of biology are very closely connected with vitamins.'

And Prof. A.Oparin, world authority on the origin of life, considers vitaminology the cornerstone of modern dietetics. Without thorough knowledge of vitamins, there can be no understanding of the fundamentals of modern biochemistry and physiology.

Honey contains vitamins B_1, B_2, B_8, B_6, B_6, B., C, E, K, and carotin. A kilogram of honey contains the following amounts: vitamin B_2 (riboflavin) up to 1.5 milligrams; vitamin B_1 (aneurine) up to 0.1 milligram; vitamin B_s (pantothenic acid) up to 2 milligrams; vitamin B_6 or PP (nicotinic acid) up to 1 milligram; vitamin B_e (pyridoxine) up to 5 milligrams; vitamin C (ascorbic acid) as much as 30 to 54 milligrams.

Although the amounts listed here are small, these vitamins are combined in honey with other substances also highly important to the organism. (carbohydrates, mineral salts, micro-elements, organic acids, enzymes, etc.).

The vitamin content of honey depends on the pollen admixture in it. Extraction of pollen by filtration also removes the vitamins. Thus honey is not just a delicious product of nature but a complete arsenal of powerful remedies. As a dietetic food it can be taken with other medicines and during other treatment.

Yet despite its obvious advantages over many other foods (sugar, jam, etc.), it is still not used as much as it should be in hospitals, sanatoria, and convalescent homes.

The ancient Egyptians and Greeks, we know, used honey to

Table 3.2: Results of Seeding of Honey No. 13 (*haematogenic*).

	Results of daily bacteriological investigations							
Bacterial culture	***1st day***	***2nd day***	***3rd day***	***4th day***	***5th day***	***6th day***	***7th day***	***8th day***
Streptococci	+	+	+	—	—	—	—	—
Staphylococci	+	+	+	—	—	—	—	—
Typhoid bacillus	+	+	—	—	—	—	—	—
Coliform bacterium	+	+	—	—	—	—	—	—
Paratyphoid bacterium A	+	+	—	—	—	—	—	—
Paratyphoid bacterium B	+	+	+	—	—	—	—	—
Breslau bacterium	+	+	—	—	—	—	—	—
Gartner bacillus	+	+	—	—	—	—	—	—
Shiga bacillus	+	+	—	—	—	—	—	—
Schmitz bacillus	+	+	—	—	—	—	—	—

embalm the dead. Abd al-Latif, a twelfth century Arab physician and traveller, found a sealed vessel in one of the pyramids at Gizeh containing the corpse of an infant, well preserved in honey.

The body of Alexander the Great, who died in the Middle East during one of his campaigns, we are told, was immersed in a vessel of honey and taken back to Macedonia for burial. The preservative properties of honey were known in Biblical times.

In the first century A. D., it is reported, the bodies of honoured Jews were embalmed by placing them in honey for a long period. The ancient Greeks and Romans also used honey to preserve meat, which kept well in it and retained its natural flavour.

Modern experiments have shown that honey inhibits bacterial growth and kills bacteria, as Giindel and Blattner[1]) found with white mice infected with haemolytic streptococci. Gonzenbach and Hoffmann[2]) infected guinea pigs through lesions on the skin and then applied honey to the wounds; the animals treated with honey outlived the controls.

Some authors (Konig) think these properties of honey are due

Table 3.3: Results of Seeding of Honey No. 37 (cocoa-milk-egg-and-vitamin).

Bacterial culture	*Results of daily bacteriological investigations*							
	1st day	*2nd day*	*3rd day*	*4th day*	*5th day*	*6th day*	*7th day*	*8th day*
Streptococci	+	+	+	—	—	—	—	—
Staphylococci	+	+	+	—	—	—	—	—
Typhoid bacterium	+	+	—	—	—	—	—	—
Coliform bacterium	+	+	—	—	—	—	—	—
Paratyphoid bacterium A	+	+	—	—	—	—	—	—
Paratyphoid bacterium B	+	+	+	—	—	—	—	—
Breslau bacterium	+	+	—	—	—	—	—	—
Gartner bacillus	+	+	—	—	—	—	—	—
Shiga bacillus	+	+	—	—	—	—	—	—
Schmitz bacillus	+	+	—	—	—	—	—	—

Table 3.4: Results of Seeding of Control Honey. (*natural Far-Eastern linden honey harvested in 1939*)

Bacterial culture	*Results of daily bacteriological investigations*							
	1st day	*2nd day*	*3rd day*	*4th day*	*5th day*	*6th day*	*7th day*	*8th day*
Streptococci	+	+	+	+	—	—	—	—
Staphylococci	+	+	+	+	—	—	—	—
Typhoid bacterium	+	+	+	—	—	—	—	—
Coliform bacterium	+	+	+	—	—	—	—	—
Paratyphoid bacterium A	+	+	+	—	—	—	—	—
Paratyphoid bacterium B	+	+	+	+	—	—	—	—
Breslau bacterium	+	+	+	—	—	—	—	—
Gartner bacillus	+	+	+	—	—	—	—	—
Shiga bacillus	+	+	+	—	—	—	—	—
Shmitz bacillus	+	+	+	—	—	—	—	—

to its high sugar content; others (Hauduschka, Kaufman) ascribe them to the organic acids in honey, and others still (Giindel and Blattner, Helfman) to the combined effect of the enzymes and sugar.

The discovery of photolabile and thermolabile antibiotics or inhibitors in honey, reported by Dold *et al.s*), is of great interest. Milan Prica considers the antibiotic substances in honey to be the product of the secretory activity of worker bees 4) Experiments carried out by the present writer with Prof. M.Neshchadimenko and A.P. Moroz at the Kiev Medical Institute showed that new honeys obtained by the 'express method' had stronger disinfecting properties than either natural or artificial honeys.')

Ten types of honey out of 63 obtained were investigated. Of these, special mention should be made of No. 2 (a vitamin honey), No. 13 (a haematogen honey), No. 17 (a mammin-vitamin honey), and No. 37 (a cocoa-milk-egg-and-vitamin honey). As can be seen from their descriptions these honeys contained substances which in normal conditions are perfect media for bacterial growth (milk, white of egg, animal blood, etc.).

Experiments were carried out with streptococci, staphylococci, typhoid bacilli, paratyphoid A and B, and Breslau, Gartner, Shiga, and Schmitz bacilli. A 24-hour culture was washed in a millilitre of saline solution, and two drops of the emulsion added to three millilitres of honey. Control samples were taken in equal amounts.

The bacterial emulsion was evenly mixed, with honey and kept in an autoclave at 37° C. Samples were seeded on agar plates and serum-agar plates and broth each day for eight days. The cultures obtained (a total of 2080) were observed for bacterial growth.

The experiments were repeated twice with the same results. The bacteria concerned grew after incubation in media with a high sugar content (40 per cent glucose and 30 per cent laevulose), with 0.02 per cent formic acid, and in saline solution.

As for the new kinds of honey and ordinary linden honey (used as a control), both exhibited high bactericidal properties, the linden honey being less effective than the new types.

Data for honeys 13 and 37 and for linden honey are given in Tables elsewhere in this chapter. The experiments, and the 85 new honeys we obtained by express methods, indicate that the antibiotic properties of honey arc undoubtedly the result of the secretory activity of worker bees.

THE ANTIMYCOTIC PROPERTIES OF HONEY

The air around us contains vast a number of mould spores. In favourable conditions, i.e. when temperature and humidity are right, these spores germinate in the presence of food. The developing mycelia penetrate several millimetres into the food.

As a result, foodstuffs like flour, macaroni, sugar, jams and preserves of all kinds, unglazed sweets, fruit, and beverages acquire an unpleasant odour and flavour, and alter in appearance. Bearing in mind the enormous wastage caused by moulds, we investigated honey, which we found to possess antimycotic properties.

The remarkable thing about the honey found in the pyramid at Gizeh was that after more than 3300 years it retained the characteristic aroma of honey. Experienced beekeepers have long said that honey, unlike other foodstuffs, does not go mouldly if stored properly.

F. Kaganova-Ioyrish, working in the Mycology Laboratory of the Kiev Dietetic Research Institute, investigated the antimycotic properties of honey for us, using two natural honeys (a 1939 linden honey from the Far East and a 1940 buckwheat honey from the Ukraine) and 20 samples of honey we had obtained by the 'express' method.

All samples were infected with ten varieties of mould isolated from food. Despite the fact that honey contains all the protein, carbohydrate, and substances necessary to sustain living cells (vitamins, minerals, etc.), the moulds not only did not proliferate in it, but perished (in our opinion because honey contains substances with antimycotic as well as antibacterial properties).

NATURAL HONEYS

Every bee's honey is sweet, says the Proverb. The majority of natural honeys have a wonderful flavour. The commonest types are the following.

Abkhazian honey (see rock honey).

Acacia (*or black locust*) honey is one of the best kinds. When runny it is transparent; when crystallized it beeomes white and fine grained, resembling snow. Acacia honey contains 35.98 per cent glucose and 40.35 per cent laevulose or fruit sugar.')

From the nectar collected from the fragrant flowers of a hectare of the false acacia or locust tree (*Robinia pseudoacacia L.*) bees make 1700 kilograms of honey.

Bees also make honey from the nectar of the yellow acacia (*Caragana arborescens* Lam.). It is very light in colour; when crystallized it becomes waxy, white, and medium grained. Yellow acacia honey is one of the best sorts. Bees gather 350 kilograms from a hectare of the flowering trees.

Alfalfa honey (see lucerne honey).

Angelica honey is gathered from the flowers of garden angelica (*Archangelica officinalis* Hoffm). It has a pleasant aroma and flavour.

Apple honey is pale yellow with an exceptionally pleasant aroma and a delicate sweetness. It contains 31.67 per cent glucose and 42 per cent laevulose. It is collected from apple blossom. A hectare of blossoming apple trees (*Pyrus malus L.*) yields 20 kilograms of honey.

Balm honey (see melissa honey).

Barberry honey is golden yellow with a pleasant aroma and a delicate sweet taste. Bees readily forage blossoming barberry bushes (*Berberis vulgaris L.*), which grow about three metres high.

Barberry is extensively cultivated in the Soviet Union because of the haemostatic qualities of the fruit. Its curative properties were known to the ancient Babylonians and Indians. In the library of Assurbani-pal there were 2600 year-old clay tablets with inscriptions indicating that barberry could 'cleanse the blood'.

In Russia, at the end of the last century, the selectionist Ivan Michurin interested himself in the barberry and in 1893 evolved a seedless variety.

Bilberry or *whortleberry* honey is reddish with an excellent aroma and pleasant flavour. It is produced from the nectar of the low bilberry undershrub (*Vaccinium myrtillus L.*), a very good nectariferous plant that can yield 2.5 kilograms of honey a day.

Bitter orange honey is one of the best kinds and has an exquisite aroma similar to that of citrus blossom, and an excellent flavour. It is gathered from the bitter orange tree (*Citrus aurantium*).

E.R.Root reported in 1938 that Alin Caillas, the French chemist, had established that bitter orange honey from Spain had a high content of calcium phosphate and phosphate of iron, and that he considered it should be given special attention from the aspect of its medicinal value.

Blackberry honey (see dewberry honey).

Black locust honey (see acacia honey).

Blueweed or *bugloss* honey is a first-class kind, light amber in colour, with a pleasant aroma and a very good flavour. It is very viscous and crystallizes slowly.

Bees collect it from the pink and bright blue flowers of the blueweed or viper's bugloss (*Echium vulgare L.*), *a* member of the Borage family. Viper's bugloss is a valuable honey plant yielding 300 to 400 kilograms per hectare.

Borage honey comes from the nectar of the beautiful big blue flowers of borage (*Borago officinalis L.*), which is cultivated as a valuable nectariferous and medicinal plant. A hectare yields 200 kilograms of this excellent honey.

Bramble honey (see dewberry honey).

Buckwheat honey is dark, ranging from dark yellow with a reddish tinge to dark brown, and is very like honeydew honey in appearance. In contrast to other honeys it has a distinctive aroma and specific flavour. Some tasters say it 'tickles the throat'.

When crystallized buckwheat honey becomes a pulpy mass. Buckwheat honey contains 36.75 per cent glucose and 40.29 per cent laevulose. Its protein and iron content is higher than that of light honeys and for that reason it is recommended in treating anaemia. There is a folk saying that 'dark honey is good for pale faces'.

This honey is made from the nectar of buckwheat (*Fagopyrum esculentum*) which is widely grown in orchards and as a field crop. A hectare yields up to 60 kilograms of honey.

Bugloss honey (see blueweed honey).

Burdock honey has a dark olive colour and a sharp, spicy aroma. It is extremely viscous. It is collected from the small dark-pink flowers of the hairy burdock (*Lap pa tamentosa* Lam.) and the greater burdock (*Arctium lappa major* Gaertn.). A hectare of burdock would yield an average of 600 kilograms of this delicious honey.

Carrot honey is dark yellow, with a pleasant aroma. It is made from the nectar of the fragrant white umbelliferous flowers of the wild and cultivated carrot (*Daucus carota L.*).

Chestnut honey is dark, has a faint aroma and an unpleasant flavour. It is produced from the flowers of the sweet chestnut (*Castanea sativa L.*).

Bees also produce honey from the nectar of the white or pink flowers of the ornamental horse chestnut (*Aesculus hippocastanum L.*). Unlike sweet chestnut honey, horse chestnut honey is colourless and runny. It crystallizes easily and is sometimes bitter. Chestnut honey is considered an inferior sort.

Clover honey is considered one of the best. It is colourless and clear and has a fine flavour. When crystallized it becomes a solid white mass. Clover honey contains 34.96 per cent glucose and 40.24 per cent laevulose. One hectare of white clover (*Tri folium repens L.*) yields 100 kilograms of honey.

Coriander honey has a pungent aroma and a specific flavour. It is collected from the white or pinkish flowers of the umbelliferous *Coriandrum sati vum L.* A hectare in bloom yields 500 kilograms of honey.

Cornflower honey is greenish yellow in colour and has a pleasant aroma reminiscent of that of almonds and a distinctive, slightly bitter smack. The cornflower or bluebottle (*Centaurea cyanus L.*) is an excellent nectariferous plant.

Cotton honey is light with a specific aroma and a delicate flavour. It usually crystallizes rapidly into fine grains and turns white. Cotton honey contains 36.19 per cent glucose and 39.42 per cent fructose.

The flavour of honey collected from the leaf (extra-floral) nectaries of the cotton plant (*Gossypium L.*) in no way differs from that collected from the flowers.

A hectare of cotton in bloom yields between 100 and 300 kilograms of honey. Cross-pollination increases the yield of cotton by 40 to 56 per cent.

Dandelion honey is golden yellow, very thick, and viscous. It crystallizes rapidly and has a strong smell and sharp flavour. It is made from the nectar of the common dandelion (*Taraxacum of ficinale* L.) which grows everywhere in great profusion. Dandelion honey contains 35.65 per cent glucose and 41.50 per cent laevulose.

Dewberry honey comes from the nectar of the flowers of the dewberry (*Rubus caesius L.*). It is clear as water and has a pleasant flavour. Bees make 20 kilograms of honey from a hectare of dewberry in bloom. A related honey is bramble or blackberry (from R. *fructiosus*).

Dragon's head honey is gathered from the bluish purple flowers of the annual essential-oil ' plant *Dracocephalum moldavicum L.*, which grows wild in the USSR in the Caucasus, Altai, Crimea, and other areas. It is light and clear and has a pleasant aroma and taste.

Dragon's head is a valuable nectariferous plant because its flowers contain large quantities of nectar with a high sugar content and a faint lemonish fragrance.

A hectare yields as much as 290 kilograms of honey.

Eucalyptus honey has an unpleasant flavour but is highly valued in folk medicine for treating tuberculosis of the lungs. It comes from the large, solitary, multi-stamened blossoms of the evergreen eucalyptus or blue gum (*Eucalyptus globulus* Labill.), which is cultivated mainly in the subtropics.

The data in the literature on its curative properties are contradictory. Some authors (L.Gdansky) are enthusiastic about it, while others (N.Ilyin) consider it overestimated. Seeing that eucalyptus oil and other eucalyptus pharmacological substances are extracted from the leaves of the tree rather than the blossoms, we may assume that the therapeutic value of eucalyptus honey has been greatly overrated.

Heather honey is made from the nectar of the delicate purplish flowers of the evergreen, branching shrubs of the common heather [*Calluna vulgaris* (*L.*) Salisb.]. It may be dark, dark yellow, or reddish brown, has a faint aroma and a pleasant or astringent, slightly bitter flavour. Heather honey is very viscous and takes a long time to crystallize. Bees make 200 kilograms of honey from a hectare of heather.

Hemp-mallow honey when freshly extracted is dull yellowish in colour. It has an extremely unpleasant flavour. A hectare of hemp-mallow (*Hibiscus cannabinus L.*) yields 40 kilograms of honey.

Honey-dew honey is not produced from floral nectar but mainly from the sweet sticky exudate of plant bugs like green fly or plant lice (Aphididae), scale insects (Coccidae), and leafhoppers (Psyllidae).

These insects feed on plant sap; their excretion is found on the stems and foliage of plants and trees and used to be thought of similar origin to dew. It was known in antiquity; Pliny thought it fell from the stars, a belief that was held for centuries.

Chemical analysis has shown that honey-dew differs greatly from nectar; whereas floral nectar consists almost entirely of sugars, honey-dew is about 70 per cent nitrogenous substances and dextrin. Bees forage energetically for it and make honey from it.

Honey-dew honey is usually dark and viscous; it has a faint aroma and frequently an unpleasant flavour. Experiment has shown that it possesses weak bactericidal properties compared with floral honey. If left in the hive as winter food honey-dew honey kills the bees.

Honey-dew honey is used in the food industry (mainly in the confectionery and fermentation industries). Research has established that honey-dew undoubtedly deserves careful study. The Czech researcher O.Gargasim established by chromatography that honey-dew contained raffinose, maltose, melzitose, saccharose, glucose, fructose, and seven undetermined sugars.

It is rich in amino acids, the following free amino acids having been noted in it: alanine, arginine, aspartic acid, cystine, glutamic acid, glycine, histidine, leucine, lysine, methionine, proline, serine, threonine, tryptophan, tyrosine, and valine.

Information on the biochemical composition and results of microscopic investigation of honey-dew and honey-dew honey is given in the beautifully illustrated book by Werner Kloft, Anna Maurizio, and Walter Keser *Das Waldhonigbuch* (The Forest Honey Book).

Several methods have been proposed for detecting whether natural honey contains honey-dew. The simplest employs a spirit reaction. Six parts of 96 per cent rectified alcohol are added to a 1 : 1 solution of the honey and distilled water; cloudiness indicates the piesence of honeydew.

Horehound honey is light in colour with a delicious aroma and flavour. Bees collect it from. the greyish white flowers of the perennial white horehound (*Marrubium vulgare L.*), which they forage readily as the nectar is fragrant and has a high sugar content. A hectare of this plant will yield 50 kilograms of excellent honey.

Hovenia honey resembles linden honey but is darker. It has a strong aroma and a very agreeable flavour. Bees collect it from the flowers of the subtropical hovenia tree (*Hovenia dulcis* Thubg.) which is cultivated for its fruit and beauty.

Hyssop honey is highly regarded for its organoleptic qualities. It is produced from the nectar of the dark-blue flowers of the medicinal shrub-like plant *Hyssopus of ficinalis L.* (which grows wild in the Ukraine, Central Asia, the Crimea, Caucasus and Altai, and other areas). Hyssop is cultivated as an essential-oil plant and a valuable nectariferous growth for bee-gardens.

Lavendar honey is a first-class sort, golden in colour, with a delicate aroma. Bees produce it from the nectar of the pale blue or bluish purple flowers of the perennial essential-oil shrub (*Lavandula vera DC*).

Linden or lime honey is one of the best kinds and is highly valued for its exceptional flavour. When freshly extracted it is very fragrant, clear, and yellowish or pale green in colour. It contains 36.05 per cent glucose and 39.27 per cent fructose.

Ufa (or Bashkir) linden honey is colourless and becomes a - white, coarse-grained mass with a golden tinge when crystallized. Amur (or Far Eastern) linden honey is dull yellow. All linden honeys have a specific and delicious flavour, in spite of a faint smack of bitterness (which, however, quickly disappears).

Linden honey is widely used in folk medicine as a remedy against colds (mainly as a diaphoretic). It is produced from the nectar of the greenish yellow blossoms of the lime or linden tree (*Tilia*), the fine nectariferous qualities of which have earned it the soubriquet of queen of honey plants. Its reputation is deserved for bees can make as much as 16 kilograms of honey from one tree; a hectare of limes will yield over 1000 kilograms of honey.

Lucerne or *alfalfa* honey is collected from the lilac or purple flowers of lucerne (alfalfa) (*Medicago sativa L.*). Newly extracted it varies in shade from colourless to amber. Lucerne honey crystallizes quickly and forms a white mass similar to condensed milk.

The honey has a pleasant aroma and a specific flavour. It contains 36.85 per cent glucose and 40.24 per cent laevulose. A hectare of irrigated Lucerne yields 380 kilograms of honey.

Maple or sycamore honey is light with an excellent flavour. Bees forage energetically for nectar from the yellowish green blossoms of the ornamental Norway maple (*Acer. platanoides L.*), the common maple (*A. campestre L.*), and the sycamore (*A. pseudoplatanus*).

The Norway maple yields 200 kilograms of honey per hectare and the common maple up to 1100 kilograms. (Maple honey is not to be confused with the maple honey of North America, which is the uncrystallized part of the sap of *A. saccharium*, the sugar maple.)

Meadow honey is golden yellow or yellowish brown with a fine aroma and flavour. It is produced from the nectar of various meadow flowers.

Melilot (peaflower) honey is a superb type, famous for its fine flavour. It is light amber to white in colour and has a very delicate, pleasant aroma reminiscent of vanilla. Bees make it from the bright yellow flowers of the common melilot (*Melilotus of ficinalis* Desr.).

It contains 36.79 per cent glucose and 39.59 per cent laevulose. The flowers and leaves of melilot (Herba Meliloti) are used medicinally and for making melilot or green plaster. Bees make 200 kilograms of the honey from a hectare of wild melilot and 600 kilograms from a hectare of the cultivated variety.

Melissa or *balm* honey has an excellent flavour. It is produced from the nectar of the fragrant flowers of balm (*Melissa officinalis L.*), which is a widely cultivated herb, grown in the Caucasus, the Crimea, and the Ukraine in the USSR as a medicinal and essential-oil crop. A hectare yields 150 kilograms of honey.

Mignonette honey is a top class variety and is rivalled only by linden honey for its exceptional aroma and pleasant flavour. It is gathered from the flowers of mignonette (*Reseda odorata L.*), which yield a nectar as clear as crystal and a beautiful reddish orange pollen. Mignonette has a yield of 200 kilograms of honey per hectare.

Milkweed honey is produced from the fragrant nectar of the extremely valuable nectariferous plants (*Asclepias syriaca L.* and *A. cornuti* Desc). It has been estimated that a hectare of milkweed yields an average of 600 kilograms of honey.

The honey is light with a yellowish tinge, has a fine aroma and excellent flavour. In hot dry weather it becomes so condensed in the comb that it can hardly be extracted even when heated.

Motherwort honey has a pale golden colour not unlike that of straw, a faint aroma, and a specific, good flavour. It is made from the nectar of the pale violet flowers of motherwort (*Leonurus cardiaca L.*), which grows on waste ground, rubbish dumps, etc. Each plant has more than 2500 flowers in thick clusters, which yield much nectar with a high sugar content. Motherwort, a former medicinal herb, is a valuable nectariferous plant on which bees readily forage in all weathers.

Mountain ash honey (see rowan honey).

Mustard honey is golden yellow, taking on a yellowish cream shade when crystallized. The nectar for it comes from the large yellow flowers of white mustard (*Sinapis alba L.*). Bees make 40 kilograms of honey from one hectare of mustard.

Peafower honey (see melilot honey).

Peppermint honey is produced from the nectar of the aromatic flowers of the perennial essential-oil *plant*(*Mentha piperita* L.),which is widely cultivated and is an abundant source of nectar. The honey is amber-coloured and has a pleasant aroma of peppermint.

Phacelia honey is light green or white and has a delicate aroma and fine pleasant flavour. It crystallizes into a pasty mass. This honey is considered one of the top sorts and is in great demand.

It is produced from the nectar of the blue blossoms of *Phacelia tanacetifolia* Benth., which is one of the most valuable and important honey plants. A hectare in blossom can yield 500 (and in southern latitudes even 1000) kilograms of honey.

Pumpkin or *squash* honey is a golden yellow with an agreeable flavour. It crystallizes quite quickly. A hectare of pumpkin (*Cucurbita pepo L.*) or squash (C. *malopepo*) yields 30 kilograms of honey. *Rape honey* is white, sometimes yellow.

It has an agreeable aroma but is unpleasantly sweet. It is very thick, crystallizes easily, dissolves poorly in water, and quickly ferments when stored too long. Bees make it from the nectar of the yellow blooms of that remarkable essential-oil plant, the rape (*Brassica napus* var. *oleifora* Metzg.).

Instances have been reported of a bee colony making as much as eight kilograms of rape honey in a day. A Hectare of rape yields 50 kilograms of honey.

Raspberry honey is white, with a very pleasant aroma and a delicious flavour. The comb honey is so tasty that it seems to melt in the mouth. Raspberry honey comes from the blossoms of the raspberry (*Rubus idaeus L.*).

When the canes are in bloom bees will pass over other nectariferous plants to forage on them; since the flower hangs down the bee working it is protected by a kind of 'umbrella' and can go on collecting nectar even in the rain. Forest raspberries yield 70 kilograms of honey per hectare and garden raspberries 50 kilograms. Raspberry honey contains 33.57 per cent glucose and 41.34 per cent laevulose.

Rhododendron honey has an unpleasant flavour and causes poisoning (general weakness, headache, vomiting, loss of consciousness, etc.). There is evidence that the poisoning is due to the presence of the alkaloid andromedotoxin. Rhododendron honey comes from the blossoms of the evergreen rhododendron shrub (*Rhododendron pon.ticum L.*).

Rock honey is a rare and distinctive type gathered by wild bees and deposited by them in crevices in rocks. It is pale yellow and has a pleasant aroma and flavour. The honeycomb contains little wax and forms a solid crystallized mass.

Pieces must be broken off in order to eat it. Unlike ordinary honey, rock honey is not sticky and does not require special packaging. It can be stored for years without losing its properties.

Because it comes from Abkhazia in the Caucasus rock honey is sometimes called Abkhazian. In Bashkiria a rock honey used sometimes to be produced from crystallized linden honey, the moisture being evaporated in special kilns so that the honey became rock hard. Its food value, naturally, suffered as it lost many of its most valuable substances (enzymes, vitamins, etc.).

Rosebay honey (see willow-herb honey).

Rowan honey is reddish in colour and has a strong aroma and a pleasant flavour. Bees produce it from the nectar of the blossom of the rowan or mountain ash (*Sorbus aucuparia L.*), which yields 40 kilograms of honey per hectare.

Sage honey is light amber or dark golden in colour with a delicate aroma and pleasant flavour. Bees collect it from the bluish purple flowers of the perennial shrub garden sage (*Salvia of ficinalis L.*), which is widely cultivated. Sage in bloom yields 650 kilograms of honey per hectare.

Sainfoin honey is golden yellow, very aromatic, and has a pleasant flavour. It is produced from the pink and red blooms of the perennial fodder grass sainfoin (*Onobrychis sativa* Lam. and 0. *vicii folia* Scop.). A hectare of sainfoin yields between 100 and 600 kilograms of fine honey.

Sallow honey (see willow honey).

Salt-tree honey is light-coloured, with a yellow tinge. It crystallizes fairly easily. It is produced from the nectar of the large pink blossoms of a small prickly tree -(*Halimodendron halodendron* Pall. Voss.) that grows in Kazakhstan. Salt-trees in bloom yield over 190 kilograms of honey per hectare.

Squash honey (see pumpkin honey).

Sowthistle honey is a first-class honey, white in colour, with a pleasant aroma and flavour. It' is made from nectar from the numerous purplish red flowers of the weed sowthistle (*Sonchus oleraceus Scop.*).

Sunflower honey is golden yellow but turns a light amber, sometimes with a greenish tinge, when it crystallizes. It has a faint aroma and a pleasant, rather astringent flavour.

It is produced from the golden yellow flowers of the sunflower (*Helianthus annuus L.*), a staple oil-seed crop. Sunflower heads are made up of around 1500 flowers. In foraging on them bees cross-pollinate the flowers, thereby greatly increasing their fertility. It has been estimated that the crop yield is nearly doubled when bees actively work sunflowers. A hectare yields 50 kilograms of honey.

Sycamore honey (see maple honey).

Thistle honey is a first-class sort, colourless or greenish or golden (light amber), with a pleasant aroma and flavour. When crystallized it becomes fine grained. Bees actively forage nectar from the beautiful raspberry flowers of the musk thistle (*Carduus nutans L.*) with its prickly stem and greyish leaves.

Tobacco honey varies in colour from light to dark, has an unpleasant aroma and a bitter flavour. Its poor organoleptic properties make it unsuitable for human consumption. It is used, however, for curing high-grade aromatic types of tobacco.

It can safely be used as a winter food for bees. The honey is produced from the nectar of the flowers of the tobacco plant (*Nicotiana tabacum L.*). Tulip-tree honey is reddish and has a pleasant aroma and flavour. Bees collect it from the greenish-red flowers of the beautiful ornamental tulip-tree (*Liriodendron tulipifera L.*), which is a good honey plant as its blossoms secrete more nectar than any other subtropical nectariferous plant.

One tree yields a kilogram of honey. Vetch honey is made in the USSR from the nectar of the thin-leafed vetch (*Vicia tenui folia* Roth.), which grows in Siberia and the steppe region. It is clear and has a delicate aroma and flavour. It is on record that a Siberian bee colony makes as much as five kilograms of vetch honey a day.

Wild parsnip honey is light and has a fine flavour. It is made from the nectar of the yellow flowers of the biennial wild parsnip (*Pastinaca sativa L.*). (In Bashkiria wild parsnip is second only to the linden as a honey plant.)

Willow or sallow honey is golden yellow, becoming a fine-grained creamy mass when crystallized. It has a good flavour. Bees readily forage nectar from the various shrubs and trees of the willow family (*Salix*) of which there are around 170 species.

Some species of willow secrete an abundance of nectar, and a bee colony can sometimes produce as much as three or four kilograms of honey a day; a hectare yields 150 kilograms.

Willow-herb or *rosebay* honey is transparent, with a greenish tinge, and crystallizes into white grains like snow, or into a creamy or suet-like mass. When heated willowherb honey turns yellow. It has a delicate aroma and a pleasant flavour.

It is made from the nectar of the showy pinkish purple flowers of the rosebay or willow-herb (fireweed) (*Epilobium* or *Chaemaenaerion angustifolium L.*). A hectare will yield 600 kilograms of honey.

Wintercress honey is greenish yellow, has a faint aroma and a good flavour, but is unsuitable for long storage. It is produced from the nectar of the golden yellow flowers of the wintercress (*Barbarea vulgaris R.Br.*), which grows on river banks, around lakes, in swamps and flooded meadows, etc.

A hectare of wintercress will yield 40 kilograms of honey.

POISONOUS OR 'HEADY' HONEY

Poisonous (toxic) or 'heady' honey was well known in antiquity, and was mentioned by Xenophon, Strabo, and Pliny. In his *Anabis or Expedition of Cyrus*, Xenophon described in detail how the Greek army was delayed in Colchis (i.e. present-day Soviet Georgia) on account of honey.

Having passed the summit, the Greeks encamped in a number of villages containing abundance of provisions. As to other things there, there was nothing at which they were surprised; but the number of beehives was extraordinary and all the soldiers that ate of the combs lost their senses, vomited, and were affected with purging, and none of them were able to stand upright; such as had eaten only a little were like men intoxicated, and such as had eaten much were like mad-men, and some like persons at the point of death.

They lay upon the ground, in consequence, in great numbers, as if there had been a defeat; and there was general dejection. The next day no one of them was found dead; and they recovered their senses about the same hour that they had lost them on the preceding day; and on the third and fourth days they got up as if after having taken physic.

Pliny mentioned two sorts of honey with intoxicating qualities, one produced at Heraclea in Pontus, and the other among the Sanni or Macrones. 'The peculiarities of the honey arose from the herbs to which the bees resorted; the first came from the flower of a plant called aegolethron, or goat's-bane; the other from a species of rhododendron.")

Maxim Gorky described the 'heady honey' of the Caucasus in his short story *The Birth of a Man:* 'To the left, above the mountain peaks, hung smoky, heavy, rain-laden clouds; they cast shadows over the green slopes dotted with boxwood, "the dead tree".

Here in the hollows of old beeches and linden is found that "heady honey" the intoxicating sweetness of which nearly caused the downfall of the soldiers of Pompey the Great long ago, having overcome a whole legion of iron Romans. The bees make it from laurel and azalea blossoms, and tramps get it out of the hollows and eat it, spreading it on what the natives call *lavash, a* flat cake made of wheat flour. ...'s)

Beekeepers in various areas around Batumi (near the scene of the episode described by Xenophon) are often forced to use only the beeswax from their hives as the honey, when used in food, induces dizzy spells, intoxication, and vomiting.

In the United States poisonous honey was first mentioned by Burton in 1794; subsequently there were reports from New Jersey, Virginia, North Carolina, Florida, and other states. It was established that poisonous honey was made from the nectar of the broad-leaved mountain laurel (*Kalmia lati folie*), a member of the heath family (Ericaceae), yellow or Carolina jasmine or gelseminum (*Gel seminum sempervirens*), the soapberry (*Sapindus marginatus*), rhododendron (*Rhododendron*), and other plants.

Honey produced in the mountains of Central and Northern Japan often causes indisposition owing to the toxic effect of the nectar of a plant of the Heather family known locally as *hotsutsayi.*

Azalea, monk's hood (wolfbane), and andromeda honeys are also poisonous; but honey from such poisonous plants as foxglove, hemlock, henbane, and oleander can be safely eaten.

In thc Far East of the Soviet Union, according to Z.I.Gutnikova, bees produce poisonous honey by collecting the nectar of bog heather (*Chamaedaphne calyculata* Moench). This shrub forms a thick carpet over thousands of hectares, blooms for 20 to 30 days, and yields nearly three kilograms of honey per day per bee colony.

The honey is yellowish, rather bitter, and crystallizes easily. It produces a cold sweat, shivering, nausea, vomiting, and violent headache. It has been observed that 100 to 200 grams leads to loss of consciousness and delirium.

It is interesting, however, that though poisonous for man the honey does not affect bees, and colonies fed on it in summer or winter have suffered no ill effects.

In the Khabarovsk Territory, I. S. Molochny found, bees produce a 'heady honey' from the flowers of wild rosemary or marsh tea (*Ledum palustre L.*), a low shrub growing in swamps and peatbogs. Its white flowers have an intoxicating scent that attracts bees.

Molochny suggests a way of rendering 'heady honey' harmless by heating it for three hours at a temperature between 80° and 90° C, stirring continuously so that it does not boil. The prolonged heating breaks down the poisonous substances and makes the honey fit to eat, but destroys its organoleptic properties.

ID this connection K.Sharashidze has developed a method of heating 'heady honey' to a temperature of 46° C at a pressure of 67 mm Hg, which decomposes the poisonous substances without affecting the flavour of the honey.

Many examples could be cited to show that bees transfer toxic substances from the nectar of poisonous plants to the honey they produce from it. In 1951 Sharashidze carried out a series of interesting experiments at the Sanitation Research Institute of the Ministry of Health of the Georgian SSR and showed that the toxic properties of 'heady honey' were due to poisons in the nectar of azalea and rhododendrons.

Feeding doses of this honey to guineapigs he found that ten grams caused quivering of the jaws, vomiting, and convulsions, while 14 grams killed the animals. Controls fed ordinary honey remained healthy.

In another series of experiments guinea-pigs were given an alcohol and aqueous extract of azalea and rhododendron flowers (after the alcohol had been removed) and the nectar from these flowers.

They showed the same signs of poisoning as those fed 'heady honey'. The toxin in 'heady honey' is not stable and becomes less toxic when stored for a long time, even in ordinary conditions.

MULTIVITAMINIZED HONEY

Very small doses of vitamins (thousandths of a gram) not only protect the human organism against various diseases (avitaminoses) but also build up its resistance to infections and other harmful external influences.

It has been demonstrated experimentally that concentrated vitamin C extracted from rosehips and other plants is more effective than synthetic ascorbic acid, the reason being that the concentrate obtained from vegetable raw materials contains other biologically active substances (e.g. flavonoid, catechol, etc.) that are not in the synthetic product.

Clinical observations have shown, too, that synthetic vitamins are assimilated better when they are taken with natural foods. In this respect multivitaminized honey is particularly valuable.

Multivitaminized honeys are not types obtained by the express method described below but are mechanical mixtures of honey, calcium, and some of the following vitamins: A (axerophtol), B_1 (aneurin), B_2 (riboflavin), C (ascorbic acid), PP (nicotinic acid), and D (calciferol). Two types are marketed in the USSR-No. 1 for adults, and No. 11 for children.

The honeys are mixed in special electric mixers at the factories where honey is packed. Mixing distributes the vitamins and calcium evenly among the crystals of invert sugar and the other components of the honey. Honey can be enriched in this way because it is so hygroscopic (containing approximately 20 per cent water in which vitamins C, B_1, B_2, and PP readily dissolve).

The fat-soluble vitamins A and D form tiny balls that also become evenly distributed among the crystals of glucose and fructose (at microscopic analysis), giving it an even, uniform, light yellow colour.

Our experiments have shown that the viscosity of the honey prevents these minute balls of fatsoluble vitamins from blending fully into the mixture. Multivitaminized honey is a little more expensive than the ordinary kind, but considerably cheaper than honey and preparations of calcium and vitamins taken separately.

Preservation of Vitamins in Honey

When foodstuffs are stored the vitamins in them deteriorate and lose much of their potency. We decided to check, therefore, how well they were preserved in vitaminized honey. As a test we accordingly vitaminized honey with ascorbic acid (vitamin C) in the analytical chemistry laboratory of the AllUnion Vitamin Research Institute of the USSR Ministry of the Food Industry), and kept it under observation for six months.

Our findings were that ascorbic acid retained its activity better in linden honey than in buckwheat honey, and that linden honey was best in this respect. There was, however, another very interesting point.

After six months the honey retained approximately 50 per cent of its natural ascorbic acid and 60 to 90 per cent of that artificially added. This made us believe that it possesses stabilizing properties preventing oxidation of vitamin C.

In addition, the physico-chemical properties of the honey have a very favourable effect.

We used ascorbic acid (vitamin C) in these experiments because it is the most unstable of the vitamins. It can be taken, not without -justification, that other vitamins (B_1, L_2, PP, D, and A) also keep well when added to honey.

Mulultivitaminized Honey and Diabetics

The Moscow docto A. Davydov described in 1915 how he had used honey with success in treating diabetics. After giving eight patients honey he concluded that honey can be very useful in treating sugar diabetes in many cases:

(1) as a tasty substance;

(2) as a nutritious addition to the diabetic diet since there is almost no desire, when it is taken, for other sweet things not permitted in the illness:

(3) as a means of preventing acetonaemia, for which sugar always has to be prescribed, so upsetting the diet;

(4) as a sugar that not only does not increase excretion of glucose but even greatly reduces it.")

The combination of vitamins B_1, PP, and C with laevulose (fructose) (of which honey contains 41 per cent) can have a beneficial effect on normalizing the conversion of carbohydrates in diabetics, since these vitamins are not only involved in their conversion but also lower the sugar level of the blood.

Honey, moreover, has been found to contain hormone substances akin to insulin. It would therefore -seem desirable for clinical tests to be made with a multivitaminized honey of special composition containing thiamine, ascorbic acid, and nicotinic acid in considerable doses. A honey of this kind would add variety to the diabetic diet. Multivitaminized products for diabetics were made experimentally from honey on the writer's initiative at the Marat Vitamin and Confectionery Factory in Moscow: multivitaminized honey, honey and blackcurrant paste, blackcurrant paste, honey and peanut butter, and honey and sesame halva (bennet butter).

Samples of these products were tasted and judged by experts at the All-Union Vitamin Research Institute, given a positive evaluation, and recommended not only for diabetics but also for small children, schoolchildren, and patients with various ailments.

Multivitaminized Honey and Glutamic Acid

Glutamic acid was discovered by Liebig over a hundred years ago but has only comparatively recently begun to be used in medicine to treat certain disorders of the central nervous system.

In view of its unpleasant taste and the fact that it often causes vomiting when taken by mouth, it is prescribed in a thick sugar syrup or with jam, preserves, or fructoglucose. In this respect honey has several advantages over other sweet substances in that it itself has curative properties.

Honey enriched with vitamins and glutamic acid can be of great value. Not only does the honey mask the unpleasant taste of riboflavin and glutamic acid, but it also stabilizes the activity of vitamin C. We recommend the following recipe for multivitaminized honey and glutamic acid:') best monofloral honey 100 g; glutamic acid 6 g; vitamin C 200 mg; vitamin B, 4 mg; vitamin B_2 4 mg; vitamin PP (B_5) 20 mg.

The amounts are based on accepted dosages of glutamic acid and the vitamin doses recommended by the Committee on Pharmacology of the USSR Ministry of Health.

ARTIFICIAL HONEYS

'The sugary substances produced by plants are not honey,' the great chemist A.M.Butlerov, who was also an outstanding beekeeper (and is called the father of rational apiculture in Russia), wrote. 'Only when they have undergone reworking in the stomach of insects and been condensed through evaporation of some of the water, do they become real honey.'

Thus nectar only becomes honey after it has been processed in the honey stomach of worker bees. 'Honey' obtained without the involvement of worker bees is therefore to be considered artificial, and not natural (or bee's) honey.

Artificial honeys are made from various fruits. The flesh of the fruit is removed from the skin or rind and the juice extracted by means of a press or juice extractor. The pressed juice is filtered through muslin or cheesecloth and then evaporated (in open copper pans) to the consistency of thick treacle or honey.

Artificial honey is a nutritious food, containing mainly invert sugar. In 1887 Lyle made artificial honey by mixing equal parts of glucose and fructose with cane sugar, fruit esters, and colouring matter. The analysis made by Gayner showed that it differed from honey in containing no phosphoric acid.

The *Beschuit Honig* (biscuit honey) popular in Holland has the following composition: margarine 30 per cent, cane sugar 29 per cent, glucose 4 per cent, dextrin 7 per cent, water 29 per cent, soda 0.5 per cent, other ingredients 0.5 per cent.

A syrup similar to honey, and considered an artificial honey, was made in Germany. Analysis gave its composition as: cane sugar 29.40 per cent, invert sugar (glucose and fructose) 40.80 per cent, mineral salts 0.1 per cent, water 29.7 per cent.

Several kinds of artificial honey are made in the USSR, as follows.

Watermelon honey from the fruit of *Citrullus vulgaris* Schrad. The pulp of watermelon contains 88 to 90 per cent water, 5.5 to 10.5 sugar (mainly fructose), 0.97 per cent nitrogenous matter, 0.6 per cent fats, 0.4 per cent cellular tissues, and 0.36 minerals.

Watermelon honey contains 41.6 per cent invert sugar (mainly fructose), 14 per cent saccharose, 1.86 per cent minerals, and 0.34 per cent organic acids. A centner (100 kg) of watermelons yield seven to ten kilograms of watermelon honey.

Musk-melon honey is obtained from the melons of *Cucumis melo L.* Its sugar content depends on the type of melon and varies between 4.5 and 14 per cent, although one variety in Central Asia, which ripens late, contains 17 per cent. Up to 80 per cent of the melon crop in Central Asia is made into honey. Musk-melon honey contains 60 per cent sugar.

Pumpkin honey is made from pumpkins (*Cucurbita pepo* L.), which contain up to 11 per cent sugar. The pumpkins harvested from one hectare will yield 25 to 30 centners of 'honey'.

Date honey is made from the juice of fresh dates, 'the bread of the desert'. It can be stored for over two years without spoiling.

STORAGE OF HONEY

Honey can be stored for a considerable time, and has been known to keep for centuries. It should be noted, however, that it is highly hygroscopic, so that it easily absorbs water and consequently ferments. Experiments indicate that the weight of honey can increase by 33 per cent in a humid atmosphere, through moisture absorbed from the air.

Under the microscope a drop of honey is seen to contain a certain amount of yeasts, which can, at definite temperatures, cause fermentation (mainly, it has been found, yeasts of the genus *Zugosaccharomyces*). Why, then, is comb honey free from fermentation in the hive where the humidity is quite high? The explanation is that in the hive the temperature is 30° C, a level at which yeast cannot cause fermentation.

The optimum temperature for fermentation of honey is 11° to 19° C, so that it should therefore be stored at temperatures between 5° and 10° C, in dry, well-ventilated premises. (Honey, incidentally, easily picks up foreign odours and should not be kept in premises where there are such items as herring, sauerkraut, and the like, or substances with strong odours like paraffin, tar, or petrol.)

The packaging and packing of honey requires careful consideration. The best and most convenient way of storing it is to keep it in glass jars or glazed earthenware vessels.

Thick waxed-paper or parchment can be used for crystalJized honey. To induce fresh honey to crystallize it is sufficient to add to it one part in a thousand of grated crystallized honey; within one or two days it will have crystallized.

When stored in large quantities honey is kept in barrels made of lime, aspen, alder, poplar, or other woods containing not more than 20 per cent moisture-the moisture content of honey. This is a very important point. The wood of coniferous trees cannot be used, because the barrels will give the honey an odour of pine. Oak barrels, too, are unsuitable because honey turns black in them. It is dangerous to store honey in metal containers, because iron combines with the honey sugars, while zinc reacts with its organic acids and produces toxic substances.

From the literature we know that honey kept in iron or zinc vessels has been found to contain 19.79 per cent of these metals. The normal content is 0.16 per cent.

The marking and labelling of honey is most important for consumers. The label should indicate the kind of honey (linden, buckwheat, black-locust, etc.), the time and place of production, the colour (light-golden, dark-brown, etc.), the weight (gross and net) and the name of the producing organization.

4 Chapter
EXPRESS METHOD OF OBTAINING VITAMINIZED AND MEDICINAL HONEYS

One sunny day in May 1939 I arrived in the village of Nikitovka in the Maritime Territory, in the depths of the taiga, where in a large bee-farm with several hundred hives, I was to carry out certain experiments. The beekeeper Ivan Bezrodny and I immediately set about what we had planned to do.

We had to select several hives, five or so average bee colonies, replace the honeycombs with empty frames, prepare feeding troughs, and try to feed the bees our prepared solutions.

During the night I crept up to one of the hives; to my horror, when I pressed my ear to its wall, I heard loud buzzing. I went up to a second and a third hive; the story was the same, the bees were in a state of excitement and were not sleeping. In the hives we had not touched everything was quiet. I went back to bed much distressed.

Early next morning Ivan Bezrodny and I went to the bee-garden.

I only had one idea and that was to find out how the bees had reacted to the artificial solution they had been fed. When we opened the first hive, we found the feeding trough as clean as if it had been licked. We began removing the honeycombs.

The cells glistened with amberlike drops of honey. We examined the other trial hives; in all of them the feeding troughs were quite empty and the honeycombs contained fresh golden honey. During the night the worker bees had been occupied on the combs. Now I understood the buzzing. Instead of resting, they had tirelessly toiled away, turning the prepared solutions into honey.

More syrup was immediately prepared and poured into the feeding troughs. Wide wooden feeding troughs attached to the top of the hive seemed to be most convenient as a great many bees could feed from them at the same time.

And they had the other advantage that the bees could easily descend with their loads without expending much energy. When I was sure that the bees readily prepared honey from the solutions we gave them, I decided to increase the number of bee colonies in the experiment to fifteen.

Eleven were left in the bee-garden, and four were taken into the office where the apiary staff worked and placed so that their bee-entrances faced a window opening onto the garden. This experiment convinced us that when hives are placed in premises where people are working, it does not disturb their work at all, and does not interfere with the activity of the bees.

Consequently, hives could be kept inside premises in town, for example, if there is no garden. I filled the feeding trough with a syrup to which egg, milk, and a rosehip extract had been added, spilling a few drops in the space between the frames.

The bees reacted to this in the appropriate manner. The first reconnaissance bees appeared in the space between the frames and set off in the direction of the feeding trough. They stopped at the rim of the trough, examined this unusual sight, cautiously putting out their probosces. A moment later they a-lighted on little 'boats' made of thin dry pieces of wood covered with wax and tried the new food.

Then, after looking over the trough containing the 'nectar', they flew back between the comb frames informing the other bees about this unusual incident and tremendous find in the hive it self. Dozens of other bees hurriedly followed them. Buzzing away, they soon filled the feeding trough.

Even when all the 'boats' were occupied it did not stop them, for those that could not find room stood on the backs of others or hooked onto one another by their legs to form a living chain, in order to get at the solution. There were so many bees in the trough that it appeared to be covered with a velvety carpet.

At first sight, the bees seemed to be stationary, but in fact they were extremely busy. Using their probosces like pumps, some had already drav'n up the nectar-solution and descended to the combs.

Others, which had already given up their loads, returned to the trough. Working energetically, the thousands of bees emptied the trough in three or four hours; and some returned to it fruitlessly though it was already quite empty.

In time I noticed that whenever I removed the roof of a hive the bees flew upward, whereas in the first experiment reconnaissance bees had been the first to appear at the feeding trough.

They had already become accustomed to the new way of life, to the fact that they no longer needed to leave the hive in search of lectar, that there was a source within the hive itself, and that their job was to turn it into honey.

Whenever we took the top off a hive it meant we were going to fill the feeding trough. The artificial nectar undoubtedly stimulated the bees. The noise when the hive was opened, the light that penetrated into the hive and the smell of the solution that accompanied filling of the feeding trough all acted as stimuli and signals.

When a find is so rich all the bee3 in the hive begin to collect nectar and make honey from it. The queen has nowhere to lay her eggs since almost all the cells are full of honey, and in those which have not yet been taken up, the bees place a drop of honey, reserving it, as it were.

There are no offspring, no nannies, no teachers in the hive during this period; the bees are only involved in the vital process of turning the solution into honey. Our experiments have convinced us that it is most important, when using the express method, to have a convenient and easily accessible feeding trough, as this facilitates the work of the beekeeper and makes it easy for the bees to take up the artificial nectar.

The trough may be made of wood or plastic, and provided with thin sticks or 'boats' coated with wax, so that the bees do not drown in the syrup. We have found that a plastic trough is best, not only for experimental purposes but also for feeding in spring and autumn, especially in the autumn when the bees turn sugar syrup into sugar honey for their hibernation.

The plastic trough designed by us is hygienic and convenient for both experiments and for production in collective farm and state farm apiaries. The way in and out of the bee space between the frames, leading to the big reservoir, is always kept open for the bees. The plastic raft has slits so that the bees can obtain syrup without drowning. Troughs must be kept clean and in good repair. They should be filled at a definite time each day (morning and evening), and filled quickly, 'without spilling, so as not to attract bees from neighbouring hives.

Strict cleanliness must be observed when honey is made by the express method. The beekeeper should wear a white overall and always wash his hands thoroughly with soap and water before preparing the artificial nectar.

The solution should be mixed in glass or enamelled vessels, dissolving the sugar in boiling water to form a 50 to 55 per cent solution, then cooling it to room temperature (16° to 21°C). The desired ingredients of the artificial nectar should be added to the cooled syrup and stirred in rapidly.

If the. sugar content is higher than 55 per cent (for example, 60 per cent), the syrup will be too viscous and the bees will be less eager to make honey from it (though Prof. Karl von Frisch, who has examined the contents of the bee's stomach, considers a 68 per cent solution could be used).

When solutions are prepared from milk, fruit juices, vegetables, fruit, and various medicinal herbs, their sugar content must be taken into consideration. The prepared solution is most effective if it is tepid when poured into the feeding trough.

The honey made from artificial syrup should not be removed from the hive for at least 7Z hours after filling of the trough, and preferably not until the bees have sealed the cells containing it. Honey removed earlier than that still contains 10 per cent saccharose, as the bees have not yet managed to convert all the sugar into glucose and fructose.

Cleanliness must be observed when extracting the honey and packing it. Express honey should be stored in a dark, dry place where there are no foodstuffs or other products with a strong odour (e.g. sauerkraut and pickled cabbage, kerosene, petrol, pine tar, etc.).

Beekeepers who employ the express method without medical inspection are not permitted to feed their bees artificial nectar containing medicines or drugs. The basic ingredients of the artificial nectar must be indicated by the name of the honey.

For instance, if the bulk of the artificial nectar consists of carrot juice, the honey should be called 'carrot honey', and so on. If vitaminized honeys obtained in this way are to be sold commercially, a permit is required from the competent authority and a certificate from an analyst stating the quantity and quality of the vitamins contained in the honey.

THE BEEHIVE AS A PHARMACY

Beehives have become chemist's shops of a kind, where remarkable little pharmacists make medicinal sorts of honey from solutions containing drugs: streptocide, phytin, convallaria, pepsin, ovarin, mammin, spermatocrine, hepatocrine, adoniside, gitalin, etc.

One bee colony was given a solution of calcium chloride, from which it readily produced talcum honey. In the bee's honey stomach the calcium becomes bound organically with the numerous biochemical elements in the honey, so that calcium honey differs considerably from the sweet calcium solution.

The types of honey obtained by feeding bees solutions of foxglove (*Digitalis purpura*), adonis (*Adonis vernalis*), and lily of the valley (*Convallaria majalis*) should possess double properties. On the one hand, they have an effect on the cardiovascular system, and on the other hand, they have a general tonic effect on the patient's organism as a whole.

We have obtained honey containing a great deal of phytin, a substance rich in phosphorus, which is administered in cases of weakness, mental fatigue, rickets, and other illnesses where the organism needs extra phosphorus. Phytin honey is better than either phytin or ordinary honey in that it possesses the properties of both.

Some bees were given solutions containing several medicines; and just like a pharmacist who makes up a prescription from the doctor for a complex medicine containing several ingredients, they made honey of a complex composition.

The bee pharmacists also have the knack of preserving such perishable organic substances as white of egg, egg yolk, milk, blood, etc. Four bee colonies were given solutions containing various colouring matters. They readily emptied feeding troughs filled with a sugar syrup to which emerald green, purplish blue, eosin, carmine, or other dyes had been added, and converted it into honeys of corresponding colour.

Our purpose in this series of experiments was to obtain honey that possessed definite curative properties. Some dyes are known to be neurotropic (i.e. having a tendency toward nerve fibres), and others to have an affinity for tumour cells, microorganisms (especially pyogenic cocci), and the plasmodia of malaria.

The fact that they possessed this property suggested the idea of using them as conductors of certain medicines, on the assumption that, in combination with various drugs or medicines, they would facilitate the passage of antibacterial substances to the affected organ.

Blue honey containing methylene blue, glucose, and a whole arsenal of important remedies could have a considerable future. The same can be said of other coloured honeys.

Three bee colonies were given syrup containing endocrine and other preparations from internal organs: viz. thyroid (thyroid gland), hepatocrine (liver), ovarin (ovaries), and mammin (the mammary glands). Spermatocrine, parathyrocrine, pantocrine, pituitrin, etc. were also tried.

The express method is now an accepted technique for obtaining honey that has been used in the USSR and other countries, and is being employed by many researchers.

The task now is to study the pharmacological properties of the honeys obtained. The French researcher Alin Caillas, for one, has not only obtained a new kind of honey in this way, but has studied its effects on children clinically.

Carrot honey (No. 59). The writer experimented to obtain carrot honey at the bee-farm of the Ukrainian Apicultural Experimental Station. Juice from red carrots was added to a sugar syrup. The bees quickly emptied the feeding trough as in other experiments.

Carrot honey is of particular interest as it possesses extremely valuable nutritive properties. Carrot juice has been used for centuries as an analeptic in folk medicine.

Since the discovery of carotene or provitamin A, it has acquired new significance, and is considered a definite vitamin concentrate. In addition to carotene carrots contain vita= mins B, C, D, and K. Their provitamin A content is 18 times that of blood, and their vitamin D_2 content double that of pig's liver.

They also contain much sugar and mineral salts. All these valuable components are incorporated into carrot honey by bees, along with various enzymes, amino acids, inhibitors, and so on of honey.

Milk Honey

Since time immemorial almost all nations have used milk and honey to treat diseases of the lungs, anaemia, and exhaustion. Avicenna wrote: 'Milk should be used straight from the cow before any change has had time to occur in it.

If it is taken with honey it cleanses internal ulcers, makes them come to a head more quickly and washes them out. Milk is also good for old people, since it moistens and frequently stops the itching from which they often suffer. But if old people are to digest milk, then they must take it with honey.

Milk possesses important nutritive and curative properties. Pavlov considered milk to have a special place among the various foods available to man. It is not just a simple mechanical mixture of various substances, but a harmonious system designed to take the place of the living tissues of the mother's organism, i.e. her blood.

Both milk and blood contain the proteins, carbohydrates, fats, mineral salts, and vitamins necessary for the normal functioning of the organism. But, while milk contains around a hundred different nutritive substances, it soon turns sour and cannot be stored.

When boiled it can be kept longer, but some of the enzymes and other important components are thereby decomposed. A second disadvantage is that milk contains water. When bees make honey from a milk syrup they remove a great deal of water from it, while preserving its valuable components.

Any beekeeper can obtain milk honey, for it is simple to make. Granulated sugar is dissolved in fresh milk, until a thick solution is obtained, and this milk syrup is fed to the bees, who readily make honey from it. Milk honey has a whitish yellowish colour and a pleasant fragrance. Its taste is reminiscent of fruit-drops.

The results of chemical and bacteriological analyses carried out at the Kiev Food Research Institute present great interest: the specific gravity of milk honey is 1.1126 (at 15° C); it contains 20.8 per cent water, 79.2 per cent dry substances (1.622 per cent nitrogenous substances-casein, albumin, globulin; 1.33 per cent fats; 74.7 per cent sugar, including 37.2 per cent glucose and lactose; and 25 per cent fructose; and 1.4 per cent mineral salts).

When inoculated on such media as bile and Boullier's medium the milk honey was found to contain no intestinal bacilli, and no bacteria of the typhus and paratyphus group. Milk honey is extremely nutritious, especially for the growing organism. It can be eaten plain or taken in the form of a beverage.

Two spoonfuls of honey dissolved in a glass of water (warm or cold) make an extremely pleasant drink., tasting of milk and honey. Milk honey can .be stored for a long time, even in an open vessel. The sweet medium of the honey is a splendid preservative for vitamins, especially vitamin C.

Haematogenous (blood) honey. When it was discovered that the new types of honey obtained by feeding bees artificial solutions possessed antibiotic properties, the question arose whether honey could be used for internal infusion.

Experiments showed that repeated intravenous injections of a sterile solution of urotropin honey (No. 4) into rabbits did not give rise to pathological phenomena, apart from the fact that respiration increased immediately after the injection.

It was noted that, when the honey solution was injected directly into the blood, it had a beneficial effect on the general condition of the rabbits, in particular on the development of erythrocytes.

Experimental intravenous injection of blood honey (No. 13), prepared by the bees from a solution of sugar and citrate blood, gave even more intriguing results.

Transfusion of erythrocytes together with honey should have a beneficial effect on the organism, and we suggested that intravenous injection of honey No. 13 into dogs would be more effective than an injection of glucose, could temporarily change the composition of the blood, and bring about regeneration.

Experiments were carried out at the Bogomolets Institute of

Experimental Biology and Pathology in the Ukraine, under the supervision of D.Brusilovskaya. At the end of the experiments the condition of the dog given honey was satisfactory.

Dogs were injected at the same time with glucose as controls. When the results were compared it was evident that honey No. 13 promoted regeneration of the blood more than glucose, which is quite understandable, since the honey consists of a whole set of substances with a complex composition and structure that affect the organism as a whole and are needed by the cells and fibres.

There can be no doubt that blood honey will be given intravenously to treat farm animals, and possibly, later, for treating humans.

Honeys from fruit and vegetable juices and medicinal substances. In September and October 1946 in a bee-garden in the mountains of Kirghizia we induced bees to make honey from fruit and vegetable juices containing many vitamins. The following types of honey were obtained in this way:

(1) bacteriophage multivitamin honey No. 63, containing a bacteriophage that destroyed the germs of dysentery, and a complex of vitamins A, B, PP, C, and D;

(2) penicillin multivitamin honey No. 64, from feeding a solution of penicillin and vitamins A, B, PP, C, and D;

(3) carrot and cabbage honey No. 65, produced from carrot and cabbage juices;

(4) egg yolk-calcium-multivitamin honey No. 66, by feeding bees a solution of egg yolk, calcium chloride and vitamins C, PP, B, and K;

(5) protein multivitamin honey No. 67, made from a solution of white of egg and vitamins C, PP, B, and K;

(6) chocolate multivitamin honey No. 68, made from a solution of chocolate, milk, and vitamins A, D, and E;

(7) rosehip and cabbage honey No. 69, prepared from a brew of rosehips and cabbage juice;

(8) blackcurrant honey No. 70, prepared from blackcurrant juice.

We managed to obtain highly nutritive types of honey by giving the bees sweet syrups made from the juices of the cheapest kitchen garden crops, and even weeds. These artificial solutions contained many substances that were good for the bees themselves.

Pumpkin juice contains as much vitamin C as carrot juice, and more than ten times as much vitamin A as blood or human milk. There is nearly 17 times as much provitamin A in beetroot tops as in pure cow's milk. In addition to provitamin A, the juice of cabbage leaves contains approximately four times more vitamin K (a haemostatic) than pig's liver.

Fresh new nettle leaves have a provitamin A content almost twice as active as that of butter and 56 times more active than that of pure cow's milk. Highly nutritive honeys were obtained from the juice of apples, the outer leaves of cabbage, from watermelons, tomatoes, maize stalks, and rosehips.

Beetroot and rosehip honey was prepared by the bees from an artificial nectar containing beetroot juice, an infusion of rosehips, and a brew of cherry leaves. Instead of sugar, food wastes were used (sugar gumption, processed glucose, etc.). Honey No. 82 made in this way was red in colour, but had a pleasant flavour and tasted of cherries; many tasters thought it prepared from sweet cherry juice.

Ginseng Honey

In Chinese medicine the root of the ginseng (*Panax ginseng*) *is* considered an invaluable remedy and is called 'a wonder of the world and a gift of eternity'. In Chinese ginseng means 'the man root'. Another name is *gin-bao* or 'heavenly herb'. Ginseng belongs to the Araliaceae, and looks rather like parsnip. It differs considerably in its properties from all the other known plants.

The Chinese, Koreans, and other Asian peoples have been using ginseng for thousands of years. A brew of ginseng is used as an analeptic, stimulant, and tranquillizer. It has a beneficial effect in the treatment of almost all illnesses.

In China and Tibet ginseng and honey are recommended as a remedy for diseases of the nervous system. The addition of honey improves the flavour, for an infusion of ginseng on its own has an unpleasant, bitter taste.

We supposed that ginseng honey obtained by the express method would have a greater effect on the organism than honey and ginseng separately.

In a bee colony given ginseng nectar, the queen began laying eggs in the comb cells more energetically than usual. Initially this was a nuisance since the cells were filled not with honey, but with eggs, and because the bees were busy building new honeycomb instead of making the honey.

For that reason we removed the queen from the hive. The worker bees then made honey from the artificial ginseng nectar for several days, without apparently noticing the absence of the queen; in normal conditions, they would almost immediately have noticed and begun looking for her.

This makes us think that ginseng contains some sort of hormonal substance, possibly of a gonadotropic character.

Dr. I. I.Brechman is probably correct in his opinion that the roots of wild ginseng contain substances that have a gonadotropic effect. Ginsburg is of the same opinion and concluded that ginseng does have a gonadotropic effect and speeds up the development of the sexual organs in infantile male and female white mice. The effect appears to be greater in the winter and autumn months.

Ginseng honey crystallizes in the comb, because the artificial nectar is prepared with glucose. Unlike other honeys, it is not sticky and can be stored in paper cartons. It has a pleasant taste and a delicate aroma. It has to be broken off in pieces and forms a kind of honey and wax wafer that has to be chewed.

Pine Honey

This is a variety made from a sugar syrup prepared from an infusion of pine needles. The experiments were carried out in greenhouses in winter at an air temperature of 21° C. The bees readily processed the sweet infusion and put the honey prepared into the honeycomb. Seven days later they had already sealed parts of the comb.

The honey was removed from several combs in the usual manner. It was amber-coloured with a slightly greenish tint and had a pleasant taste and a faint smell of pine tar.

Bees can be made to work right throughout the winter, but must be placed in a hothouse from the autumn onwards so that there is no break in their activities. Once a bee colony is in hibernation, it cannot be induced to make honey in the winter.

As a result of the pine feed, there were four times more offspring in the experimental hives than in controls not given the..pine solution; and young worker bees appeared in March.

The needles of coniferous trees are a vitamin concentrate. Pine needles contain ten times more vitamin C than potatoes, seven times more than apples, and four times more than lemons. There is twice as much vitamin K in pine needles as in pig's liver.

The provitamin A content of pine needles is more than a hundred times that of pork, and almost eight times that of blood.

The abundance of pines, firs, and spruces everywhere means that there is no difficulty in preparing an infusion of high vitamin content, and makes rapid and easy processing of vitamin preparations by bees tempting.

THE ADVANTAGES OF THE EXPRESS METHOD

Any kind of honey of a definite chemical and biological composition can be obtained using the express method. Bees will even make honey from medicinal substances like quinine, antibiotics, etc. that have an unpleasant taste and odour.

To accustom them to the taste and smell of drugs, small amounts are added initially to the sugar solution and then gradually increased. Bees rapidly develop a conditioned reflex to the (to our minds) unpleasant sweet solution and readily make honey from it.

Experiments carried out in the Far East, the Ukraine, Central Asia, the Urals, and other regions of the Soviet Union indicate that the express method can be used to obtain honey everywhere, no matter what the climate,what the strain of bees, or what the season.

The method is extremely economical, for bees given artificial nectar in the hive itself require much less feeding than when they fly out in search of nectariferous plants in flower. In the autumn months the method makes it possible not only to obtain honey of the required composition but also to save tons of natural honey that would normally be required for feeding the bees throughout the winter.

Beekeepers have observed that artificial nectar prepared from various vitamins and from medicinal, antibiotic, and edible substances has a beneficial effect on the bees themselves, increasing their ability to work and their resistance to illness and harmful external factors. In 1959, R.Chernigovskaya, describing the experiments carried out on a mass scale by the beekeepers of Irkutsk Region, communicated the results obtained by G.S.Timofeev, the beekeeper of the Kalinin Collective Farm, which were the best for the Region.

Twenty of the farm's 70 bee colonies were used in the experiment. The test hives were divided into four groups of five each; three were given supplementary feeding from May 20 to June 15 while the fourth (the control group) was given nothing extra.

Group I was given 200 grams daily of a sugar syrup containing penicillin (1 kg sugar and 50 000 I.U. of penicillin per litre of water); Group II was given 200 grams daily of a sour feed (a 1:1 sugar syrup containing 700 mg of citric acid per litre); while Group III was fed the same amount of pure sugar syrup.

The average yield for the 70 hives overwintered had been 50.5 kg of honey and 1.5 kg of wax. The yields for the test hives were as follows (with a late cold spring): 1-82 kg of honey and 2 kg of wax; 11-63 kg of honey and 1.1 kg of wax; 111-53 kg of honey and 1.0 kg of wax; and IV-25 kg of honey and 0.5 kg of wax.

During experiments carried out with 12 hives (six controls) by the department of zoology of the Moscow Veterinary Academy in 1959[1]), it was ascertained that, when bees were fed three times in one week with a sugar syrup containing 30 000 I.U. of antibiotics (penicillin, biomycin, dehydrostreptomycin, or terramycin), the yield of honey rose from 19 kilograms per hive for the controls (given only the sugar syrup) to between 41.6 and 52 kilograms.

Similar results were obtained in 1960 at the bee-farm of the Timiryazev Agricultural Academy, and in 1961 in the apiaries of state and collective farms in Siberia and Moldavia. It was also found that the queens in the hives given antibiotics laid more eggs than normal while the bees lived longer.

HONEY AS MEDICINE AND REMEDY

Honey has long been used in medicine not only as a valuable item in the diet but as a remedy and a means of healing. In the oldest medical papyri of Egypt, dating back to 15531550 B.C., there are indications that honey was used to heal wounds, 'in order to cause urination', and 'as a means of easing the belly'.

In Mesopotamia and Assyria, too, honey was used for healing and is mentioned among remedies on the tablets found in the library of Ashur-bani-pal.

In Indian medicine it was considered that honey could be used both as a remedy and as an analeptic. The tonics prescribed 'to give pleasure' and 'to preserve youth' were mainly prepared from honey. And a diet in which honey and milk were the main items was thought to prolong life.

In ancient Greece honey was considered one of nature's most precious gifts. The Greek philosopher Democritus, creator of atomic theory, said, when asked for advice on how to live and how to keep in good health, thgt one should anoint one's interior with honey and one's exterior with oil.

Hippocrates, the great Greek doctor, prescribed honey extensively and successfully for many diseases. Honey taken with other food, he said, was nutritious and improved the complexion.

Galen, the great Roman physician, considered honey an all-purpose remedy, recommending it to treat many kinds of poisoning, and intestinal ailments, in particular gangrenous stomatitis. Later, in the Arab East, honey was extensively used by doctors.

The greatest medical authority of mediaeval times, Ibn-Sina (or

Avicenna), gave dozens of recipes in his *Canon* that included honey and beeswax among the ingredients.

Of the medicinal gruel that was eaten by scholars and philosophers he wrote: 'It helps you when you have a runny nose, cheers you up, make you feel fit, facilitates the digestion of food, gets rid of wind, and improves the appetite.

It is almost a provision for retaining youth, making the memory better, sharpening the wits, and loosening the tongue. . . .' He considered honey to have absorbing properties and recommended a wafer *(tapitma)* made of honey and wheat flour without water to treat wounds.

The wafer was placed on the surface of the wound and changed every twelve hours -until healthy tissue grew. Ibn-Sina also wrote that honey had a beneficial effect on deep, contaminated ulcers.

Honey is also considered an important remedy in folk medicine. 'There is no need to be afraid of asking simple people what they think is a good cure,' Hippocrates wrote, 'for I believe that the art of medicine was on the whole discovered by so doing.'

Through observation and folk wisdom people made many valuable discoveries down the ages which furthered the development of medicine and the art of healing.

Remedies like foxglove, adonis, quinine, opium, atrophine, cocaine, and others were all borrowed from folk medicine.

Modern experiments and observations indicate that there is every reason to consider honey a remedy. To what does it owe its curative properties?

Mainly to the glucose it contains, which has an invigorating effect on the cardiovascular system, but also to its many other substances that improve the resistance of the organism.

TREATMENT OF WOUNDS

In folk medicine, and in antiquity, honey was used to heal wounds. Pliny wrote that fish fat mixed with honey had a beneficial effect on infected wounds and on sores in the mouth. And in mediaeval times, as we said above, Avicenna used wafers containing honey to treat wounds.

In mediaeval Russia a honey ointment containing pine tar was used to heal wounds; old Russian manuscripts on cures often said: 'Honey takes away the stench from wounds'. Later honey and fish oil were used to treat extensive wounds, the treated wound healing after ten or twelve days, leaving a large scar.

In 1938 the Soviet surgeon Ya.M.Krinitsky obtained good results from using an ointment of honey and fat to treat 48 patients with infected, necrotic wounds.')

After five days the dead tissues began to come away in 90 per cent of the patients and a new epithelium to replace them. Krinitsky concluded from his observations that the honey helped the wounds to heal more quickly by bringing about a marked increase in glutathione in the wound. (Glutathione plays a most important part in oxidation-reduction processes in the organism and stimulates cell growth and division.)

In 1946 Prof. S.A.Smirnov (Tomsk Medical Institute) used honey to treat gunshot wounds in 75 patients, and concluded that it stimulated growth of tissue in slowhealing wounds?)

Many other examples could be cited from the experience of doctors and surgeons. The highly respected Ukrainian .doctor, A.S.Budai, treated slow-healing wounds and ulcers in his rural practice with an ointment containing 80 g honey, 20 g fish oil, and 3 g xeroform.

The honey and xeroform were pounded together in a mortar, the fish oil added, and the mixture stirred until uniform.[3]) More recently I have tested a similar ointment containing honey and seabuckthorn oil, which proved more effective. Many people become allergic to fish oil and xeroform.

In 1946 A.E.Gel'fman reported having treated patients with torpid wounds at an evacuation hospital by means of honey electrophoresis.) His observations of 35 patients with fractures due to gunshot wounds, complicated by osteomyelitis (inflammation of the bone marrow), indicated that honey electrophoresis induced active development of granulation.

After treatment the wounds, which had been covered with flaccid anaemic granules full of pus, became—cleaner, blood flowed freely in them, and they began to heal.

HONEY INHALATIONS

Good therapeutic effects have been obtained when honey is inhaled into the upper respiratory tract. The observations of Dr.Ya.A.Kiselstein, reported in 1938, are of special interest in this respect. He employed an ordinary inhalation apparatus adapted to atomize aqueous solutions, and used a 10 per cent solution of honey.

Each session of treatment lasted five minutes. One of his cases, 32 years of age, had suffered for several years from a feeling of dryness in the pharynx and loss of voice.

The nasal mucosa and the back of the pharynx were more or less normal, but the laryngeal mucosa and the upper sections of the trachea were covered with suppurative scabs. After seven inhalations the patient felt better and the scabs and hoarseness disappeared.

Of 20 patients treated by honey inhalation, only two felt no improvement at all. Before beginning honey inhalations all the patients concerned had been under observation and had been treated with ordinary conservative remedies, from which they derived no noticeable improvement.

When inhaled honey not only has an effect on the mucous membrane of the nose and throat, but also on the alveoli of the lungs (through which it enters the blood). Thus it not only acts as a local bactericide, but also helps to build up the organism generally.

Dr.Kiselstein incorrectly attributed the therapeutic effect obtained from inhalation to the vitamin content of the honey, though its vitamin content, in fact, is low. We therefore decided to test 10 per cent and 5 per cent solutions of honey enriched with vitamins C, B_1, and A.

The results far exceeded our expectations. The patients treated were soon free of their complaints. In 1967 the Bulgarian doctor Stoimir Mladenov reported having used honey inhalation extensively and successfully to treat patients with diseases of the upper respiratory tracts.') Inhalation with honey can easily be carried out at home, but only under the supervision of a doctor.

Since olden days honey has been reputed an all-purpose remedy for colds, not simply on its own, but mixed with other foods and medicines. People with colds are recommended to take honey with warm milk (one tablespoon of honey to a glass of milk) or with lemon (the juice of one lemon to a hundred grams of honey). A good remedy is a 1:1 syrup of horseradish juice and honey.

When honey is taken for a cold the patient should stay in bed, or at least at home, for honey causes one to sweat a great deal. Linden honey is a particularly good diaphoretic.

Honey has also been used since time immemorial for diseases' of the lungs. Hippocrates wrote that 'honey gets rid of sputum and soothes a cough'. Avicenna recommended a mixture of honey and rose petals in the early stages of tuberculosis, considering it more effective when taken before noon.

He also believed that hazel nuts and honey helped in cases of chronic coughing and facilitated expectoration. 'Honey is juice with heavenly dew', we read in a seventeenth century Russian manual on medicine, 'which the bees collect in fine weather from fragrant flowers and which possesses many curative properties in the treatment of various illnesses.

'Honey rids a wound of its stench, prevents people from going blind when smeared on the eyeball, heals sores in the mouth, causes urination, eases the bowels, soothes a cough, heals poisoned bites and the bites of mad dogs. It has a good effect on deep wounds and is a remedy for the lungs and the inner joints.'

These old manuals describe honey as a remedy exerting a beneficial effect on people of all ages. 'We need not be afraid to give wild honey to children and old people and even to pregnant wives, for eating wild honey is without harm to what is conceived in the womb.'

In Russian folk medicine, honey was used for certain skin complaints.')

Despite numerous examples that honey is an excellent remedy for pulmonary tuberculosis, no specific curative properties can be attributed to it in this disease. It can merely be noted that honey is generally a restorative and thus helps the organism to fight the tuberculous infection.

This is our own observation from a comparison of various methods of treatment of abscess of the lung, and our own observations of patients in Prof. F.A.Udintsev's clinic at the Kiev Medical Institute.') Three patients were given 100 to 150 grams of honey a day. As a result considerable improvement was noted. They began to feel better, their appetites improved, and they began to put on weight. Their haemoglobin increased, while the erythrocyte sedimentation rate (E.S.R.) decreased.

The patients coughed less and the amount of sputum decreased; they began to urinate more during the day thar at night (the opposite being the case before honey was given); and a beneficial effect was noted on the gastrointestinal tract.

HONEY AND THE HEART

The muscle of the heart is working continuously and needs glucose in order to make up the energy expended. When a very small quantity of glucose (0.1 per cent) is added to the physiological saline in which an isolated heart is immersed, the heart will continue working outside the body for four days.

Honey has a beneficial effect on the heart because it contains much easily assimilated glucose. It has been noted (Theobald) that it has an invaluable effect on the weakened muscle of the heart in various types of cardiac diseases. Even diabetics can take honey, since cardiac activity is improved by the injection into the organism of fructose or honey.

In all cases where a cure depends on the activity of the heart, honey should not be forgotten, so that the heart will not only be stimulated, when given digitalis, but also receive nutrition: Honey causes the veins to expand and improves circulation through the coronary arteries.

With prolonged prescription of honey (50 to 140-on an average 70-grams of honey daily for one to two months) patients with heart trouble feel better in themselves, the composition of their blood returns to normal, their haemoglobin level increases, and cardiovascular tonus improves.

HONEY AND DIGESTION

An old saying has it that honey is the stomach's best friend. The medical literature indicates that honey has a beneficial effect on digestion. It is particularly good as a laxative, and when eaten regularly helps keep the gastrointestinal tract in normal working order.

Food remains in the stomach for two to three hours, even longer, after eating, during which time it is subjected to the action of the gastric juices. Many authors think, on the basis of clinical observations, that honey reduces hyperacidity of the stomach when taken with other food.

Our own investigations') showed that a barium meal with honey remained in the stomach an hour or two longer than barium sulphate on its own; and the outline of the organ was much sharper on the X-ray plate. The passage of a barium meal with honey through the small and large intestines in no way differed from that of barium sulphate on its own or with sugar.

Honey can be used as a remedy, or as part of the diet, in the treatment of several gastro-intestinal ailments, for instance in cases of gastritis or gastric ulcer in which there is hyperacidity. In 1924 Dr. V.P.Grigoriev had a patient under clinical observation for whose hyperacidity the only effective remedy was honey.[2])

In the period 1944-9, 600 patients with ulcers of the stomach were treated with honey at the clinic of the Irkutsk Medical Institute. M.L.Khotkina (1953) described 302 cases with the most typical course: 76 (34.3 per cent) had hyperacidity; 67 (30.2 per cent) were normal; in 54 (24.7 per cent) acidity was subnormal; and in 24 (10.8 per cent) there was no acidity.

When the normal diet and medicines were prescribed 61 per cent of the patients recovered and 18 per cent still felt pain; but when honey was prescribed 79.7 to 84.2 per cent recovered and only 5.9 continued to,feel pain at the end of treatment. X-ray established that, with normal treatment, the ulcers healed in 29 per cent of patients, but in 59.2 per cent of those taking honey.

The average period of hospitalization was shorter for patients prescribed honey. A general tonic effect was also noted: weight increased, the composition of the blood improved, gastric acidity became normal, and there was a tranquillizing effect on the nervous system. Patients became calm, cheerful, and full of life.

Muller and Arkhipova, of the dietetic department of the Ostroumov Hospital in Moscow, studied the effect of honey on 155 patients with ulcers.') Their observations indicated that honey brought acidity and the secretion of gastric juice back to normal, and saved patients from heartburn and belching, ended cramps, and so on.

When honey is used to treat ulcers it has a dual effect: (a) a local effect helping the surface of the gastric mucosa to heal; and (b) a general effect building up the organism as a whole, and particularly the nervous system (which is extremely important since gastric and duodenal ulcers develop when the receptors of these organs cease to function properly).

For ulcers honey should be taken 90 minutes to two hours before meals, or three hours afterward, preferably an hour and a half or two hours before breakfast and the midday meal and three hours after the evening meal.

The honey should be dissolved in warm, boiled water. In this form it dilutes the mucus in the stomach and lowers acidity, and is rapidly assimilated without irritating the intestine.

A cold solution, on the other hand, increases acidity, slows down digestion of the contents of the stomach, and irritates the intestine. When taken just before meals, honey stimulates secretion of gastric juice.

The liver is rightly called the organism's main chemical laboratory, since it takes an active part in all its vital processes, namely, the conversion of carbohydrates, proteins, fats, vitamins, hormones, etc. Enzymes are formed in the liver and carotene is transformed there into vitamin A.

Prothrombin (a substance involved in coagulation of the blood) is formed there with the help of vitamin K and the hormones produced by the endocrine glands acquire new properties in the liver.

Honey has long been used in folk medicine to treat complaints of the liver. Its beneficial effect is due to its chemical composition, in particular to its high glucose content.

Glucose not only feeds the tissue cells of the liver, but also increases its reserve of glycogen and improves the process of tissue replacement.

The liver acts as a filter, rendering bacterial poisons harmless; glycogen helps it to carry out this function more effectively and so builds up the organism's resistance to infection. Diseases of the liver are frequently treated clinically with intravenous injections of glucose.

Honey mixed with curd (cottage cheese), porridge, boiled buckwheat or barley, apples, etc., is not only good for the sick, but also for the healthy.

Doctors recommend the following for people with kidney trouble: either honey and rosehip tea (15 grams of rosehips to 0.5 litre of water) or honey and radish juice (100 to 200 grams daily). People suffering from gravel in the kidneys are advised to take a tablespoon of olive oil, honey, and lemon juice three times a day, but only under the supervision of a doctor.

Since olden days honey has been reputed an all-purpose remedy for colds, not simply on its own, but mixed with other foods and medicines. People with colds are recommended to take honey with warm milk (one tablespoon of honey to a glass of milk) or with lemon (the juice of one lemon to a hundred grams of honey).

A good remedy is a 1:1 syrup of horseradish juice and honey. When honey is taken for a cold the patient should stay in bed, or at least at home, for honey causes one to sweat a great deal. Linden honey is a particularly good diaphoretic.

Honey has also been used since time immemorial for diseases' of the lungs. Hippocrates wrote that 'honey gets rid of sputum and soothes a cough'. Avicenna recommended a mixture of honey and rose petals in the early stages of tuberculosis, considering it more effective when taken before noon.

He also believed that hazel nuts and honey helped in cases of chronic coughing and facilitated expectoration. 'Honey is juice with heavenly dew', we read in a seventeenth century Russian manual on medicine, 'which the bees collect in fine weather from fragrant flowers and which possesses many curative properties in the treatment of various illnesses.

'Honey rids a wound of its stench, prevents people from going blind when smeared on the eyeball, heals sores in the mouth, causes urination, eases the bowels, soothes a cough, heals poisoned bites and the bites of mad dogs. It has a good effect on deep wounds and is a remedy for the lungs and the inner joints.'

These old manuals describe honey as a remedy exerting a

beneficial effect on people of all ages. 'We need not be afraid to give wild honey to children and old people and even to pregnant wives, for eating wild honey is without harm to what is conceived in the womb.'

In Russian folk medicine, honey was used for certain skin complaints. Despite numerous examples that honey is an excellent remedy for pulmonary tuberculosis, no specific curative properties can be attributed to it in this disease.

It can merely be noted that honey is generally a restorative and thus helps the organism to fight the tuberculous infection. This is our own observation from a comparison of various methods of treatment of abscess of the lung, and our own observations of patients in Prof. F.A.Udintsev's clinic at the Kiev Medical Institute.

Three patients were given 100 to 150 grams of honey a day. As a result considerable improvement was noted. They began to feel better, their appetites improved, and they began to put on weight. Their haemoglobin increased, while the erythrocyte sedimentation rate (E.S.R.) decreased.

The patients coughed less and the amount of sputum decreased; they began to urinate more during the day thar at night (the opposite being the case before honey was given); and a beneficial effect was noted on the gastrointestinal tract.

HONEY AND THE HEART

The muscle of the heart is working continuously and needs glucose in order to make up the energy expended. When a very small quantity of glucose (0.1 per cent) is added to the physiological saline in which an isolated heart is immersed, the heart will continue working outside the body for four days.

Honey has a beneficial effect on the heart because it contains much easily assimilated glucose. It has been noted (Theobald) that it has an invaluable effect on the weakened muscle of the heart in various types of cardiac diseases.

Even diabetics can take honey, since cardiac activity is improved by the injection into the organism of fructose or honey. In all cases where a cure depends on the activity of the heart, honey should not be forgotten, so that the heart will not only be stimulated, when given digitalis, but also receive nutrition: Honey causes the veins to expand and improves circulation through the coronary arteries.

With prolonged prescription of honey (50 to 140-on an average 70-grams of honey daily for one to two months) patients with heart trouble feel better in themselves, the composition of their blood returns to normal, their haemoglobin level increases, and cardiovascular tonus improves.

HONEY AND DIGESTION

An old saying has it that honey is the stomach's best friend. The medical literature indicates that honey has a beneficial effect on digestion. It is particularly good as a laxative, and when eaten regularly helps keep the gastrointestinal tract in normal working order.

Food remains in the stomach for two to three hours, even longer, after eating, during which time it is subjected to the action of the gastric juices.

Many authors think, on the basis of clinical observations, that honey reduces hyperacidity of the stomach when taken with other food. Our own investigations') showed that a barium meal with honey remained in the stomach an hour or two longer than barium sulphate on its own; and the outline of the organ was much sharper on the X-ray plate.

The passage of a barium meal with honey through the small and large intestines in no way differed from that of barium sulphate on its own or with sugar. Honey can be used as a remedy, or as part of the diet, in the treatment of several gastro-intestinal ailments, for instance in cases of gastritis or gastric ulcer in which there is hyperacidity. In 1924 Dr. V.P.Grigoriev had a patient under clinical observation for whose hyperacidity the only effective remedy was honey.

In the period 1944-9, 600 patients with ulcers of the stomach were treated with honey at the clinic of the Irkutsk Medical Institute. M.L.Khotkina (1953) described 302 cases with the most typical course: 76 (34.3 per cent) had hyperacidity; 67 (30.2 per cent) were normal; in 54 (24.7 per cent) acidity was subnormal; and in 24 (10.8 per cent) there was no acidity.

When the normal diet and medicines were prescribed 61 per

cent of the patients recovered and 18 per cent still felt pain; but when honey was prescribed 79.7 to 84.2 per cent recovered and only 5.9 continued to,feel pain at the end of treatment.

X-ray established that, with normal treatment, the ulcers healed in 29 per cent of patients, but in 59.2 per cent of those taking honey. The average period of hospitalization was shorter for patients prescribed honey.

A general tonic effect was also noted: weight increased, the composition of the blood improved, gastric acidity became normal, and there was a tranquillizing effect on the nervous system. Patients became calm, cheerful, and full of life.

Muller and Arkhipova, of the dietetic department of the Ostroumov Hospital in Moscow, studied the effect of honey on 155 patients with ulcers. Their observations indicated that honey brought acidity and the secretion of gastric juice back to normal, and saved patients from heartburn and belching, ended cramps, and so on.

When honey is used to treat ulcers it has a dual effect: (a) a local effect helping the surface of the gastric mucosa to heal; and (b) a general effect building up the organism as a whole, and particularly the nervous system (which is extremely important since gastric and duodenal ulcers develop when the receptors of these organs cease to function properly).

For ulcers honey should be taken 90 minutes to two hours before meals, or three hours afterward, preferably an hour and a half or two hours before breakfast and the midday meal and three hours after the evening meal.

The honey should be dissolved in warm, boiled water. In this form it dilutes the mucus in the stomach and lowers acidity, and is rapidly assimilated without irritating the intestine. A cold solution, on the other hand, increases acidity, slows down digestion of the contents of the stomach, and irritates the intestine.

When taken just before meals, honey stimulates secretion of gastric juice. The liver is rightly called the organism's main chemical laboratory, since it takes an active part in all its vital processes, namely, the conversion of carbohydrates, proteins, fats, vitamins, hormones, etc. Enzymes are formed in the liver and carotene is transformed there into vitamin A.

Prothrombin (a substance involved in coagulation of the blood) is formed there with the help of vitamin K and the hormones produced by the endocrine glands acquire new properties in the liver.

Honey has long been used in folk medicine to treat complaints of the liver. Its beneficial effect is due to its chemical composition, in particular to its high glucose content. Glucose not only feeds the tissue cells of the liver, but also increases its reserve of glycogen and improves the process of tissue replacement. The liver acts as a filter, rendering bacterial poisons harmless; glycogen helps it to carry out this function more effectively and so builds up the organism's resistance to infection. Diseases of the liver are frequently treated clinically with intravenous injections of glucose.

Honey mixed with curd (cottage cheese), porridge, boiled buckwheat or barley, apples, etc., is not only good for the sick, but also for the healthy.

Doctors recommend the following for people with kidney trouble: either honey and rosehip tea (15 grams of rosehips to 0.5 litre of water) or honey and radish juice (100 to 200 grams daily).

People suffering from gravel in the kidneys are advised to take a tablespoon of olive oil, honey, and lemon juice three times a day, but only under the supervision of a doctor.

HONEY AND THE NERVOUS SYSTEM

Honey is known to have a favourable effect on the nervous system. Clinical observations are that hypertonic solutions of glucose take effect rapidly in the treatment of some diseases of the nervous system. And usually, after two or three injections, headaches lessen, the sight improves, and so on.

Prof. N.K.Bogolepov and V.I.Kiseleva (1949) reported treating two cases of St. Vitus' dance with honey. After. three weeks' treatment with honey alone the patients began to sleep normally, their headaches ceased, they felt stronger and less irritable and became cheerful and active again.

People with nervous conditions or suffering from exhaustion are recommended to drink a glass of water in which. honey and the juice of half a lemon have been dissolved, or to eat two tablespoons of honey, before going to bed. In 1938 Prof. E. Zander noted that there is no less harmful soporific than a glass of honeyed water, taken at night.

Honey is undoubtedly better than powders that irritate the stomach. Bran soaked in water and mixed with honey is considered an excellent remedy for strengthening the nerves; or vitamin B_1 can be taken instead of bran.

A preparation of honey from which the proteins have previously been extracted is frequently used to prevent the radiation sickness that often develops in patients during radiation therapy, an intravenous injection of 10 ml of a 20 to 40 per cent solution of this preparation being administered before each session of the course of treatment. Once the properties of protein-free honey in the treatment of this illness had been established, it began to be used in the patented preparation Melcain, which contains a 1 to 2 per cent solution of procaine in protein-free honey for therapeutic and prophylactic purposes in diseases normally treated with procaine and honey.

HONEY AND THE EYES

Honey has long been considered a most effective remedy for many eye diseases. An ancient Egyptian papyrus gives the recipe for a honey ointment and instructions how to use it. Ibn-Sina recommended honey mixed with onion juice, clover, or wheatgrass for the eyes.

In the last century honey was held by some writers to be a good remedy for burns, especially those affecting the eyes, and an excellent cure for inflammation of the eye. It has not lost its importance today, even when medicine has been enriched with a host of new preparations (sulphonamides, antibiotics, etc.), and is, in fact, highly effective for certain diseases of the eye.

A.Kh.Mikhailov reported having used eucalyptus honey as an ointment to treat swelling of the eyelid, conjunctiva, and cornea, sores on the corneal membrane, and other complaints.') The honey was made by bees from a mixture of honey with an infusion of eucalyptus leaves (since it is the leaves and not the flowers of this tree that possess curative properties).

A honey ointment has been widely used in the eye department of the Odessa Regional Hospital to treat various lesions of the corneal membrane. At first honey was merely added to a 3 per cent sulphapyridine ointment (replacing vaseline). This ointment was highly effective on very slowhealing sores and speeded up the rate of cicatrization.

A 30 per cent solution of sodium sulphanil acetamide given in drops, or sulphapyridine ointment containing vaseline, brought no relief to patients with inflammation of the cornea, their condition only improving when the honey and sulphapyridine ointments were administered.

Quite a few patients with keratitis or sores on the corneal membrane were cured with honey on its own. Honey has also been used extensively in the eye clinic of the Omsk Medical Institute (Maximenko')) to treat herpetic and ulcerous keratitis, and as a means of resorption in cases of opacity of the cornea or vitreous body, immature or initial cataract, and burns affecting the eye.

Only sterile honey from honeycomb should be used in the eyes, and then only under the supervision of a doctor or ophthalmologist.

HONEY AND CHILDREN

A sensible diet is most important in a child's development. As we have already mentioned it is better for children to take honey with their food than sugar. It is advisable to give them a teaspoon of honey two or three times a day, but the dose should not exceed 30 to 40 grams daily.

N. B. Some people are allergic to honey. In them it may cause a rash, shortness of breath, vomiting, and diarrhoea. They should not, on any account, be given even tiny doses of honey.

It has been noted' in the literature that children prefer honey to sugar. We ourselves made the following experiment once at the Istra Rest Home for children. Each morning and evening the children were given an extra three lumps of sugar (30 to 35 grams).

After a couple of days, however, we were forced to alter the test, as the children were giving the sugar to the dog, throwing it away, or leaving it. The effect was quite different when we gave 60 of them a spoonful of honey morning and evening. All were eager to get their ration of honey first and were always anxious to know whether there would be any the next day.

Dentists have no doubts about the harmful effect of sugar on the teeth. It has been established that the remains of sugar in the mouth break down, under the effect of bacteria, to form acids, particularly lactic acid, which leads to slow but considerable decalcification of the teeth and to caries. Honey, on the other hand, has active antibiotic properties and in fact disinfects the mouth.

HONEY WITH MEDICINAL HERBS

Honey has a beneficial effect when taken with medicinal herbs.

Agrimony *(Agrimonia eupatoria L.)* was used in folk medicine as an all-purpose remedy, and for treating rheumatism, haemorrhoids, gastric disorders, and other illnesses.

Ertel and Bauer recommend drinking a small cup of agrimony tea and honey three times a day, and using an agrimony infusion as a lotion. Agrimony tea and honey can be used in cases of chronic rheumatism, blood-spitting, serious indigestion, and inflammation of the pharynx.

It is'a most effective remedy for complaints of the liver and spleen, as it helps prevent diarrhoea and weakness in the intestines. It dissolves and rids the organism of kidney sand, and has a beneficial effect on cancerous tumours.

Aloes

The resinous sap of aloe leaves *(Aloe spp.) is* frequently used for medical purposes. It is dark brown, has a distinctive, unpleasant smell, and a bitter taste. In folk medicine the juice of fresh aloe leaves was used, mixed with fat and honey in the following proportions, for pulmonary tuberculosis:

A tablespoon of the mixture is taken in a glass of warm milk twice a day (morning and evening).

Blackthorn (*Prunus spinosa L.*)

The flowers are used in folk medicine as a mild laxative..Ertel and Bauer consider that tea made from blackthorn flowers is invaluable for inflammation of the respiratory tract, clearing it of sputum.

The tea is prepared by boiling a tablespoon of dried blackthorn flowers in 250 g of water for one minute. The liquor is poured off, honey added to it, and then boiled again. One. cup a day should be taken and sipped slowly.

Barnet saxifrage (*Pimpinela saxifraga L.*)

A decoction of saxifrage in water and wine (1:1), or in the form of an infusion (10 g of the root to 200 g of water) with honey is considered to be an extremely good expectorant, and also acts as an analeptic after illness. It is taken a tablespoon at a time, three to five times a day. Two glasses of a saxifrage tea with rosehips and honey are recommended to dispose of stones in the bladder; A.Raff considers this a real remedy for stones.

The Swiss specialist in medicinal herbs, I. Kiinzle recommended a tablespoon of powdered saxifrage root, mixed with honey, every four hours for children with diphtheria (in the 24th edition of his almanac, 1945).

Coltsfoot

The leaves and flowers of *Tussilago farfara L.* have been widely used in the form of a brew or tea as an expectorant. The Romans considered coltsfoot an effective remedy for cough, as is indicated by the Latin name for this plant Tussilago (from *tussis* cough).

The leaves of coltsfoot contain a bitter glucoside (tusilagin), gallic acid, indulin, essential oils, mucus, tannin, and other substances. The Pharmaceutical Committee of the USSR Ministry of Health has approved the following coltsfoot remedies for general use:

Chest tea No. 1, containing two parts coltsfoot leaves, two parts marshmallow root, and one part marjoram.

Diaphoretic tea No. 2, containing two parts of coltsfoot leaves, two parts raspberries, and one part marjoram.

In folk medicine the fresh juice of coltsfoot leaves, or a brew (15 g of leaves to 200 g of water) with honey, was used as an expectorant. Several authors indicate that coltsfoot and honey preparations are very effective in several illnesses.

Raff recommends a cup of coltsfoot tea and honey once a day for pulmonary tuberculosis. Ertel and Bauer maintain that two cups a day of a tea prepared from the leaves and flowers of coltsfoot and lungwort *(Pulmonaria of ficinalis)* with honey have a beneficial effect on the nervous system and gastro-intestinal tract, and help ward off fatigue.

The fresh juice of coltsfoot leaves with milk and honey can also be used for the same purpose. K.Apinis recommends the following remedy for cough: boil 15.g of coltsfoot root and flowers in 500 g of water for six minutes; soak 90 g of sage and 120 g of centaury in four litres of boiling water, strain off the liquor, and mix it with the clotsfoot brew. The mixture is taken with honey four to six times a day.

Cowberry or red bilberry (*Vaccinium vitis-idea L.*)

The leaves of this evergreen underbush are used for medicinal purposes, and are extensively employed in folk medicine as a brew for treating kidney stones, rheumatism and gout.

An infusion (20 g of leaves to a glass of water) or a tea ntade from the leaves with honey (one tablespoon of honey to a glass of the infusion or tea) is usually taken.

Dyer's greenweed *(Genista tinctoria)* was used in folk medicine as a remedy for scrofula, fractures, venereal diseases, mange, and skin lesions. Its seeds contain the alkaloid cytisine ($C_{11}H_{14}N_2O$), which eases breathing.

According to S. E. Zemlinsky, tea made from the greenery of greenweed has been successfully tested clinically on patients with disorders of the thyroid gland.

Ertel and Bauer report that tea made from greenweed, taken with honey, is effective in cases of loss of strength, and weakness of the heart accompanied with low blood pressure.

Elder flowers and berries *(Sambucus nigra L.)* are used for medicinal purposes. Tea made from the flowers is a good diaphoretic. The fresh berries are used to treat rheumatism and neuralgia.

The root is a very effective diuretic. Elder contains tannin and proteins, malic acid, valeric acid, wax, resin, and other substances.

Elder tea, made by infusing 1 or $1^1/_2$ tablespoons of flowers in a glass of water, to which a spoonful of honey is added, is considered an effective diaphoretic for people with fever, influenza, or rheumatism in the joints.

A tablespoon should be taken five times a day, or half a glass morning and evening, for a month.

Elecampane or inula (*Inula helenium L.*)

The roots are extensively used in both folk and scientific medicine as an effective diuretic and as an expectorant.

Raff recommends a cupful of tea made from elecampane root with honey (one tablespoon of honey to a glass of tea) morning and evening for catarrh of the bronchi and bad coughs.

He also notes that an infusion made by boiling one tablespoon of the ground root for ten minutes with a glass of water is extremely effective-one tablespoon three times a day an hour before meals. The patient should lie on his right side for 15 minutes after taking the infusion.

A decoction of the root *Eucommia (Eucommia)* is widely used in Abkhazian folk medicine to treat cardiac sclerosis. Eucommia infusion and extract injected intravenously into cats and rabbits lower blood pressure.

This effect has been confirmed by tests carried out on patients at the Institute of Experimental and Clinical Therapy of the USSR Academy of Medicine. There we tested a tincture of eucommia with honey. Twenty drops of the tincture were given three times a day with a teaspoon of honey to patients suffering from hypertension.

It had a good therapeutic effect and lowered blood pressure significantly. Lemon juice *(Citrus medica L.)* and honey can be used in treating hypertonic and other illnesses. A.Raff recommends the juice of half a lemon and a tablespoon of honey in a glass of boiled water as a beverage extremely good for the organism and ensuring relaxed repose.

G. Hartwig recommends honey and lemon juice for catarrh of the throat. K.Apinis writes that an infusion of lemon juice and honey helps cure colds. Ertel and Bauer recommend lemon juice with honey and olive oil as an effective remedy for diseases of the liver and gall bladder.

Linden or lime (*Tilia*)

The flowers of the common lime are one of the most ancient and popular remedies known in folk medicine. The flowers mainly used for medicinal purposes are those of the small-leaved lime *(T. cordata* or *T. cordi folia Mill., T. parvi folia* Ehrh.) and the large-leaved lime *(T. cordifolia* Bess. or *T. platyphyllos Scop.)* (both of which are included in the USSR State Pharmacopoeia).

The Committee on Pharmacology of the USSR Ministry of Health approves the following for production: Diaphoretic tea No. 1, prepared from equal parts of linden flowers and raspberries; Mouthwash No. 1 containing one part lime flowers and two parts oak bark; Mouthwash No. 2 containing two parts lime flowers and three parts camomile.

A number of authors recommend lime tea with honey for various illnesses. Ertel and Bauer say that a cup of lime tea with honey is extremely good for old people as it 'cleanses the lungs of sputum', and is highly effective in treating diseases of the lungs and kidneys.

D.Swiekule considers that tea prepared from lime flowers, taken with honey and wine, cures anaemia and improves the complexion of women whose skin has a pale yellowish-green tinge. G. Hartwig recommends lime tea with honey and milk to quench the thirst during measles.

He also believes it is good for patients suffering from spasms of coughing and influenza to take a brew of lime flowers (one cup) with honey morning and evening.

Lungwort *(Pulmonaria officinaits L.)* was used in folk medicine as an astringent. A.Raff recommends the following for diseases of the lungs: 20-30 g lungwort leaves, honey, and a handful of wheat bran boiled in 1.25 litres of brown ale until half the liquid has evaporated. The remaining liquor is well strained, bottled, and taken before meals.

Ertel and Bauer recommend tea prepared from a mixture of dried lungwort leaves, plantain, sage, centaury, and wormwood with honey as an effective remedy for bronchitis, disorders of the throat and bladder, haemorrhoids, and other illnesses.

Marshmallow *(A lthaea officinalis L.)* has been known to have curative properties since ancient times (Greek *althein* to heal). Avicenna valued it highly. It has been established that marshmallow does in fact possess various curative properties.

It has been successfully used in treating inflammation of the respiratory organs and the urinary tract, and for diarrhoea. A tablespoon of tea made from marshmallow flowers (one tablespoon of flowers to a glass of water) can be taken several times a day for inflammation of the respiratory or urinary tracts.

The Committee on Pharmacology of the USSR Ministry of Health approved Tea No. 4 for chest complaints. This consists of two parts marshmallow root, two parts coltsfoot, and one part marjoram. Its curative effect is improved by adding a tablespoon of honey to a glass of the tea.

Mustard *(Sinapis).* K. Apinis says that a brew of mustard seeds, honey, and lily flowers is an extremely good means of getting rid of freckles and softening the skin.

Nettles *(Urtica diotica L.)* were used for centuries in folk medicine for haemorrhages of the womb, intestines, and lungs, and for haemorrhoids. They have been found to contain vitamins C and A (carotene) and vitamin K, which explains their haemostatic properties.

Prof. A.S.Tomilin writes: 'It has been demonstrated experimentally that nettles are able to restore haemoglobin and increase the number of erythrocytes at least to the same extent as iron preparations, and that they have a considerable effect on the conversion of carbohydrates.

In folk medicine nettle has long been used as a haemostatic, besides being a remedy for jaundice, rheumatism, and sweating during the night in those suffering from consumption. French doctors say that netties are extremely effective in treating severe and chronic enteritis, and diarrhoea in patients with tuberculosis.'

Nettle was widely used in folk medicine as an all-purpose remedy in the form of the fresh juice, a brew, extracts, and tea made from the leaves. Raff recommends nettle-leaf tea with honey for haemorrhoids, and particularly advises those who have been ill for some time to use honey.

Oak *(Quercus robur L.).* The acorns, bark, and leaves are used for medicinal purposes. Oak bark (Cortex Quercus) contains approximately 20 per cent of tannic substances and is mainly used as an astringent for gargling and in cases of looseness of the gums, stomatitis, and so forth.

K.Apinis claims that tea prepared from oak leaves, acorns, and bark, taken with honey, is an excellent remedy for diseases of the lungs, stomach, and liver. Ertel and Bauer recommend tea made from oak bark and acorns with honey for scrofula.

Onion *(Allium cepa L.)* mixed with honey was used as a remedy at the time of Hippocrates. Avicenna pointed out its highly bactericidal properties.

Today onion is used variously as a remedy. In 1949 the Committee on Pharmacology of the USSR Ministry of Health approved production of *Allilchep* (a spirit infusion of finely chopped onion), which has been used with success in treating intestinal diseases (colitis with a tendency to constipation and atonia of the intestine), and arteriosclerosis with and without hypertonia.

K. Apinis recommends onion and honey in the following form for a bad cough: 500 g finely chopped onion, 50 g honey, and 400 g sugar, boiled in a litre of water on a low flame for three hours. The liquor is then cooled, bottled, and tightly corked.

The patient takes four to six tablespoons a day. Raff advises gargling a sore throat with honey and onion brew or onion juice five or six times a day; and for chest complaints, coughs, and hoarseness in the elderly an onion and honey prepared as follows: a grated onion is soaked in a glass of vinegar and the mixture strained through wool, and mixed with an equal amount of honey.

A teaspoonful is taken every half an hour. Ertel and Bauer say that raw onion with honey and apple helps ease inflammation of the throat, and that a gruel of grated onion and apple with honey taken, daily is good far a weak bladder.

According to Raff, a tablespoon of onion brewed in water with honey is an effective diuretic.

He also advises a teaspoon of onion juice boiled with honey several times a day for whooping cough. V.A.Lukashev used onion with success to treat patients with cerebral arteriosclerosis.

Plantain's *(Plantago)* curative properties were known in ancient times. The Greeks and Romans used its seeds to treat dysentery.

A thousand years ago it was used as an all-purpose remedy in Arab and Iranian medicine; Avicenna recommended the seeds for skin infections in children.

Indian doctors found plantain seeds effective in treating bacillary and amoebic dysentery; they are mentioned in the Indian Pharmacopoeia. Plantain seeds contain oil, mucus, protein, tannin, and other substances. Plantain leaves contain a great deal of citric acid, plus calcium, enzymes (invertase, emulsin), provitamin A (carotene), vitamin C, phytoncide, bitter principles, tannin, and other substances.

They were widely used in folk medicine for cuts, lesions, grazes, dermatitis, bronchitis, nephritis, haemorrhages, etc. An infusion of plantain leaves (6 g of leaves to 200 g of water) is an excellent expectorant; a tablespoon is taken three times a day.

Prof.A.Tomilin writes that the plantain leaves have been effectively used by French doctors to treat severe and chronic enteritis, dysentery, and diarrhoea in patients with tuberculosis or chronic nephritis.

D. Swiekule recommends the juice of fresh plantain leaves (P. *major* and P. *lanceolata)* as an effective remedy for bronchitis, pleurisy with effusion, pulmonary tuberculosis (even with coughing of blood). An infusion or brew of plantain leaves and honey can also be taken, three tablespoons a day (6 g of leaves, 200 g of water, and 30 g of honey).

Radish *(Raphanus sativa)*. Several authors speak of radish having highly curative properties in combination with honey. K.Apinis recommends patients with rheumatism to rub themselves with an embrocation consisting of 300 g of radish juice, 200 g of honey, 100 g of vodka, and a tablespoon of salt.

Ertel and Bauer say that radish juice and honey (100 g to 400 g a day) prevent the formation of stones in the bladder and kidneys. Radish juice and honey also help to prevent arteriosclerosis, sand in the liver, and dropsy.

A good way of obtaining the juice is to remove the flesh from the centre of the radish, fill the cavity with honey, leaving it for three or four hours. Adults take two or three tablespoons of juice an hour, and children one teaspoon.

Radish juice and honey is also good for cough and hoarseness as it stimulates the secretion of sputum. Raff recommends a tablespoon of radish juice and honey three times a day for cough.

Raspberries *(Rubus idaeus L.)* have been known to possess curative properties since antiquityy when its dried berries were used to treat fevers, and an infusion of its flowers was considered an antidote for snake bite. According to Zemlinsky, raspberry contains ethereal oil, malic and citric acid, sugar, colourings, mucus, vitamin C, and other substances.

Dried raspberries are used as a most effective diaphoretic during colds. Some authors have had success using raspberry juice or tea with honey. Raff says that raspberry juice and honey is both a refresher and an analeptic during measles. Two or three cups of warm raspberry tea with honey daily are recommended for erysipelas.

Red clover *(Tri folium pratense L.)* was used in folk medicine in the form of an infusion or a tea made from the flowers as an expectorant and a diuretic, and also as a poultice for treating burns and lesions. D. Swiekule says that warm tea from clover flowers is extremely effective in bronchitis and asthma as an expectorant and diuretic.

Sweet violet *(Viola odorata L.)* is used as a remedy for coughs and as an expectorant. Ertel and Bauer recommend a tea made of violet leaves and honey for consumption and bronchial asthma. Other authors consider that this tea is effective in treating pulmonary tuberculosis. Three teaspoons are taken every three hours, especially for a bad cough.

Thyme *(Thymus vulgaris L.).* Zemlinsky says that galenical preparations for whooping cough and colds can be made from the dried leaves and flowering tops of thyme.

Galen and Avicenna attributed important curative properties to thyme in treating diseases of the gastro-intestinal tract. Ertel and Bauer say that thyme tea with honey is effective against tapeworms, and recommend it to be taken daily for four to six weeks (20 g of thyme, 250 g of water, and 30 g of honey).

Valerian drops *(Valeriana of ficinalis L.)* are an extremely popular remedy as a tranquillizer for people suffering from nerves, insomnia, etc. Sebastian Kneips recommends a tea made from valerian root and rue, with honey, for hysteria: one tablespoon every two hours.

OTHER HERBAL AND HONEY REMEDIES

Elderberry and Honey Jam

Sebastian Kneip (the wellknown advocate of hydrotherapy) recommends a curative jam made of honey and elderberries for people leading a sedentary life. A spoonful of the jam in a glass of water makes a pleasant beverage that has a good effect on the stomach and kidneys.

Horseradish and Honey

Horseradish and honey, according to Raff, eases bronchial asthma. Equal parts of grated horseradish and honey are mixed, and a teaspoonful taken during the day and another when going to bed.

Herbal Tea

Raff recommends a tea made from lungwort, coltsfoot, althaea, and honey as a remedy for cough in illnesses affecting the respiratory tract.

A tablespoon of the herbal mixture is steeped in a litre of boiling water for three or four hours. One or two glasses of the tea (or infusion) are drunk daily, with a teaspoon of honey.

Lemon Juice and Honey

Lemon juice and honey is a good remedy in cases of hypertension, insomnia, and nervous conditions. Dissolve a spoonful of top quality honey in a glass of mineral water and add the juice of half a lemon. The beverage is pleasant and nutritious. Bauer recommends lemon juice with honey and olive oil for complaints of the liver and gall bladder.

Linseed Tea

Ertel and Bauer recommend linseed tea with aniseed, fennel, and honey as an effective laxative. A teaspoonful of the mixture is boiled with 250 g of water for three or four minutes, using ground linseed, fennel, pharmaceutical dill, and good quality honey.

Tea with Honey

V.V.Pokhlebkin gives a recipe for tea with honey and other ingredients that was widely used in folk medicine.') Fairly strong, warm tea, taken with lemon, black pepper and honey is an effective diaphoretic for treating catarrhal illnesses of the respiratory tract, and a diuretic.

Tea contains no less than 120 to 130 chemical substances. Pokhlebin writes, including essential oils (0.0k per cent), tannin (15-30 per cent), albumin (16-25 per cent), alkaloids (1-4 per cent), vitamins B;, B_2, PP, C, R, K, and provitamin A.

Dr.D.F.MacLeadon (U.S.A.) contends that tea contains fluorine and can therefore be used as an effective means of averting tooth decay. But this property is lost when tea is drunk with sugar, which encourages caries. MacLeadon therefore strongly recommends sweetening tea with honey instead of sugar. Pokhlebkin, too, concludes that tea should be drunk with honey..

Yarrow tea. Raff maintains that a tea made by steeping 20 grams of yarrow in 500 g of boiling water (and mixed with 50 g of honey after infusing) is very good for influenza. One coffee cup of the tea is drunk, three times a day.

Old Wife's Remedies

A teaspoon of honey before bed is recommended for babies cutting teeth. It reduces the amount of phosphorus in the blood and so eases the pain.

A. similar dose of honey prevents bed-wetting, as it causes dehydration and reduces the amount of calcium in the blood.

Two tablespoons of honey taken regularly instead of supper help in cases of insomnia. The honey (50 g) is best taken on rye or wholemeal bread an hour or hour and a half before going to bed. It has a soothing effect on the nerves and a beneficial effect on normal intestinal function.

HONEY IN THE HOME

COOKING WITH HONEY

For curative purposes honey is best taken in its natural form or diluted with water (drinking water or mineral water), or eaten with bread, milk, cereals, or fruit. Honey improves the taste and increases the calorific value and digestibility of dishes.

It can be used as a substitute for sugar in making mousses and jellies, stewing fruit, and making vitamin drinks and other beverages. Honey-cakes apart, cakes, cookies, and biscuits made with honey have a pleasant flavour and are much more nutritious than when made with sugar.

Honey jams from fruits or berries (cranberries, damsons, rowan berries, and so on) are also delicious. In this chapter we give some recipes that can be made with honey.)

Honey Cakes and Sweetmeats

Apple Cake

100 g clear honey	½ cup sugar
500 g apples (preferably a winter variety)	100 g butter
	½ teaspoon bicarbonate of soda)
1 cup plain flour)	2 eggs

1 tablespoon butter for greasing tins

Add the honey, sugar, and eggs to the softened butter and beat well. Sieve the flour and soda together and mix all the ingredients into a dough. Core, but do not peel, the apples, cut them up into small pieces, and add to the dough. Fill buttered biscuit tins or paddy pans with the mixture and bake in a moderate oven (170°C or 350°F).

Armenian Arishta

1 kg flour   200 g sugar
600 g honey   whites of 20 eggs
700 g clarified butter   yolks of 10 eggs

Beat the egg whites until stiff. Cream the yolks with the sugar. Then blend the two together and fold in the sieved flour. Mix thoroughly for 20-25 minutes. Divide the dough into pieces and place on a floured table.

Roll out the pietas to form a thin layer and cut into noodle shapes. Sprinkle the shapes with flour and fry in clarified butter. Place the fried noodles in a sieve to drain. When drained immerse them in a syrup of boiling honey and again drain. Arrange on a plate in vertical and horizontal rows to form a lattice work, and cut into squares.

Armenian Gozinakh

500 g shelled walnuts   100 g sugar
500 g honey

Boil the honey and sugar together. Sprinkle the lightly roasted and finely chopped walnut meats into the syrup and boil for 15 minutes. While still hot, place in a dish, and sprinkle with cold water, level the surface, and leave to cool. Then warm the dish, remove the *gozinakh,* cut into diamond-shaped pieces, and arrange on a plate. Almonds may be used instead of walnuts.

Armenian Puffed Pakhlava

750 g flour   50 g yeast
1 cup water

filling:

300 g chopped nuts   300 g sugar
175 g clarified butter   3 g cardamon

glaze:

yolks of two eggs

sauce:

150 g honey   110 g clarified butter

Dissolve the yeast in warm water in a mixing bowl and gradually add the flour. Knead the dough for 15-20 minutes, then cover with a towel and allow to stand in a warm place for 30-40 minutes. Prepare the filling, first mincing the walnuts and then mixing with the sugar and grated cardamon. When the dough has risen turn it out on a pastry board and divide into fourteen equal pieces.

Roll out each piece on a floured pastry board and brush with melted butter. Place three pieces of dough on top of each other on a greased baking sheet, spread the top one with onefifth of the prepared filling, and cover with another two pieces of dough.

Again spread the top piece with filling, and repeat the procedure three times. Finally cover with three layers of pastry, brush the top one with egg yolk, and made diamond-shaped cuts in it. Bake in a hot oven for 30-35 minutes.

After the first ten minutes pour melted butter (110 g) into the cuts. When the *pakhlava is* ready, remove from the oven and pour the honey, warmed, into the slits.

Armenian Rich Pakhlava

750 g plain flour 175 g clarified butter

2 eggs 35 g yeast

200 g water

filling:

500 g walnuts 500 g sugar

5 g cardamon 110 g clarified butter

175 g honey

Dissolve the yeast in the water in a large mixing bowl. Beat in the eggs and mix thoroughly. Gradually add the flour and stir well. Pour in the melted butter and knead the dough for 10-15 minutes. Allow to stand in a warm place for 90 minutes.

While the dough is rising prepare the filling, mincing the walnuts and mixing with the sugar and grated cardamon. When the dough is ready turn it out on a pastry board and divide into two halves. Roll each half out thin. Place one piece on a greased baking sheet and spread with the prepared filling.

Place the other piece of pastry on top of the filling and pinch the edges of the two pieces together. Brush the top with the egg yolk and make diamond-shaped cuts. Bake in a hot oven for 35-40 minutes. After the first ten minutes pour the melted butter into the slits and return the ***pakhlava*** to the oven. When ready pour the honey into the slits and cut into squares.

Armenian Yugatert

1 cup plain flour)	2 eggs
1 kg flour	200 g clarified butter (150 g for coating)
1 cup of hot milk	1-2 g bicarbonate of soda
6 eggs	300 g honey

Sift the flour into a mixing bowl. Make a hollow in the flour and pour in the beaten eggs and hot milk (in which the soda has been dissolved) and 50 g of butter.

Knead the mixture and roll out as thin as possible. Brush with melted butter and sprinkle lightly with flour. Fold into an envelope, roll out again, brush with butter, sprinkle with flour, and fold again into an envelope. Repeat the procedure six times.

Place the final envelope in a greased pan and bake in a hot oven for 10-15 minutes. Cut into squares, arrange on a plate, and pour hot melted honey over them.

Bulgarian Honey Cake

250 g honey	$^1/_3$ cup water
1 cup sunflower oil	$^1/_3$ cup ground walnuts
$^1/_3$ cup raisins	4-5 glace fruits, finely grated
1 teaspoon cocoa	1 teaspoon cinnamon
4-5 cloves, ground plain flour	1 teaspoon bicarbonate of soda

Dilute the honey with the water and pour in the sunflower oil. Then add the ground walnuts, raisins, glace fruits, cocoa, cinnamon, clove, soda, and sufficient flour to make a mixture of soft consistency.

Roll out to a thickness of two centimetres. Place on a greased baking sheet and bake in a moderate oven for about an hour. Serve cold and iced with white-of-egg frosting or thickly dredged with icing sugar. The icing may be coloured, if desired, with cocoa, chocolate, or food colouring.

Butlerov Honeycake

5 egg whites	120 g plain flour
200 g honey (buckwheat preferred)	200 g lightly roasted almonds
	3 egg yolks
2 g cinnamon	2 g grated nutmeg
	pinch of aniseed

Beat the egg whites with the egg yolks and honey. Add the flour, and spices. Mix thoroughly and add the almonds, coarsely chopped.

Roll the mixture out to a thickness of one centimetre. Cut into shapes or bake whole.

Cheesecake

500 g cottage cheese	50 g clear honey
½ cup sugar	2 eggs
3-4 teaspoons semolina	1 tablespoon butter (for greasing cake. tin)

Sieve the curd and add the honey, sugar, eggs, and semolina. Mix thoroughly. Place in a well-greased cake tin and bake for 35-40 minutes.

Favourite Honeycake

300 g clear honey	¾ cup strong tea
60 g butter	½ cup sugar
1 egg	550 g plain flour
½ teaspoon bicarbonate of soda	10-15 cloves (ground)

20 g butter (for greasing baking tins)

Add the softened butter, sugar, egg, tea, ground cloves to the honey and mix thoroughly. Sprinkle in the flour and soda, and knead the dough. Place the mixture in a well-greased tin (either a gugelhupf mould or a round cake tin) and bake in a fairly hot oven (200°C or 400° F).

Halvoiter (*Soft honey halva*)

6 cups plain flour	2 cups clarified butter or
2 cups honey	lamb dripping
2 cups water	½cup shelled walnuts (ground)

Brown the flour in a copper pan with clarified butter or lamb dripping until an even, crumbly, light brown mixture is obtained.

Add the honey and water and boil for a few minutes (not more than five). When ready place the halva on a serving dish or platter, sprinkle with the ground walnuts and cut into pieces of different shapes. Makes two kilograms of soft, sticky halva.

Honey Baba *(Steamed cheesecake with honey and nuts)*

200 g cottage cheese	20 g plain flour
100 g honey	30 g shelled walnuts (ground)
1 egg	
20 g butter	10 g sugar

Warm the honey and add the lightly dried ground walnuts, egg yolk, flour, and butter. Beat thoroughly. Pass the curd through a sieve and mix with the other ingredients.

Carefully fold in the beaten egg white. Place the mixture in buttered metal cones or cylindrical tins, sprinkled with sugar. Steam until ready. When cooked pour warmed honey over the cake and serve. Makes two babas.

Honey Biscuits

100 g honey	5 tablespoons sugar
2-3 eggs	1 tablespoon butter
1 teaspoon bicarbonate of soda	1 teaspoon ground cloves
1 teaspoon cinnamon	shredded dried peel of one lemon

plain flour (to make a thick dough)

Make a syrup of the sugar and honey. Add flour to the hot syrup and whisk together quickly to a thick consistency. Allow the mixture to cool to room temperature and add the softened butter and soda (previously mixed with one tablespoon of flour) and the shredded - dried lemon peel.

Knead for 15-20 minutes, then roll out to a thickness of one centimetre. Cut into pieces or shapes. Place the biscuits on a greased baking sheet and brush with white of egg and sprinkle to taste with poppy seed. Bake in a moderately hot oven.

Honeycake *(Medovik)*

100 g honey	5 tablespoons sugar
1 kg honey	1 cup sugar
2-3 tablespoons butter	4 cups plain flour
4-5 eggs	½ teaspoon bicarbonate of soda
½ teaspoon cinnamon	clove to taste

Bring the honey, butter, and sugar to the boil. Remove from the flame, add the flour, and knead the dough. Allow the mixture to cool, then add the eggs, bicarbonate of soda, clove, cinnamon, and mix together thoroughly.

Set the dough to stand in a cool place for two days. Then roll out to two or three centimetres thick, place on a greased baking sheet, and bake in a fairly hot oven.

Honeycake with Peel

200 g honey	100 g butter
1 cup sugar	1 g ginger
3 cups flour	¼ teaspoon cinnamon
2-3 eggs	¼ teaspoon ground clove
3 teaspoons shredded dried lemon peel	salt to taste

Warm the honey and blend in the melted butter. Add the sugar, ginger, and salt, and mix thoroughly. Then mix in the eggs, cloves, cinnamon, and lemon peel, and gradually add the flour. Knead the dough well and roll out to a thickness of one centimetre. Cut with pastry cutters or a knife. Place on a greased baking sheet and bake in a fairly hot oven.

Honey Mazurkas

50 g clear honey	¾ cup sugar
1½ cups chopped walnuts	1 cup sultanas or raisins
3 eggs	½ cup flour
¼ teaspoon bicarbonate of soda	1 tablespoon butter

Cream the yolks of the eggs with the sugar and' add the honey, nuts, sultanas, sieved flour, and soda. (If crystallized honey is used it should be warmed first in a bath of water.)

Mix thoroughly and add the beaten egg whites. Stir carefully and place on a large baking sheet or in a buttered baking tin. Bake in a moderate oven (180°-190°C; 360°F). Cut and serve while hot. Dredge with icing sugar if desired.

Honey Nutcake

200 g honey	1 cup icing sugar
3 cups plain flour	1 cup chopped walnuts
1 cup strong tea	1 teaspoon bicarbonate of soda
3 tablespoons vegetable oil	5-6 cloves, ground
1 teaspoon cinnamon	dried lemon or orange peel

Dilute the honey with the tea. Gradually mix in the icing sugar, vegetable oil, soda, cinnamon, cloves, and a small quantity of grated dried lemon or orange peel, the chopped walnuts, and the flour.

Stir thoroughly and pour into a greased, floured cake tin. Bake in a moderately hot oven. When ready turn out of the tin, dredge with icing sugar, and serve cold.

Honey Oatcakes

1 cup flour	1 cup rolled oats
½ cup sugar	½ cup honey
½ cup sour cream (smetana)	1 egg
100 g butter	½ teaspoon bicarbonate of soda

Mix and sift the flour and soda. Cream the butter and sugar together until white, then while beating add the honey, sour cream, egg, rolled oats, flour and soda. Roll out thin (3-5 millimetres), cut into various shapes, and bake in a hot oven (200°-220°C; 400°-425°F) for 10-15 minutes. Makes 750-800 grams of oatcakes.

Honey Puffs

100 g honey	100-150 g icing sugar
2 eggs	1 teaspoon bicarbonate of soda
200 g vegetable oil	
flour	several cloves, ground

Mix the honey with the icing sugar and warm. Add the vegetable oil, eggs, soda, and clove. Beat the mixture, gradually stirring in flour until the dough is fairly thick. Form into balls a little larger than a hazel nut. Bake in a moderate oven.

Honey Puffs with Nuts

5 tablespoons honey	1 cup icing sugar
1 cup chopped walnuts	5-6 cloves, ground
1 teaspoon bicarbonate of soda	3-4 black pepper corns, ground
plain flour	½ teaspoon cinnamon

Mix the honey with the icing sugar and add the chopped walnuts, soda, spices, and sufficient flour to make a fairly thick dough. Shape into balls the size of a walnut. Place on a greased and floured baking sheet and bake in a moderately hot oven.

Hungarian Honey Biscuits

300 g plain flour	140 g icing sugar
grated dried peel of one lemon	cinnamon
	clove
honey	bicarbonate of soda

Mix the flour and icing sugar and add the lemon peel with ground cinnamon and clove to taste. Then add a pinch of soda and sufficient honey to make a soft but not runny mixture.

Roll out thin (5 millimetres) and cut into rounds or rings. Bake on a buttered baking sheet. When ready ice or sprinkle with caster sugar.

Hungarian Nut Cookies

300 g plain flour	whites of three eggs
140 g honey	yolk of one egg
100 g butter	grated dried peel of one
80 g ground walnuts	lemon
1 tablespoon rum	juice of one lemon
bicarbonate of soda	

Rub the butter into the flour and add the honey, egg yolk, egg whites, ground walnuts, lemon peel, lemon juice, rum, and a pinch of soda.

Knead the mixture well, roll out, and cut into shapes or rounds. Bake until a golden brown. When cold the cookies can be iced with a chocolate icing and decorated with half a shelled walnut.

Moscow Honeybread

2 cups honey (preferably buckwheat)	4 eggs
	2 cups rye flour
2 cups plain flour	1 teaspoon bicarbonate of soda

Mix all the ingredients together thoroughly. Roll out the dough to a thickness of one centimetre and place on a greased baking sheet. Allow to stand for two hours, then bake in a fairly hot oven (200°C or 400°F).

Oatcakes with Honey

½ cup honey	½ cup sugar
1 cup flour	1 cup rolled oats
1/2 cup sour cream (sme-tana)	1 egg
100 g butter	½ teaspoon bicarbonate of soda

Cream the butter and sugar thoroughly. Add the honey, egg, sour cream, oats, flour, and soda. Mix together, and roll out thin (3-5 millimetres). Cut into diamond shapes and bake in a fairly hot oven (200°C or 400°F) for 10-15 minutes.

Russian Gingerbread *(Kovrizhka)*

250 g plain flour	50 g water
100 g sugar	5 g sunflower oil
100 g honey	5 g bicarbonate of soda
1 clove, ground	1 g cinnamon

Mix the honey and sugar with the water and boil thoroughly. Allow the syrup to cool to room temperature, then add the spices and soda. Mix well and add the flour to make a soft dough.

Knead the mixture well and roll out to a thickness of one centimetre. Place on a greased baking sheet and bake gradually raising the temperature to 200° C (400° F).

Russian honeycakes *(Pryaniki)*

250 g plain flour	yolk of one egg
100 g honey	50 g water

70 g sugar	dried peel of a quarter of a lemon
30 g butter	2 g bicarbonate of soda

Make a syrup of the sugar, honey, and water. Add threequarters of the flour to the hot syrup and whisk together quickly to a thick paste. Allow the mixture to cool to room temperature and add the softened butter and soda (previously mixed with one tablespoon of flour), and shredded dried lemon peel.

Knead the mixture until a smooth dough is formed. Roll out to one centimetre in thickness and cut with pastry cutters or a knife. Place the pieces on a greased baking sheet and brush with egg yolk before baking in a moderate oven. These honeycakes have an extremely pleasant flavour and aroma, and keep well.

Tajik Corn Puffs

1 kg popping corn   1 cup honey

Pop the corn in a popping basket or pan. Mix the popcorn with the honey and form into balls the size of an apple.

Tajik Honey and Nut Halva

1 kg honey   ½ cup sugar

1 kg shelled walnuts

Boil the honey, stirring constantly. Add the walnuts, chopped, and sugar and cook thoroughly until the mixture becomes thick and viscous (almost solid). Place on a board, sprinkle with water, and roll out to form an even layer 10-15 millimetres thick.

When cold, serve in rectangles or square pieces. Pistacchio nuts, peanuts, or almonds can be used instead of walnuts, but should be roasted lightly first.

Tajik Honey Sweets

One kilogram of honey is needed to make a kilogram of the sweets. Boil the honey thoroughly in a cast-iron pan for 15-20 min, stirring constantly, until it becomes dark brown.

Spread the boiled honey on a greased tray, press it flat, and pull as taffy to form plaits. Cut ringlets, twirls, or cushion-shaped pieces from the plaits with a knife.

Tajik Zulbieh

1 kg plain flour	4 eggs
1½-2 cups milk	½ teaspoon salt
1 cup honey	600-800 g cooking oil

Prepare a stiff, unleavened dough from the flour, milk, and eggs, and leave to stand for 40-50 minutes. Then place the dough in a bowl and gradually dilute with milk until an even mixture of the consistency of thick cream is obtained.

Pour the mixture gradually criss-cross in a thin stream into a frying pan or copper pan containing a large amount of hot cooking oil (or fat), so as to form a lattice. Fry until both sides are brown. When ready, put the *zulbieh* into a previously prepared syrup of honey and sugar and leave for five to seven minutes before serving. *Zulbieh* can be served with honey and fruit juice.

Uzbek Halva *(B adrok)*

200 g roasted maize	½ cup honey
(Indian corn)	1 teaspoon clarified butter
200 g shelled walnuts	

Mince the roasted corn and walnut kernels and place in a china vessel lightly greased with clarified butter. Boil the honey in an alumin-ium pan for five to seven minutes, then pour it over the ground corn and nuts, mixing thoroughly.

Pour out onto a plate or platter, press down to about one centimetre thick. Cut the *badrok* into diamonds and serve with hot tea (black or green).

Uzbek Noodles *(Chak-chak)*

500 g plain flour	150 g lamb dripping
500-600 g honey	350 g vegetable oil (cotton
100-150 g sugar	seed oil by preferen
5-6 eggs	ce), or 500 g clarified butter

Break the eggs into the flour and work into a stiff paste. Roll out the dough as thinly as possible and cut into narrow strips four or five centimetres long.

Shake off surplus flour and fry in a mixture of lamb dripping and cottonseed oil (or dripping and clarified butter). Place the fried noodles on brown paper to drain and cool. While they are cooling melt the honey in a metal bowl, stirring all the time, and add the sugar (which is to harden the noodles).

Remove the bowl from the flame as soon as the sugar is melted. Put several handfuls of fried noodles into a deep bowl and gradually pour the honey and sugar syrup over them. Stir, adding more noodles and syrup.

The resulting mixture should be transferred quickly to a dish lined with greaseproof paper and pressed down with the hands (moistened with water) and shaped. Put the shaped *chak-chak* in a refrigerator or cool place to set. When properly set decorate with small coloured sweets or fruit drops. Cut into small neat pieces to serve.

Yugoslav Honey Halva

1 kg plain flour 400 gclarified butter

400 g honey

Sift the flour and put in a frying-pan, add the clarified butter, and mix, stirring well. Fry the mixture until it becomes uniform, crumbly, and yellow. Add the honey and continue to fry for five minutes more. Put the halva on a plate, form it into an even shape, and cut into squares.

SALADS AND HEALTH DISHES

Creamed Rice with Honey

To make one helping (200 grams):

50 g rice 70 g water

50 g milk 20 g honey

10 g butter 1 g salt

Prepare the rice with milk and butter in the usual way. Add the honey before serving.

Fresh Cucumbers and Honey

For one helping:

120 g cucumber 25 g clear honey

Wash and peel a medium-sized cucumber and cut lengthwise

into segments. Pour the honey over the segments and serve. Makes a dish that is both delicious and nourishing.

Grated Carrot with Sour Cream and Honey

To make one portion (100 grams):

200 g roasted maize	½ cup honey
60 g carrot scraped and washed	20 g honey
	20 g sour cream (Smetana)

Shred or grate the carrot and mix with the honey and sour cream before serving.

Fresh Tomatoes and Honey

Select tomatoes that are only just ripe. Wash and cut them into halves. Pour honey over the halves and serve as a dessert.

Honey and Yeast Paste

This is an invaluable dietetic food for people of all ages, but especially for the elderly, recommended by Prof. K. I. Parhon, late president of the Romanian Academy of Sciences, in his book *The Biology of Age.*

The paste is prepared by mixing equal parts of honey and baker's yeast, or one part honey and two parts yeast. A daily portion of 50-75 grams is an excellent health booster.

Pickled Cucumber and Honey

Cut a pickled (salted) cucumber or gherkin lengthwise into four pieces. Pour honey over the pieces and serve as a dessert. (Quantities as for fresh cucumber and honey.)

Polish Curd and Honey

450 g cottage cheese	3 tablespoons honey

Pass the curd through a sieve and mix with the honey until smooth. Dish up and serve.

Russian Salad with Honey

For one portion (100 grams):

10 g cooked carrot	15 g cooked beetroot
20 g boiled potato, diced	30 g salted or pickled cucumber
15 g spring onion	10 g honey

Prepare Russian salad in the usual way, dicing the vegetables and mixing them together (salting to taste). Before serving pour the honey over the salad and mix it in.

PRUNE AND HONEY STEW

For each helping:

83 g stewing beef	10 g honey
15 g chopped onion	5 g cooking fat
15 g stoned prunes	1 g spices and salt

tomato to taste

Cut the raw meat into pieces, fry, and place in a casserole. Add lightly browned onions, tomato, and washed, stoned prunes. Simmer over a low flame until ready. Before serving add the honey. Serve from the casserole or in a small earthenware pot, or from the frying pan with the juice from the fried meat. Garnish with stewed vegetables if desired.

HONEY DRINKS AND BEVERAGES

Honey drinks are extolled in national epics, folk tales, legends, and songs. The story of their preparation is age old, and both ancient and modern poets and writers have devoted fine passages to it.

Greek mythology tells that Zeus, the king and ruler of the gods, was nursed by the honey nymph Melissa, who taught him how to make a delicious wine from it. With the help of his mother Rhea, Zeus saw to it that his father Cronos drank heavily of this honey wine, and usurped the throne while Cronos was sleeping it off.

In the twenty-fifth rune of the Finnish *Kalevala,* it says of the wedding-feast:

Beer of barley ceaseless flowing,
Honey-drink that was not purchased,
In the cellar flows profusely,
Beer for all, the tongues to quicken,
Mead and beer the minds to freshen.

Mead figures largely in Scandinavian sagas, in Scottish legends, in Welsh customs. Down to the fifteenth century in Russia, and among the Slavs generally, the honey drink, or mead, was considered the national alcoholic beverage. Russian epics attributed supernatural curative powers to honey drinks.

In the *Kalevala,* Wainamoinen, 'wise and wonderful enchanter' heats a honey-bath in order to kill the nine diseases children, of Louhi, and sings:

When I pour the sacred waters
On the heated blocks of sandstone,
May the water turn to honey,
Laden with the balm of healing.
Let the stream of magic virtues
Ceaseless flow to all my children.

Blackcurrant and Honey Milk

3 cups milk   300 g blackcurrants
4 tablespoons honey

Boil the milk and mix with the honey. Leave to cool. Remove the stalks from the blackcurrant, wash the berries and rub them through a sieve. Add the milk slowlyy to the puree and then stir quickly to prevent curdling. Serve cold in small glasses.

CENTRAL ASIAN BAL

In many of the languages of Central Asia, *bal* means *honey,* or drinks made from honey. For one litre of *bal, you will* need the following:

125 g honey   1 litre water
25 g cinnamon   5 g ginger
5 g cloves   ¼ bay leaf
0.25 g black pepper

Put the spices and bay leaf in hot water and bring to the boil. Remove from the flame, cover tightly, and leave to infuse for five to ten minutes. Then add the honey, mix thoroughly and strain. Serve hot.

Honey Cocktail *(Gogol-mogol)*

2 cups -milk   ½ cup orange juice
6 tablespoons honey   1 egg
60 g brandy

Beat the egg until thick and add salt to taste. Add the beaten egg and honey to the cold milk, then the brandy and orange juice. Serve in tall glasses with straws. Makes three to four portions.

Honey Table Beverage

Per portion:

1 cup boiled water 25 g honey

1 g citric acid

Add the honey to the hot water and boil for four minutes. Then add the citric acid. Strain and serve cold.

HONEY AND YEAST MILK

This is a very nourishing drink for people of all ages. It meets all the requirements of the growing (child) organism, as it contains all the amino acids needed, is rich in monosaccharides, vitamins, minerals, micro-elements, etc.

The milk is particularly useful for the elderly as it has a beneficial effect on the cardiovascular system and gastrointestinal tract. Honey and yeast milk can be prepared as follows.

1 kg fresh baker's yeast	400 g icing or granulated sugar
3.6 litres of water (18 cups)	200 g flour (preferably whole meal)
200 g butter	300 g clear honey (preferably buckwheat)

Mix the yeast briskly with the sugar in an enamel saucepan until smooth. Add one litre (5 cups) of water and boil for two hours. Dilute with the remainder of the water (13 cups) and boil again for 18-20 minutes.

Then pour onto a boiling paste of the flour and butter. Add the honey to the strained yeast milk while it is still warm and stir thoroughly to obtain an even mixture. Keep the milk in a refrigerator. Take warm (room temperature), two tablespoons two or three times a day.

Honey Grog

75 g brandy 20 g honey slice of lemon

Put the honey in a warmed glass, add the brandy, and fill up with boiling water. Add the slice of lemon.

Hungarian Honey Cream

4 tablespoons fresh cream   2 liqueur glasses of brandy
2 tablespoons honey

Fill a glass a quarter full with crushed ice. Pour in the honey, brandy, and cream. Shake well to mix and serve.

MEAD

Of all the various drinks and beverages made with honey, one of the tastiest and most satisfying is mead. Mead is most nutritious, containing many elements needed by the organism, quenches the thirst quickly, and has an excellent effect on the digestion and metabolism.

It is particularly good for those suffering from or recovering from anaemia or chronic illnesses of the gastro-intestinal tract (gastritis with hypoacidity, colitis with flaccid peristalsis, etc.).

The following ingredients are required for meads: pure honey, hops, spices (cinnamon, clove, cardamon, orris root, ginger, vanilla, mint), cranberries, juniper berries, raspberries, cherries, currants (red, white, or black), rose petals, lemons, oranges, or other fruits, raisins or sultanas, brewer's or baker's yeast.

Since honey is an ingredient, alcohol is formed during fermentation. A must or wort is prepared in making mead. If honey in the comb is used, the honeycomb should be immersed in simmering water; the wax will float to the top and can be skimmed off. When honey out of the comb is used, the scum formed during boiling should be skimmed off.

Honey that has not been boiled produces a more aromatic and tasty must but the mead tends to sour more quickly than when made with boiled honey. In preparing the must the honey should be diluted with six parts of water and flavoured with spices.

Fruit juices, however, can be used instead of part of the water. As soon as the honey, water, spices and fruit juices are mixed together they begin to ferment. The must for boiled-honey mead should be boiled for two to four hours, until it becomes light in colour, before being left to cool and ferment.

When hops are used they should be added to the must 15 to 25 minutes before boiling is completed; and pure fruit juices should only be added after the honey has been boiled and cooled.

When the must is ready it should be strained through muslin and left to ferment. Fermentation can be said to have begun when a white foam appears on the surface, and the must becomes bubbly. When the foam disappears the main, or initial, fermentation is completed.

The unmatured mead should be covered and kept in a refrigerator or a cold cellar to continue fermenting slowly for one or two months. This lengthy fermentation and maturing in a cool place makes the mead clearer and more flavoursome and aromatic; and it keeps better.

It is not recommended to mature mead at a temperature above 12°-15° C; and the final stage of fermentation is best done at a temperature of 2°-4° C as by-products that could spoil the quality of the mead are not formed at such a temperature.

When fermentation is completed the mead is strained through muslin. The matured mead is bottled, preferably in champagne bottles., corked, and wired to hold to eight weeks after preparation began. After bottling the mead should stand for another two weeks before drinking. Bottles are best stored lying on their sides, either on ice or in the ice (freezer) compartment of an ice box or refrigerator.

When stored in the cold mead will keep for at least three or four months and will become lighter in colour during that time, without the addition of white of egg or isinglass.

Mead made with yeast does not keep as well as that made without. With yeast a pure culture (100 grams for 18-20 litres -of must) is used (with raisins), and added to the must before the main fermentation takes place. With yeast fermentation takes from one to three days, and after fermentation and maturation another two weeks.

If a lighter colour is desired, the mead can be lightened by adding the white of an egg for every three to five litres (one gallon) of mead (or 1 g of isinglass for every five litres).

Latvian Mead

5 litres of water   800 g honey

25 g yeast 2 lemons

Boil the water and add the honey. When the liquid has cooled to 20° C add the yeast, the juice of the lemons (or the equivalent of citric acid) and leave to stand for 10-12 hours. Cool, bottle, and cork well.

Lemon Mead

2 kg honey 100 g hops

6-8 lemons 100 g yeast

3 g isinglass

Boil the honey and hops in 12 litres of water. The cooled mixture is honey must. Add the yeast and allow to ferment. Then store in the cool (refrigerator or cold cellar) for two or three weeks.

Strain out any remaining honey and bottle. Keep the corked bottles in a cool place until needed.

Red Mead

4 kg honey 25 litres of water

100 g hops 6 g orris root

1 tablespoon burnt sugar 2-3 grains of cardamon

Makes 23 litres.

Russian Mead

4 kg honey 15 litres water

200 g yeast 200 g hops

Follow the general directions given above. Makes 15 litres.

Tatar Mead *(bal)*

2.5 kg honey 8 litres boiled water

100 g yeast

Remove the honey from the honeycomb, warm it, pass through a sieve, and pour into a small oak cask (10 litres). Add the boiled water and yeast.

Allow the cask to stand at room temperature for eight to ten days. When fermentation is over, store the cask in a cool place.

The mead or *bal will* keep for up to six months. Serve cold. Makes ten litres.

White Mead

4 kg honey 25 litres water
100 g hops 6 g orris root
2-3 grains of cardamon
Makes 23 litres.

Other Drinks

Moldavian Honey Wine *(Tineretse)* For one serving:

70 g white wine 30 g honey
80 g soda water 20 g ice
1 g citric acid (or lemon juice)

Add the honey and citric acid to the white wine and bring to the boil. Cool, add the ice, and splash in the soda water.

Polish Blackcurrant Syrup

600 g blackcurrants 5 tablespoons honey
2 glasses soda water

Remove the stalks from the blackcurrants and wash thoroughly. Rub through a fine sieve and mix with the honey. Pour the puree into several glasses, add ice and top up with soda water.

Polish Gooseberry and Raspberry Drink

300 g gooseberries 3 tablespoons honey
300 g raspberries 2½ glasses of boiling water

Wash and clean the berries and pass through a sieve. Dilute the honey with the boiling water and mix with the sieved berries. Strain through muslin. Serve cool in tumblers.

Polish Carrot and Lemon Drink

1 kg carrots 2 tablespoons honey
juice of one lemon 1 glass of boiled water
salt dill to taste

Scrub the carrots thoroughly and shred finely. Squeeze out the juice and mix with the cooled water. (A juice extractor may be used instead of shredding and squeezing.) Add salt to taste, the lemon juice and honey. Finely chop= ped dill may be added before serving.

Polish Mint and Camomile Tea

1 teaspoon dried mint   1 teaspoon dried camomile

1 glass water   honey to taste

Steep the mint and camomile in boiling water, cover for ten minutes. Strain, add honey, and serve instead of tea.

Rosehip Syrup

1 litre water   2-3 tablespoons rosehip

4 tablespoons honey   puree

Boil the water and allow to cool. Mix the rosehip puree (or equivalent in rosehip syrup) with the honey and cooled water. Serve chilled in tumblers with an ice cube.

Rosehip and Camomile Tea

1 tablespoon dried rose hips   1 teaspoon dried camomile

1 glass of water   honey to taste

Wash the rose hips, cover with the water and boil for five minutes. Add the camomile, cover, and allow to draw for ten minutes. Strain, add the honey, and serve instead of tea.

RUSSIAN HONEY KVASS

Normal Russian kvass is a fermented but non-alcoholic drink. When honey is used, however, alcohol is formed during fermentation.

3 kg rye malt flour   100 g honey (or treacle)

4 kg medium ground rye flour 200 g flour for fermentation

3 tablespoons liquid yeast

Add the rye flour to the malt flour and mix together with cold water. Knead the dough well until free of lumps and place in an enamel dish. Place on the back of a well heated stove or oven for a day. Next day re-heat the oven and put the dough in it for another 24 hours. (The oven, of course, is allowed to cool once the dough has been put in.)

At the end of the two days the dough is put into a kneading trough and 12 litres of warm water poured over it, stirring constantly. The diluted must is covered and left to stand in a warm place for 15 to 20 hours.

A fermenting must is made from 200 g of flour and the yeast and a glass of water. After the main must has stood for the requisite time, pour it carefully into a prepared cask (which has been steamed and thoroughly washed) or into an enamel vessel to ferment. Immediately add the yeast mixture and the honey (or treacle).

After stirring thoroughly, leave the must to ferment for 12-16 hours in a warm place. When it has ceased to ferment, leave to stand for a time (as to lighten for mead). The lightened liquor is bottled and stored in a refrigerator or cold cellar.

Russian Kvass with Honey and Horseradish

1 litre kvass 25 g honey

5 g horseradish

Shred the horseradish root. Warm the honey and mix with the kvass. Add the grated horseradish and leave to stand in the refrigerator for 24 hours. Strain, and serve. (Bottled Russian kvass can be used if draught kvass is not available.)

Strawberry Milk

$1^1/2$ cups of milk 1 tablespoon honey

100 g fresh wild strawberries

Mix the milk with the honey and mashed strawberries. Add a pinch of salt and beat to obtain a smooth mixture.

HONEY PRESERVES AND JAMS

Armenian Marinated Grapes Per kilogram of grapes:

200 g water 200 g vinegar

50 g sugar 50 g honey

20 g salt 5 cloves

5 grains cardamon

Wash the grapes (medium-sized bunches) and arrange in layers in a jar. Mix the ingredients and pour the marinade over the grapes.

Plums, apricots, and other fruits and berries can be marinaded in the same way. Berries should be blanched first and left to cool in cold boiled water.

Blackcurrants and Honey

Blackcurrants are rich in vitamins [provitamin A (carotene), vitamin B_1 (thiamine), vitamin P (rutin), vitamin C_2] . Because of their vitamin C content it is advisable to preserve them uncooked, which can be done as follows. Remove the stalks and wash the berries well.

Then mash them with a wooden pestle to make a puree. Mix the puree thoroughly with honey (weight for weight). Store in jars sealed with paraffin wax and keep in a cool dark place. The mixture will keep better if the jars are sterilized and sealed with metal lids.

Cranberry and Apple Jam

1 kg cranberries 1 kg apples

3 kg honey 1 cup walnuts

Sort and wash the cranberries, then boil them in a covered saucepan with half a cup of water until soft. Mash the stewed berries and rub through a sieve. Boil up the honey in an enamel pan; add the apples (peeled, cored and sliced) and walnuts, and simmer for an hour. When ready, bottle as for any jam.

HONEY PRESERVES

Fruit may be preserved in honey instead of sugar. The fruit are prepared in the usual way for bottling, packed in jars, covered with a honey syrup, and sealed.

The following syrups can be used.

A. Mix two kilograms of honey and 100 grams of milk together and add the stiffly beaten white of an egg. Bring the mixture to the boil, and skim. Pour the hot syrup over the fruit, and continue as when bottling with sugar.

B. Dilute one kilogram of honey with a litre of water and' boil thoroughly. Pour over the fruit and proceed as when bottling with sugar.

C. If the fruit is being bottled under pressure a thicker syrup is required (700 grams of water per kilogram of honey).

Quinces in Honey

Honey gives the normally astringent quince a particularly pleasant taste and aroma. Prepare as follows: using two kilograms of honey per kilogram of quinces.

Peel and core the quinces and cut into slices. Place in a saucepan, cover with cold water and boil until tender. Remove the boiled quinces and strain the juice.

Pour the honey into a preserving pan with 1½ cups of strained juice, and prepare a syrup. Add the quinces to the boiling syrup and simmer over a low flame until the pieces of quinces become transparent.

HONEY COSMETICS

Since the skin protects the organism against harmful external influences, care and preservation of a healthy skin are an important part of personal hygiene. As we age the skin begins to lose its ability to absorb and retain moisture and tends to become dry and wrinkled as its fat glands function less efficiently.

But regular care can slow down the physiological process, give the face a fresh velvety texture, ana smooth away wrinkles and roughness. Honey has a high place among the prophylactic means for preserving the beauty of the skin and improving its tone.

It is, in fact, a remarkable 'cosmetic since, because of its permeability, it feeds the muscle layer of the skin with glucose. Its hygroscopic properties enable it to absorb skin secretions, while its inhibitors and bactericidal properties protect the skin and have an antiseptic effect.

Honey can be used as a cosmetic in the form of face packs, lotions, baths, etc., that can be prepared at home. But many commercially produced creams contain honey and/or beeswax. Those produced in the USSR are listed below, with their main ingredients.

Face Packs

Beauty specialists advise the use of honey in various face packs. Packs consisting of pure honey, or honey mixed with equal parts of yolk of egg and sour cream are recommended for strengthening and softening the skin.

Before packs are applied the skin should be thoroughly cleansed with due account of its type (dry, greasy, normal), and a hot compress applied for two or three minutes to open the pores, improve lymph and blood circulation, and increase the skin's ability to absorb moisture.

After the compress apply the face pack in a thin layer with cotton wool, and leave for 15-20 minutes. Wash off with warm or tepid water. Dry and lightly powder the skin.

For dry skin the honey and flour pack below is recommended; it should be used as follows. Wash the skin with warm water and then apply a hot compress.

After the compress smear the face with vegetable oil (olive, peanut, etc.) and cover it with a thin layer of cotton wool (leaving holes for the eyes and nose). Smear the face pack over the cotton wool with a tampon of cotton wool and leave for 20 to 25 minutes.

Remove the cotton wool and face pack, and apply three hot compresses to the skin. Rinse the face in tepid water (room temperature).

Honey and alcohol face pack (this is the honey face pack most widely used): mix 100 grams of honey with 25 grams of alcohol (surgical spirit) and an equal quantity of boiled or distilled water;' if the honey is crystallized it should be warmed slightly. Shake thoroughly before using. Leave on for 20 minutes.

Honey and flour face pack (for dry skin): mix 30 g wheat flour, 30 g water, and 50 g pure honey. Apply as described. *Honey and glycerine face pack*: make a smooth mixture from one teaspoon of honey, the same amount of glycerine, and the yolk of an egg.

Honey and oatmeal face pack: beat the yolk of one egg, add a teaspoonful of honey and a tablespoonful of fine oatmeal. Mix thoroughly until smooth.

Honey and sour cream face pack: make a smooth mixture of equal parts of honey and sour cream (smetana), and the yolk of a hen's egg.

Honey Baths

We have found that the addition of 200 to 250 grams of honey to the bath water has a beneficial effect on the organism.

Honey Water

Honey water is a convenient, easily prepared, and effective means of combating premature deterioration of the skin of the face and neck. Cleansing the skin with honey milk daily helps to preserve its elasticity, freshness, and velvety texture.

To prepare honey water dissolve two tablespoons of high quality single-flower or multifloral honey in a litre of warm water in a large bowl (three litres or more).

Add another two litres of warm water and wash the face and neck for 10-15 minutes. Rinse with clean warm water.

Honey and Cucumber Lotion

100 g cucumber juice 100 g vodka
100 g high quality honey

This is a moistening mixture with an excellent prophylactic effect. To prepare add the cucumber juice (from fresh cucumbers) to the vodka (or 40 per cent alcohol), and put the mixture in a sealed bottle in a cool dark place for eight days to infuse.

Filter the infused liquor and mix with the honey (single-flower or multifloral). The mixture is then ready for use.

Wash the face and neck with tepid water (room temperature), then moisten a piece of muslin with the lotion and apply to the skin. It is rapidly soaked into the skin. Apply once a day, preferably in the evening an hour or so before retiring.

BEESWAX COSMETICS

Beeswax (which is usually white) is an ingredient of many cosmetic preparations and makes an excellent thick base for creams, lip salves, face packs, and lotions. Beeswax is readily absorbed by the skin, giving it a smooth, soft appearance, and whitening it.

Anti-wrinkle Cream

30 g beeswax 30 g honey
30 g onion juice 30 g juice of white lily flowers

Mix in a porcelain mortar until the wax melts, then stir with a wooden spoon until the mixture is quite cold. Wash the face with warm water before using.

Apply a thick layer of the cream and leave for 25-30 minutes. Remove the excess cream with a paper tissue or clean linen towel. Allow an interval before powdering the face lightly.

Astringent Face Pack

10 g beeswax 10 g peach oil
10 g lanolin 50 g vaseline
0.5 g zinc sulphate 1 g bismuth nitrate
8 g zinc oxide

Cream for Greasy Skin

5 g beeswax 5 g ammonia water
7.5 g water

Nourishing Cream

3 g beeswax 6 g spermaceti
4 g glycerine 24 g peach oil

Nourishing Face Pack

50 g beeswax 70 g honey
juice of one white lily bulb

Peach Cream

6 g beeswax 0.5 g borax
16 g water 27.5 g peach oil

COMMERCIAL COSMETICS

A number of the creams made by the Soviet cosmetic industry contain beeswax and/or honey and other physiologically active substances. Their main ingredients are given below.

Biokrem (for normal and dry skins): beeswax, peach oil, spermaceti wax, lanolin, infusion of camomile, lime flowers, and bottle brush, and an emulsifier.

Biokrem VTO (for normal and dry skins): beeswax, lanolin, spermaceti wax, nut oil, penthol, infusions of camomile, lime flowers, and bottle brush, perfume.

Camomile (Emerald) Cream (against inflammation): beeswax, lanolin, spermaceti, nut oil, aqueous infusion of pharmaceutical camomile, an emulsifier.

Izumrud Cream (for dry skin): beeswax, animal and vegetable fats, penthol, water.

Lux Cream: nut oil, beeswax, spermaceti.

Medovy (Honey) Cream: alcohol of high molecular weight, lanolin, water.

Mindalny (Almond) Cream (for dry skin): beeswax, lanolin, spermaceti, almond oil, water.

Nektar Cream (for all skins) contains royal jelly.

Nikolaevsky Cream (for dry skin): beeswax, spermaceti, lanolin, nut oil, and an emulsifier.

Ogni Moskvy (Lights of Moscow) Cream (for dry skins): beeswax, lanolin, spermaceti wax, palm kernel oil, perfumed oil, cholesterol, water, and an emulsifier.

Spermacetovy (Spermaceti) Cream (for dry skins): beeswax, lanolin, spermaceti, palm kernel oil, perfumed oil, water.

***Trembita Cream*:** beeswax, lanolin, nut oil, cocoa butter, spirit of high molecular weight, water.

***Vesna (Spring) Cream*:** beeswax, lanolin, spermaceti wax, vaseline.

7 Chapter THE CURATIVE PROPERTIES OF BEE VENOM

Many effective remedies have been taken into medical practice from folk medicine. Among them, bee venom or apitoxin holds an important place. It is rightly called a curative toxin, since it has passed the tests and been found suitable for clinical use.

In 1957 the Learned Council of the USSR Ministry of Health sanctioned a temporary instruction for its use in the form of a bee sting for the treatment of certain illnesses.

Three of the names connected with the development of apitoxin therapy in the Soviet Union deserve particular mention. A hundred years ago, in 1864, Prof. M.I.Lukomsky, of the St. Petersburg Forestry Institute, published an article in which he demonstrated that bee venom was a valuable remedy and appealed to doctors to study it.

The army doctor I.V.Lyubarsky, who used bee venom for twenty years in the form of bee stings, and obtained good results where conventional methods had failed, published a long article in the *Kazanskii Telegraf* in 1897 entitled 'Bee Venom as a Cure', describing his experiments in treating rheumatism with bee stings.

The third name is that of M. B. Krol, Member of the Academy of Sciences. On his initiative, an experimental preparation of bee venom was made and employed with success in 1936-7 to treat patients with disorders of the nervous system.

Our own observations over many years and the data we have collected from questionnaires on the health of beekeepers indicate that bee venom is not only effective in treating certain illnesses, but also possesses prophylactic properties.

It must be mentioned, however, that incorrect use of bee venom can cause irremediable harm. In recent years, unfortunately, many articles and notes have appeared in periodicals by authors who were not qualified in apitoxin therapy, and who treated bee venom as a cure-all.

They recommended, without theoretical grounds and without practical testing in experiments and clinical observations, that bee stings should be used on closed eyelids, around the heart, on the throat, and so on. Such 'recommendations' and the application of up to a hundred stings at one session are not only dangerous to the health of the patients, but could prove fatal.

Apitoxin therapy should only be carried out by a qualified and experienced doctor and, in many cases, as part of a complex of therapeutic and prophylactic measures (e.g. with physiotherapy, dietotherapy, drug therapy, etc.).

THE COMPOSITION AND PROPERTIES OF BEE VENOM

Bee venom is transparent, has a sharp smell reminiscent of honey, and a bitter burning taste. Its specific gravity is 1.1313. When tested with litmus paper, it gives an acid reaction.

It has been established that bee venom contains formic, hydrochloric, and orthophosphoric acids, histamine, tryptophan, sulphur, and other substances. It may be supposed that magnesium phosphate $Mg,(PO_4)_2$, which makes up 0.4 per cent of the dry weight of venom, is of great curative value.

Traces of copper and calcium have also been noted. Bee venom also contains many proteins, volatile oils that evaporate when it is dried, the enzymes hyaluronidase and phospholipase, and other substances.

Some researchers think that it is the volatile oils that produce the feeling of burning and soreness in a bee sting. Bee venom rapidly dries out, even at ordinary room temperature, losing 30 to 70 per cent of its weight.

The dried venom is a transparent mass resembling gum arabic. It is readily soluble in water or acids. Bee toxin is not decomposed by caustic alkaline solutions or sulphuric acid, even after 24 hours, but its properties are subject to change, when it is heated for any time with hydrochloric acid or a caustic alkali. The effect of potassium permanganate and other oxidizing agents is to reduce its activity. Bee venom is extremely heat-resistant; when heated in the dry form to 100° C, even for ten days, no noticeable change occurs in its properties. Freezing, too, does not alter its toxic effect. When kept dry, venom retains its toxicity for several years.

As the chemical composition of bee venom has not been sufficiently studied as yet, no synthetic preparation has been created as a substitute for it.

Prof. G.F.Gauze, head of a laboratory at the Institute of Malaria and Medicinal Parasitology of the USSR Academy of Medical Sciences, considered bee venom one of the strongest antibiotic substances known. 'The third category of antibiotic substances,' he wrote, 'embraces compounds containing nitrogen and sulphur, above all bee and snake venoms. . . Gliotoxin, an antibacterial substance formed by the mildew *Gliocladium, has* the same composition...

A hundred-thousandth of a milligram of Gliotoxin in a culture medium inhibits the growth of certain gram-positive microbes. Gliotoxin, bee venom, and snake venom are among the most powerful antibiotic substances known to us.

The Soviet researchers Komarov and Erstein[2]), Balandin[3]) and others have established that an aqueous solution of bee venom is sterile (i.e. does not contain microorganisms), even when diluted to a concentration of 1 : 50 000; at strengths of 1 : 500 000 and 1 : 600 000 it stimulates the multiplication of *Paramoecium.* Koop rightly notes that bee venom deserves no less attention than antibiotics of fungoid and bacterial origin.

THE MECHANISM OF THE ACTION OF BEE VENOM

Centuries of observation and the research of recent years give us every reason to consider that bee venom has a selective effect on the nervous system.

Cleopatra, who was interested in the effects of poisons, collected every possible kind of poisonous substance, trying to find a poison that would act painlessly.

She tested their effect on prisoners condemned to death. The poison that caused the least agonizing death, it proved, was wasp venom (bee venom could not be used, as bees were considered sacred).

A person given an injection of wasp venom lost consciousness, beads of sweat appeared on his face, and he died quickly and painlessly. If an attempt was made to rouse the victim from this condition by physical exertions he resisted as if in a deep sleep.

The German naturalist Karl Krepelin wrote: 'Sand wasps attack their prey in a particularly cruel manner. They attack the caterpillars of small butterflies and inject poison into their nerve ganglia, with the result that the caterpillars become paralysed.

The wasps drag the paralysed caterpillars to the nest to their young, sometimes by the dozen. The growing larvae feed on the caterpillars and gradually eat them alive.

The action of wasp venom differs little from that of bee venom. The German research workers Neumann and Habermann[2]) published an interesting article in 1954 in which they showed that mellitin (a protein extracted from bee venom) caused a lowering of blood pressure, haemolysis (dissolving of erythrocytes), and contraction of striated and smooth muscles, and blocked nerve muscle and ganglial synapses.

The enzyme hyaluronidase, which is also isolated from the bee venom, according to their data, increased capillary permeability. The state of the permeability of the blood vessels is of extraordinary importance.

A decrease occurs as a result of functional disturbances of the vascular system caused by ageing or illness of the organism. Consequently, the conditions of intermediate exchange between organs and tissues deteriorate.

It has now been established that the permeability of the ground substance in the connective tissue and capillaries depends to a significant extent on the state of the enzyme system destroying one of its components, hyaluronic acid.

Preparations containing hyaluronidase (bee venom, hirudin, ronidase, testicle extract, spermine, etc.), even in extremely small doses, increase their permeability. The French researchers E.A.Gourt and G.Derry showed in 1958, in experiments on mice, that bee venom has an antagonistic effect on staphylococcic a-toxin and tetanus toxin, which is explained by the fact that it contains phospholipase A.

Our own observations made over many years are that bee stings or injections of apitoxin are conducive to raising immunity not only to bee venom but also to certain infectious diseases.

When used correctly, bee venom is a therapeutic and prophylactic remedy affecting the organism as a whole and not just separate organs or particular illnesses. When bee venom enters the organism it rallies all the latter's forces of resistance, which explains in part why beekeepers who have worked for many years in a bee-garden enjoy good health and live to ripe old ages.

They develop immunity to various illnesses. It is high time to study the prophylactic properties of the sera of laboratory and domestic animals that have been artificially immunized with bee venom.

This measure will undoubtedly enrich the arsenal of effective biological remedies.

MAN'S SENSITIVITY TO BEE VENOM

When a bee stings, it injects a drop of venom into the skin. This venom has curative properties. To be toxic, the dose must be ten times greater than the curative one; and to be fatal it must be a hundred times greater.

The sensitivity of the organism to bee venom varies, women and children and the elderly being most sensitive. It has been observed that a healthy person can easily stand one to five stings and even ten. Bee stings cause a local reaction only (reddening of the skin, swelling, a burning sensation, etc.); but 200-300 simultaneous stings poison the organism with characteristic signs of disturbance of the cardiovascular and nervous systems (shortness of breath, cyanosis, quickening of the pulse, convulsions, paralysis).

Five hundred and more stings cause death, more often than not as a result of paralysis of the respiratory centre. There are people, however, who are abnormally sensitive to bee venom, in whom one sting is sufficient to cause general indisposition, severe headache, a rash similar to nettle rash, vomiting, and diarrhoea.

The organism of most people soon becomes accustomed to bee

stings and reacts slightly, if at all. Numerous observations have shown that people who have worked with bees for a long time can endure stings with no harm to the organism. Some beekeepers who have worked many years with bees have tolerated being stung by as many as a thousand bees without symptoms of poisoning of any kind.

The data from a questionnaire circulated to apiaries in the Soviet Union indicate that 28.2 per cent of beekeepers become immune to bee venom within a year of starting work; 34.6 per cent become immune within two years; and 10 per cent within three years; but a very small percentage (5.7 per cent) do not become immune at all. In some (4.2 per cent) immunity is congenital.

It has been shown experimentally that specific antibodies counteracting the effect of bee venom develop in the blood of beekeepers who have worked with bees for a long time and consequently have often been stung.

Serum from beekeepers has been tested as follows: 0.2 ml of blood serum in a diluted solution of 1 : 100 and 1 : 400 was mixed with an equal quantity of bee venom and injected into a rabbit's skin.

A control animal was injected with a mixture of bee venom and blood serum from a person who had never been stung. The results indicated that the serum from the beekeeper counteracted the action of the venom, whereas ordinary serum did not have this property.

Through frequent stinging, it would seem, specific antibodies develop in beekeepers, giving rise to local and general humoral immunity. Some authors consider that the saliva of a person accustomed to bee stings acts as an antitoxin, i.e. as an antidote to bee venom.

It is frequently observed that not all members of a bee keeper's family react to stings in the same way, but we have not found any cases of inborn immunity to bee venom in the literature. In this connection we should like to mention several interesting cases of congenital or acquired immunity.

The beekeeper I.E.Pozdnyakov (from the village of Sopron in Kursk Region) described in detail in a letter how, in 1947, a large number of bees (at least 300) attacked his year-old son. The child's face and body became swollen and it was feared he would die within a few hours; but in three days the swelling had disappeared almost completely, and on the sixth day the little boy was quite well again.

It was subsequently discovered that the beekeeper's wife had been stung by bees during the pregnancy, which suggests that the son inherited immunity to bee venom from his mother and was therefore able to survive such a large number of stings.

The father also remarked that in the following years his son was seldom ill, even when other children of his age were going down with measles, scarlet fever, etc.

The beekeeper O.M.Lamonova informed us that her seven-year-old daughter, who had frequently been stung by bees, did not catch measles, although she had been in close contact with a friend who had it.

The search for antitoxins in the blood of animals and people who have been stung by bees or given injections of bee venom has not been crowned with success. Some authors believe there is no such thing as true immunity to bee venom and by way of example cite the fact that many beekeepers often lose their acquired immunity in the winter—when they are not in contact with bees.

Immunity to bee venom is indubitably of a special character, but there is no doubt that it exists since the numerous facts accumulated over the centuries of man's contact with bees point to it.

Bee stings can often do great harm to healthy people, especially if they are hypersensitive to the venom. Individual cases have been recorded, though admittedly very rarely, where a single bee sting has been the cause of death of a completely healthy person.

It must be added that even autopsy cannot always reveal how a microscopic drop of bee venom can bring about the death of a healthy person within a few minutes.

Prof. E.N.Pavlovsky, Member of the USSR Academy of Sciences, believed such cases would be explained by an allergy to bee venom, and by the location of the sting.').

Obviously, the maximum effect is rapidly observed (in a few minutes) when the sting goes right into a blood vessel and the poison is consequently taken up immediately by the blood stream.

Many ways of counteracting bee stings have been suggested, but the very abundance of such preparations merely goes to show that a reliable one has still to be found.

The Russian magazine *Weekly News o f the Free Fconomic Society* published an article in 1788 entitled 'Against Bee Stings' in which it was said: 'It is pointless to look for a general means of treating bee stings, even in books about bees.

Neither the application of vinegar, nor fresh cold earth, nor urine, nor parsley, nor crushed bee, nor scorpion oil, nor other similar nostrums prevent swelling, if the properties of the body are so disposed.'

The only remedy advisable is the extraction of the sting together with its poison sac. The longer the sting remains in the skin the more poison passes into the blood.

When a bee has stung a person, it instinctively attempts to fly away, but the barb of the sting catches firmly in the skin and the stinging apparatus is torn off with both the poison glands and poison sac and the ganglion of the abdominal nerve chain, which ensures its automatic innervation and contraction outside the bee's body.

As a result, venom continues to enter the blood. Beekeepers are, therefore, absolutely correct in advising, that the sting should be pulled out of the skin as soon as possible; the victim, however, usually uses his fingers and thereby presses the entire stock of venom out of the stinging apparatus into the skin.

By using special tweezers it is possible to remove the sting quickly, gently, and carefully, losing hardly any of the poison from the sac. Once freed of the sting, the wound should be treated with cream containing calendula, surgical spirit, and vaseline or lanolin.

The combination of calendula and spirit soon relieves the pain and the unpleasant burning sensation, and apparently neutralizes the action of the histamine and the other active components of bee venom. When poisoning by bee venom has occurred, a glass of a honey-vitamin-alcohol mixture should be taken every three or four hours (50-100 g of honey, 200 g of vodka, 1 g of ascorbic acid, and one litre of boiled water).

Honey has a beneficial stimulating effect on the heart, liver, and other organs in all cases of poisoning. Our own observations indicate that alcohol possesses specific antitoxin properties against bee venom.

For that reason a patient is forbidden alcohol during apitoxin therapy. Ascorbic acid is essential because bee venom sharply reduces the level of this vitamin in the suprarenal glands. Ascorbic acid stimulates the action of histamine so that large doses are indicated in cases of allergic reactions.

It also increases the organism's resistance, counters bacterial toxins, is involved in the formation of antitoxins, and consolidates enzymatic processes and the action of such substances as adrenaline and choline. In severe cases of poisoning, where the cardiovascular and nervous systems are seriously affected, patients should be hospitalized immediately.

When allergic symptoms occur as the result of incorrect apitoxin therapy or of bee stings, some authors recommend employment of adrenaline, calcium chloride, sodium bromide, etc.; this, of course, should be done by a doctor, and the doctor must adopt a strictly individual approach, since each patient reacts to bee venom in a different way.

Complications in the form of allergies can certainly be avoided, since the first (test) sting demonstrates quite clearly whether apitoxin therapy can be used to treat the patient concerned.

From the results obtained with apitoxin therapy, it may be concluded that bee venom blocks the conductivity of the sensory nerves and thus not only lessens but also prevents neuralgic and rheumatic pains and dilates the finer blood vessels, thereby improving blood supply to the tissues.

Apitoxin also stimulates the production of new blood cells; in 70 per cent of cases the number of erythrocytes increases from 50 000 to 500 000, and in 65 per cent of cases the amount of haemoglobin is raised to 12 per cent. The cholesterol level of the blood is lowered.

THE TREATMENT OF VARIOUS DISEASES WITH BEE VENOM

Rheumatism. In 1888 the Viennese clinician F. Tertsch described 173 cases of rheumatism that had been cured with bee stings.') He himself had suffered from rheumatism and been cured by accidental stinging; and he had subsequently begun to take an interest in bees and the healing properties of their venom, and to use bee stings extensively to treat rheumatism. In 1897 the Russian army doctor, I.V.Lyubarsky, in the article already referred to, concluded from his years of experience that bee venom was a valuable remedy for rheumatism.

In 1912 Tertsch's son Rudolph published a work describing 660 cases of the treatment of rheumatism with bee stings.

Of these 554 had been completely cured, while the condition of 99 had improved; only in 17 had no change been observed. The author divided the last into two groups: those with rheumatism in an extremely neglected form, and those who did not complete the cure.

Clinical observations have shown that bee venom is an active remedy in cases of acute rheumatic carditis or Sokolsky-Bouillaud disease. Patients tolerate treatment by bee stings without difficulty. In cases of infective arthritis resulting from syphilis, gonorrhoea, or tuberculosis, injection of bee venom causes strong local and general reactions.

For that reason clinicians have proposed using bee stings for diagnosis, in order to establish the existence of rheumatism. The mechanism of the action of bee venom in rheumatism has not been sufficiently studied, but it may be supposed that it has a beneficial effect on the central nervous system, which is impaired in this illness, as is indicated by the altered allergic reactivity of rheumatism patients.

Neuritis and Neuralgia

On the initiative and under the supervision of Prof. M. B. Krol, Kh. I. Erusalimchik used bee venom in 1938, in clinical conditions at the 2nd Moscow Medical Institute to treat neural disorders (affecting the sciatic, femoral, and other nerves).

Most of the patients treated had had rheumatism in the past; and before treatment with apitoxin almost all had been given the normal drugs or physiotherapy without result.

A solution of 2 per cent bee venom (in doses of 0.5 to 2.0 cm^3) was administered subcutaneously in the most painful spots. Easing of the pain was noticeable as early as one or two injections.

After three or four injections considerable subjective and objective improvement was observed. Complete relief was felt after eight injections.

Erusalimchik did not, however, observe or record remote results, so that there is no confirmation that the cure is lasting. Cases are known of patients suffering from neuritis, especially inflammation of the trigeminal nerve, who had undergone a course of treatment with bee stings and considered themselves completely recovered, but who had a relapse after a time (two or three months later) and got no curative effect from further courses of apitoxin therapy.

Certain Eye Diseases

In folk medicine bee venom has long been used to treat certain eye diseases. Here is an example: a patient had been suffering from keratoconjunctivitis (inflammation of the cornea and mucous membranes) for two years.

One day, after being accidentally stung by a bee, he felt an improvement in his condition. After treatment with bee stings he was completely cured. In modern medicine bee venom is extensively used with success to treat such diseases as iritis (inflammation of the iris) and iridocyclitis (inflammation of the ciliary body and the iris).

Prof. O.I.Shershevskaya, of the Novosibirsk Eye Clinic, obtained good results using bee venom in the form of bee stings. In cases of severe iritis in which vision had deteriorated to 0.001, the results were striking.

The inflammation subsided and within three to four days the patien was completely cured with his sight restored to normal. But it must not be forgotten that there is tremendous danger in applying stings even to the closed eyelid. Several operations may frequently be required to remove a tiny fragment of a sting from the eyeball.

Even when the bee stings only the eyelid, the protruding end of the sting can damage the cornea and induce keratitis on the surface of the eye, and sometimes it gives rise to a serious disorder affecting the whole eye.

Bee venom was used with success in the eye clinic of the Kirov State Medical Institute in Gorky in the form of the Czechoslovak ointment 'Virapin' (in combination with normal treatment), and hastened improvement in herpetic keratitis, rheumatic iritis, rheumatic scleritis, and episcleritis. The procedure followed the pattern recommended by us: the first day the ointment was rubbed into the left shoulder; the second day into the right shoulder in the morning, the left hip at midday, and the right hip in the evening; the third day a doubled dose was applied distally to the spots already treated on the shoulders and right hip.

On the fourth day no ointment was applied; on the fifth and sixth days the procedure for the third day was repeated. The skin was first washed with warm soap and water.

Skin Diseases

Bee venom was widely used in folk medicine to treat various skin diseases. G. Kovalev, a beekeeper, reported that one day his son, who had suffered from tuberculosis of the skin of the face (lupus) for five years, was accidentally stung in the bee-farm on the affected cheek.

The skin around the sting turned pale. It was decided to treat the boy with bee stings. After several days' treatment the skin assumed a healthy colour, and in six weeks the boy was completely cured. Unfortunately we have no further information on this case.

It would be useful if dermatologists would test bee venom clinically, especially for diseases for which no effective cure has yet been found.

EFFECT OF BEE VENOM ON BLOOD PRESSURE AND CHOLESTROL LEVEL

It is the view of Prof. N. N. Anichkov, Member of the USSR Academy of Medical Sciences, that cholesterol is one of the main causes of atherosclerosis, 'the disease of old age'.

In this respect Erusalimchik's observations cited above are especially interesting, as they established that. the blood cholesterol level of some patients fell as a result of treatment with bee venom. And in cases where the effect of bee venom was not beneficial, hypercholesterolaemia (i.e. excess of cholesterol in the blood) occurred.

These observations are all the more valuable since they serve as a warning against the use of bee venom without prior investigation of each patient's reaction to it.

K.Dier and G.Graber reported in 1936 that they had noticed an increase in cholesterol level in almost all patients with disorders of the joints when apitoxin therapy (in the form of Forapin ointment) was administered, while bee venom had absolutely no effect on cholesterol in the blood in patients with neuritis.

K. A.Forster showed that bee venom raised the cholesterol content of the blood in some patients; E.M.Alesker reported that she had been unable to ascertain whether bee venom effected the cholesterol level of the blood in 100 patients with rheumatoid arthritis and neuritis who had received apitoxin treatment.

Bee venom is known to bring blood pressure down. Research on dogs has established that an intravenous injection of the venom from a single bee causes a slight lowering of blood pressure, while injection of the venom from several bees causes a sharp drop (brought about by dilation of the peripheral blood vessels under the action of the histamine in the venom).

The Chinese doctor Fan Chu employed bee venom to treat hypertension in 12 patients, and noted one cure. There was considerable improvement in the condition of four, improvement in three, and no change in three others. Treatment of the remaining patient had been discontinued.

Many other examples could be cited in which patients with hypertensive conditions improved soon after they began to work in an apiary (where they were stung by bees). Their headaches disappeared, their fitness for work improved, and their blood pressure dropped almost to normal.

It should also be mentioned that, apart from the effect of the bee venom itself, the calm atmosphere of rural areas and salubrious air of a bee-garden have a beneficial effect on the patient's condition.

INDICATIONS AND CONTRA-INDICATIONS FOR THE USE OF BEE VENOM

Some beekeepers, and even medical workers, consider that all illnesses can be treated with bee venom and use it in gynaecological and children's diseases, and even in cases of venereal diseases. But there are diseases that cannot be treated with bee venom.

Cases taken from folk medicine, observations made in modern clinics, and the information we have assembled confirm that bee venom does possess certain healing properties, and is particularly effective in rheumatic diseases of the joints and muscles, St. Vitus' dance, inflammation of the sciatic, facial, and other nerves, hypertension (primary and secondary stages), migraine, Basedow's disease, and certain other diseases').

However, bee venom must be used with care, and only under medical supervision, especially when treating children and elderly people, who are very sensitive to it.

Bee venom cannot be used in the treatment of tuberculosis, heart failure, diabetes, arteriosclerosis, or venereal diseases. If a patient is affected by general indisposition after the first bee sting (running a high temperature, with headache, and feeling feverish and very weak, has a rash like nettle rash, ringing in the ears, and diarrhoea, etc.) treatment should be discontinued immediately.

METHODS OF EMPLOYING BEE VENOM

In recent years apitoxin therapy has been widely used in the Soviet Union and other socialist countries. Preparations made with bee venom, Virapin (Czechoslovakia) and Apisarthron (GDR) are extremely popular.

But clinical observations in Romania, the USA (Beck, Broadman, and others), and the USSR (Bessmertny, Bredikhin, Ioyrish, Okhotskaya, Okhotsky, and others) indicate that bee venom is most effective when injected intracutaneously by means of a natural bee sting.

Natural Bee Stings

The area of skin selected for treatment with bee venom should first be washed with warm water and soap (there is no need to rub it with surgical spirit). The bee is then placed on the skin by means of special tweezers.

If the sting is to be repeated in the same place, it should only be done five days later. By the fourth day the swelling, soreness, and other phenomena will have disappeared and the patient felt normal. Apitoxin therapy can then be continued.

Areas of the body where hypodermic injections are usually given (the outer aspect of the shoulders and hips) are used for bee stings.

Bee venom enters the skin slowly (taking as much as several hours) as the contractions of the stinging apparatus force venom out of the poison sac.

The sting should therefore not be removed until all the poison has been absorbed into the skin. Cessation of its contractions can usually be detected with the naked eye.

The venom absorbed is instantly taken up by the blood and on reaching the bloodstream its effect is felt throughout the organism. The procedure for treatment with stings can be as follows: first day one sting (one bee); second day two stings (two bees); third day three stings, and so on for ten days.

After a first course of treatment, i.e. after the patient has received the venom of 55 bees, a break should be made for three or four days. Treatment can then be continued with three stings daily for six weeks.

During the second course of treatment, the patient should be

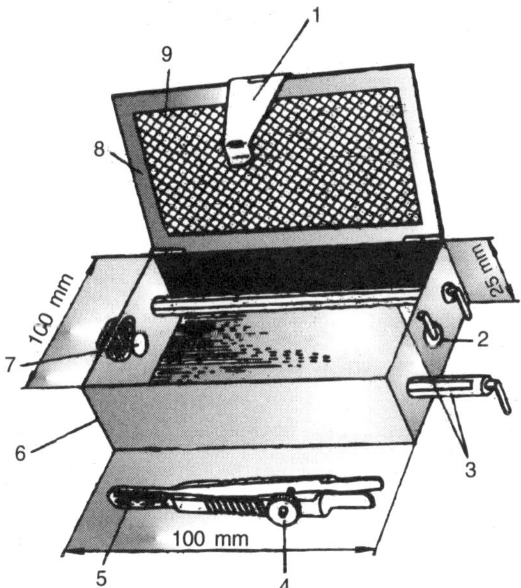

Figure 7.1: Drawing of portable box and tweezers for apitherapy. i-clasp; 2-bee exit (closed); 3-movable feeding trough; 4-limiting stop; 5-special tweezers for handling bees; 6-box- 7-bee exit (open); 8-lid of box; 9-mesh insert In lid Bees should be picked up with special tweezers.

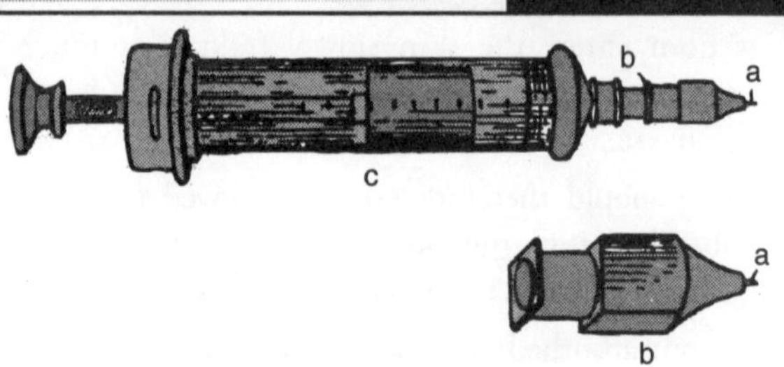

Figure 7.2: Special syringe for bee-venom therapy
(a) needle; (b) sleeve; (c) syringe

given the venom of approximately 140-150 bees, which means that over the full two courses he or she receives between 180 and 200 bee stings.

Treatment should then be stopped if the patient is not cured or there is no noticeable improvement in his (or her) condition. Experience is that treatment can be carried out in half this time, though keeping the number of stings at around 200.

On the first day the patient receives two stings, on the second day four stings, on the third six, on the fourth eight, and on the fifth and subsequent days nine stings a day. If that dose is too large, the number of stings should be limited to five.

Thus, during a normal 24-day stay at a sanatorium, the patient will receive up to 125 stings; the remainder of the 200 can then be given locally at home. It should be noted that swelling or soreness is not usually observed in patients for whom treatment with bee venom is indicated; and patients can take 20 to 30 stings and more at a time without difficulty.

But when they recover, or there is a significant improvement in their condition, several stings (or even one) sometimes elicit the usual local reaction (reddening of the skin, swelling, soreness, etc.).

Several dozen bees taken from an apiary cannot survive more than a day in an ordinary cardboard box, which precludes many patients from receiving the correct treatment, as they have to travel to an apiary for bees every day or at least every other day. For that reason, some patients set up a small hive at home, in the attic or on a balcony.

The author has designed a portable one-frame beehive for the purpose. It is similar to an ordinary hive but has certain alterations and improvements to enable it to be used at any time of the year. It is constructed in the form of a small suitcase or dressing case, is convenient for use, and can even be taken on a journey.

The hive is fitted with a feeding trough that can be filled with a sweet syrup. The trough is pulled out two or three centimetres for filling and the syrup poured through a funnel into a reservoir with a latticed wall. The syrup seeps through the lattice and distributes itself over the length of the feeding trough, while the lattice prevents bees from entering the reservoir.

The feeding trough is designed in such a way as to make it possible to feed the bees with honey or sugar syrup at times of the year when there are no nectariferous plants in flower. In order to give bees access to flowers, the hive may be placed in a copse or wood, in a field or garden; but then the bee-entrance should only be closed late in the evening. If it is closed too early and the hive removed, the bees cannot return home. In town the hive can even be placed on a windowsill with the bee-entrance toward the street or a garden.

If the patient is unable to keep a hive, a special portable box designed by us can be used, in which up to a hundred bees can live for six to ten days. The box is warm, well ventilated, with sufficient space for feed (honey or sugar syrup).

It is fitted with two convenient, removable feeding troughs that can be filled with honey without opening the box or disturbing the bees. When a bee is needed, the side hatch is opened, and one immediately crawls out.

The tweezers we suggest for the purpose are a somewhat. modified version of dissecting forceps. The free ends are three millimetres apart, which makes it possible to lift a bee gently by the thorax and place it on the skin. Young bees, which have as yet no store of poison, are smaller and cannot be picked up by the tweezers.

It is not recommended to pick bees up with ordinary dissecting tweezers since even the slightest pressure will cause the bee to release its venom considerably before it, is placed on the skin. The special tweezers have two additional metal plates which make, it possible to squeeze all the venom out of the sac immediately after the sting has been injected and then pull out the sting immediately with its stinging apparatus. This is most important as patients frequently have to waste much time waiting for the stinging apparatus to stop contracting. Tweezers save time and ensure that all the venom enters the skin.

Intracutaneous Injection of Apitoxin

A method of giving intracutaneous injections of apitoxin has been developed. Its advantage over natural bee stings is that it makes it possible to prescribe various dosages, with due regard for the patient's condition.

Moreover, a ready store of apitoxin can always be kept on hand in.hospitals and clinics. It has proved more convenient and effective to inject a solution of apitoxin intracutaneously (between the epidermis and the dermis) with a special needle in doses of 0.1, 0.2, or 0.3 millilitres of apitoxin.

As a fifth of the blood is in 'the skin, the apitoxin is immediately distributed throughout the whole organism. A considerably greater amount of apitoxin in solution (1 ml) may be given subcutaneously, but the curative effect is less satisfactory than with intracutaneous injections.

Electrophoresis of Apitoxin

Electrophoresis is widely employed clinically in the treatment of internal diseases, nervous disorders, gynaecological diseases, surgical conditions, etc. The method is based on electrolytic dissociation and is the best 'way of administering drugs and medicines through the skin. It is usually carried out in physiotherapy departments.

Experience is that apitoxin treatment by means of electrophoresis has several advantages over bee stings. Administration by electrophoresis has no unpleasant effects except for a slight hyperaemia (or reddening) of the area of skin affected.

At the 20th (Jubilee) International Congress of Apiculture, held in Bucharest in 1965, the Bulgarian doctors V. Mladenov and V. Kazanjieva reported that they had administered apitoxin by means of electrophoresis to 108 patients being treated at the Kastendil Balneological Sanatorium for disorders of the peripheral nervous system.

Of the patients treated 32 were cured, the pain disappearing completely and the nervous system returning to normal; 64 were discharged as noticeably improved (and no relapses were recorded over the next two years). No improvement was registered in 12 patients and one proved allergic to bee venom. Good results were also obtained in the treatment of rheumatoid and rheumatic arthritis, and diseases of the arteries.

The solution of apitoxin for electrophoresis is prepared as follows: 0.04 to 0.05 gram of unpurified bee venom is dissolved in a litre of distilled water. Two electrodes with hydrophilic pads (150-250 cm^2 in area) are placed on the spot where the pain is felt.

The pads are dampened with warm water and the apitoxin solution and applied to the skin. The leads are then connected to the anode and cathode and the apitoxin is administered simultaneously from both poles.

The first day 2 ml of the solution are poured onto the pads; on each successive day the amount is increased by 1.0 ml until the eighth day; from then on 8.0 ml a day are used until the end of the course. On the first day a current strength of 10 mA is used; this is increased by 2.0 mA on successive days to a maximum of 20 mA, which is maintained until the end of the course.

On the first day the time taken for the procedure is ten minutes; this period is increased by two minutes a day to a maximum of 20 minutes, which again is maintained until the end of the course. Treatment lasts for 15 to 20 days; and a. total of 200 to 250 ml of apitoxin solution is used.

Apitoxin Ointment

Bee venom can be administered by means of an ointment prepared from pure apitoxin, white vaseline, and salicylic acid. The salicylic acid softens the outer layer of skin (the epidermis) and increases its permeability. But as apitoxin can only enter the blood through damaged skin or lesions the ointment must contain minute silicate crystals, which act as an abrasive.

Treatment by ointment, which is prescribed by a doctor, can be-carried out at home. The disadvantage of the ointment is that a large area of skin is abraded when it is rubbed in. Administration of apitoxin intracutaneously or by electrophoresis is therefore much to be preferred.

Apitoxin Treatment by Inhalation

Because of the large area of vesicles of the lungs, medicines are absorbed more quickly through the lungs than from the gastro-intestinal tract.

Good results have been obtained through administering apitoxin by inhalation, a simple method of treatment that can be used in any medical institution, and it consists in the patient merely breathing in apitoxin-saturated vapour from hot water.

Apitoxin Tablets

Joseph Broadman M.D., the well-known American specialist on the use of preparations made from bee venom,') has suggested that apitoxin should be given in tablet form. The tablets contain various quantities of bee venom, from which toxic protein has been removed, and are differently coloured according to the dosage of venom (harmless vegetable colouring matter being used).

For a single course of treatment, 28 tablets containing the venom from 215 bees are recommended. The tablets are placed under the tongue and sucked. If swallowed directly the apitoxin does not have the desired effect, since it is readily digested by the enzymes in the gastro-intestinal tract.

The apitoxin tablet proposed by Broadman has an important advantage over natural bee venom in that it is quite free of toxic protein. As we see it, it is this toxic protein that not only is the cause of allergy to bee venom, but also brings about the basic symptoms of poisoning.

Work is proceeding to improve the tablets; there can be no doubt that in the near future apitoxin will be accepted in this form and will occupy the place it deserves in chemists' shops in many countries.

At presentt the tablets are being tested by the Research Institute for Rheumatic Illnesses in Prague (Czechoslovakia), in three clinics in the Georgian SSR, and in the Pharmacology Department of the Pavlov Higher Medical Institute in Plovdiv (Bulgaria). In Soviet Georgia apitoxin tablets have been approved by the Medical Council of the Georgian Ministry of Health.

METHODS OF OBTRAINING BEE VENOM

The young worker bee that has just left its waxen 'cradle' has hardly any venom. Its stock increases gradually, reaching a maximum by the time the bee is two weeks old. F.Flury has suggested an original method of obtaining bee venom.

A large number of live bees are placed in a wide-necked glass jar which is closed with filter paper dampened with ether. The ether vapour irritates the bees, and they release their venom on the walls and the bottom of the jar, as well as on other bees.

After the bees, under the effects of the ether, have fallen into a narcosis, the walls of the jar are rinsed with water. This liquor is then filtered and the water evaporated. The substance remaining is bee venom, which can be stored for several months without losing its properties.

The bees themselves are dried and returned to the hive. The method, however, has the following drawbacks: first, the bees do not release all of their venom; second, some of them do not survive the narcosis, washing and drying; third, it is difficult to purify the apitoxin obtained.

A method of obtaining bee venom by means of a weak electric current has also been suggested. For this purpose a special device is fitted at the bee-entrance of the hive.

As the bees pass through the entrance, they receive a slight electric shock and release their venom which falls onto a piece of glass placed there for the purpose. The venom rapidly dries, forming crystals similar to gum arabic.

Several other methods are known but they are all unsatisfactory; either it proves impossible to obtain pure venom, or a great many bees perish.

We suggest the following method for obtaining natural bee venom without harming the bees. The bee is picked up with special tweezers (as used in apitoxin therapy) and placed with its abdomen downward on a slide.

The bee stings the slide, i.e. releases its poison but retains its sting. We managed to get 300 units of apitoxin per slide (by units we mean the amount of venom released by one bee). Two slides can be placed together with their venom-covered surfaces in contact and sent through the post in, the ordinary way.

More recently, celluloid, plastic, and polyethylene discs have been used for the purpose instead of glass. The crystallized apitoxin is easily scraped off the disc; and it is easy to weigh it and calculate an exact dose.

Bee venom obtained in this manner retains its curative properties for two years. In order to use the apitoxin for medicinal purposes, it is sufficient to place the disc in distilled water. The solution of apitoxin obtained can be used for intracutaneous and hypodermic injections, or for inhalation or electrophoresis, or to prepare ointment, etc. The method does not harm the bees, and can be carried out in any laboratory, or medical institution.

A hundred years ago or so a decoction of dead bees was used in folk medicine with some success to treat certain diseases. A few years ago the Soviet beekeeper E.L.Hofman informed the writer that this remedy is still widely used in the Altai Territory.

DIET DURING APITOXIN THERAPY

Diet is extremely important during treatment with bee venom. And it should be noted that it is not only the content of the diet that is important but also the regularity of mealtimes. The diet should be of high calorific value, but not onerous, and should contain the normal balance of carbohydrate, protein, fat, and vitamins.

An increased intake of vitamins C and B_1 has a beneficial effect. It also helps to substitute honey (approximately 50-100 grams per day) for some of the sugar and other carbohydrates (bread, potatoes).

Alcoholic beverages and spices are not allowed during the treatment since they lessen the therapeutic effect of the venom. The use of bee venom immediately after a large meal, when there is a surge of blood to the digestive organs, is categorically forbidden.

Bee venom can provoke increased anaemia (blood deficiency) in the brain, thereby causing fainting fits. Baths, showers, and long walks are inadvisable immediately after treatment by stings.

After the sting has been removed from the skin and the wound smeared with boric acid ointment, the patient should lie down for at least 20-25 minutes. A rational diet is exceptionally important when rheumatism is treated.

SNAKE AND BEE VENOM

M. Phisalix (1932-5) demonstrated that it was possible to cross-immunize animals against snake and bee venom. It has also been established that the antivend ie known as Calmette's serum has a therapeutic effect in poisoning by bee venom.

Bee and snake venom have a great deal in common. Hedgehogs

are equally immune to snake and bee venom, while horses are extremely sensitive to both. Oxidizing agents (potassium permanganate) and alcohol neutralize the toxic effect of both. The spot where they are injected into the body is of great importance with each. And with both death occurs through paralysis of the respiratory centre.

Although bees and snakes are phylogenetically very dissimilar, their .poisons have this in common that, when correctly used, they can be used as remedies. When bee and snake venom enter the blood they are distributed throughout the organism and have a very specific effect on the nervous system. Both possess analgesic properties.

The indications for their use in certain illnesses are almost identical. Vipratox and Virapin (or Apisarthron) can be administered in cases of muscular rheumatism, rheumatism in the joints, neuralgia, etc. Treatment, however, must obviously be carried out under the supervision of an experienced doctor.

Good results have been obtained when preparations containing bee and snake venom have been used together with a procedure similar to that we recommend for bee venom (i.e. rubbing the skin of one shoulder on the first day with Vipratox, the other shoulder on the next day with Virapin, a hip on the third day with Vipratox, and the other hip on the fourth day with Virapin).

THE CURATIVE PROPERTIES OF BEEWAX AND OTHER BEE PRODUCTS

Beeswax is one of those complex substances that have still not been fully investigated. It has about 15 separate chemical components; and it has been ascertained that it contains 70.4 to 74.7 per cent complex esters of monatomic alcohols (melissyl or myricyl alcohol, ceryl alcohol or cerotin, etc.) and fatty acids, 13.5 to 15 per cent free acids (cerotinic, melissic, the oleic group, etc.), and 12.5 to 15.5 per cent saturated hydrocarbons (pentacosane, heptacosane, nonacosane, etc.).

In addition it contains colouring matter and fragrant substances that give it its colour and pleasant smell. People have been well acquainted with the remarkable properties of beeswax since ancient times. In Ancient Egypt sacrifices of beeswax were widely offered.

A scroll of the time of Rameses 11 (13th century B.C.) mentions that the Pharaoh's contribution to the sacrificial fund was 3100 *deben.* In the fourth century B.C. Aristophanes described beeswax as an invaluable and extremely useful substance, noting that it could be used for many purposes (protecting the surfaces of metals against rust, for modelling and making waxed tablets, for letters and for sealing them).

Various ancient peoples (among them the Scythians and Iranians) used beeswax to embalm the corpses of eminent leaders. Hippocrates recommended applying beeswax to the head and neck as a cure for sore throat. Centuries later Avicenna gave many interesting prescriptions containing beeswax in his *Canon of Medicine,* which are just-as valid today, although they are a thousand years old. In old Russian manuals on medicine it was said that beeswax healed wounds and eased chest complaints. In 1707 D.

Moor wrote that Pure wax, when distilled, became a most effective oil, a remedy more divine than human because it worked miracles or. wounds and internal ailments. In folk medicine bees= s ax was used to treat several illnesses, in particular lupus. (In this connection the findings of D. Rapoport, a worker at the Pyelorussian Dermato-venereological Institute, reported in 1939, are of interest.

He considered that current preparations for local therapy of lupus had certain great disadvantages in that they produced soreness and gave unsatisfactory cosmetic results. In his opinion an ointment made from beeswax and butter, which contained no harmful ingredients, was effective.) From ancient times down to the invention of paper, letters were written on flat tablets covered on one side with an even layer of wax in which the letters were cut.

The instrument or stylus used for the purpose was made of metal and had a sharpened end for writing and a blunted end for smoothing out the surface where there was already writing. Down the centuries, too, artists used wax paints, which have an attractive sheen and retain their colour well. This is attested not only by literary sources but also by archaeological finds.

During the excavation of Pompei and Herculaneum in 1706 a wax mural was uncovered that had decorated the banqueting hall of a rich citizen of Pompei. Despite the fact that it had been covered with earth and volcanic ash on 24 August in A. D. 79, during an cruption of Vesuvius, and had consequently remained buried for almost 18 centuries, it had retained its beauty and the brightness of its colours.

Even today, when new techniques have ousted wax painting, beeswax is still an important ingredient of oil paints, binding the oil and the pigment. Beeswax was extensively used in sculpture, and busts and models were still made in wax in Russia in the eighteenth century.

In 1716 Peter the Great invited the famous architect and sculptor Bartolomeo Rastrelli to St. Petersburg to make sculptures for him. In 1719 Rastrelli modelled the wax head of Peter that now stands in the Ethnographic Museum of the USSR Academy of Sciences; and in 1729 he completed a bust of Menshikov.

The many wax portraits that have come down to us retain the

freshness of their colours in a striking manner. Beeswax is also used for making models for medical purposes. Leonardo da Vinci (1452-1519), that remarkable naturalist and artist of the Renaissance, worked out a method of making anatomical preparations of the brain by injecting molten wax into the ventricles.

The preservative properties of beeswax can be seen from the anatomical preparations that Peter the Great acquired from the Dutch anatomist Rutsch for the school of the first hospital in Russia, which are kept in the museum of the USSR Academy of Sciences. Beeswax was the basic constituent of these preparations.

Blood vessels and tissues had been filled with waxes of different colours so that they could be observed more easily; the wax at the same time preserved them from decay. Beeswax retains its importance in medicine today.

The USSR Pharmacopoeia says that discs, ointments, and, creams should be prepared from it. Adhesive, mercury, melilotin, and soap plasters cannot be prepared without it' nor camphor ointment, the Spanish fly ointment used in veterinary medicine, nor spermaceti, lead, zinc, or other ointments.

It is also extensively used in the cosmetic industry for creams, as it is easily absorbed by the skin and gives the latter a smooth delicate look. In 1962 N.Yakobashvili developed a process for obtaining a scented substance from beeswax that can be used in the production of high-quality perfumes. This fragrant substance possesses properties like those of rose and jasmine oils but is much cheaper to-make.

More than five kilograms of high quality oil can be obtained from a ton of beeswax, while the residue retains the numerous industrial properties of the wax.

Beeswax is rich in vitamin A, a hundred grams of wax from the comb containing 4096 international units (compared with 60 in the same .weight of beef). We prepared vitaminized sweets that retained their value for several months, utilizing beeswax.

We took the honey sweets 'Little Bee' and 'Golden Hive' made by the Red October Confectionary Works in Moscow (which contain a small amount of clear honey enclosed in a rather large sugar casing) and covered them with vitaminized beeswax by immersing them in slightly melted wax to which we had added vitamins in the following quantities (in milligrams per cent): A 0.5, B_1 1.0, B_2 1.0, C 25, rutin 20.

The sweets improved metabolism and had a beneficial effect on circulation and the work of the muscles. The very act of chewing them in itself was beneficial since much saliva was secreted and heightened the secretory activity and motor function of the stomach, while the wax automatically cleaned the teeth of deposits and strengthened the gums.

Such sweets can be recommended for people who want to give up smoking. Beeswax has many industrial uses, and is employed extensively in foundry work, in the engineering industries, railway transport, and the textile and leather industries, as well as in the perfume, pharmaceutical, and confectionary industries.

It is an ingredient of ski wax, shoe polishes, sealing wax, glue for marble and plaster, and pencils for writing on glass. And it is used in horticulture for grafting. The legendary Daedalus, builder of the first flying apparatus, used beeswax in constructing his wings; and even today aircraft and space vehicles cannot do without it.

BEE GLUE (PROPOLIS)

When a beehive is opened on a sunny summer's day, a brownish green resin-like substance can be seen sticking to the upper edge of the honeycomb frame. This is propolis or bee glue (from the Greek *propolis*, a suburb) and is so called because in their natural surroundings bees make the entrance to their bee town smaller with bee glue to keep out unbidden guests.

Bees use their glue to fill in cracks in the hive, to attach the corners of frames to the grooves in the hive, and to polish the cells of the honeycomb. The bodies of dead lizards, snakes, and mice that have entered hives are sealed into the walls with bee glue, thereby protecting the colonies against the unpleasant odour and bacterial flora of the putrefying corpses.

It used to be thought that propolis was made from substances collected by bees from the buds of trees (willow, poplar, birch, fir, pine, horse chestnut, etc.), but research has established that it is prepared from pollen.

On average propolis contains 55 per cent resin and balsam, about 10 per cent scented ethereal or essential oils, up to 30 per cent wax, and 5 per cent pollen. Our own collection of samples from the various geographical zones of the USSR demonstrates that they differ in chemical composition as well as in colour and aroma.

Bee glue is quite a complex substance containing protein and vitamins, and various minerals (iron, manganese, calcium, aluminium, silicon, vanadium, and strontium). Spectrum analysis has shown that it is a high molecular organic compound containing minerals and volatile esters, and that it very likely acts by the physiological mechanism of phytoncides. In folk medicine propolis was reputed to have antituberculotic properties.

At our request the Moscow Tuberculosis Institute specially tested it for bactericidal properties. The mycobacteria of tuberculosis, however, grew just as quickly in thermostatic conditions on a culture medium containing propolis as on controls that had none and in fact, it is interesting to note, they grew better on a culture medium to which propolis was added in small doses than on the controls.

During the Boer War propolis was reported to be effective in healing wounds. And although it was successfully tested for this purpose during World War II, propolis therapy has not been widely adopted in medicine.

Propolis was popular in folk medicine for removing corns. A piece of propolis was softened by heating, and a thin layer smeared on the corn, which was then lightly bandaged. The corn and its root came away completely after a few days.

In 1953 N.Toporova and K.Toporina concluded that propolis ointment was effective in necrobacillosis in cattle, even without removing the infected part of the surface. In 1955 K.Gaptrakhimanova used a propolis ointment with success to heal farm animals affected by necrobacillosis.

The ointment, prepared with vaseline and sunflower and henbane oils in proportions of 1 : 1 and 1.5 : 1, was more effective than other remedies. It is obviously a mild irritant and probably promotes normal trophics.

In 1957 N.Prokopovich described experiments on the effect of propolis as a local anaesthetic. The anaesthetizing strength of its 25 per cent solution was greater than that of cocaine and procaine; stomatologists and dentists do not, however, use it.

We ourselves obtained good results using a 10 per cent spirit extract of high-quality crushed bee glue to treat dental disorders like pyorrhoea and paradontosis, and also for sore throat, inflammation of the tonsils, etc.

At the first Moscow Regional Conference on Medical Apiculture, held in 1959, G. Mukhamediarov described the anti-pruritus properties of propolis. Our own clinical observations, and communications from Yugoslavia indicate, however, that propolis in its various medicinal forms (ointment, propolis milk, etc.) gives only temporary relief against itching.

Khmelevskaya et al., of the Kiev Radiological and Ontological Research Institute, reported that, when propolis ointment was applied to the skin of patients who were to have radiation treatment, it prevented a radiation skin reaction in most cases.

Propolis ointment apparently had a beneficial effect in reducing the radiation reactions, thus shortening the period of treatment and enabling the necessary dose of radiation to be administered without interruption. The authors concluded that propolis ointment could be recommended to prevent radiation reactions and to treat radiation lesions generally.

Good results have been obtained from inhalation of propolis in diseases of the upper respiratory tract and the lungs (e.g. bronchitis and tuberculosis). The treatment is simple and can be employed at home as well as in out-patient departments.

For an inhalation 60 g of propolis and 40 g of beeswax are put into an aluminium or enamel vessel (300400 ml), which is stood in a large metal bowl of boiling water. The mixture is inhaled for 10 or 15 minutes in the morning and evening over a period of two months.

At the 20th (Jubilee) International Congress on Apiculture in Bucharest in 1965 Derevich, Popescu, and Popescu made some interesting communications on guinea-pigs. They had established that an alcohol extract of propolis and propolis ointment accelerated the healing of burns.

They considered that the entire group of flavonoids, i.e. pigments containing galangin (the active fraction in propolis), had a preserving and regenerating effect on the connective tissue. When its toxins have been removed galangin could be used as a remedy with good effect.

Of the complex of components making up propolis only the phytoncides of the ethereal oils are active. For that reason propolis loses its antibiotic properties if it is stored for a long time without being hermetically sealed.

Its properties are improved by heating as the antibiotic ethereal oils organically combined with wax, resin, balsam, and pollen are thus freed for action. That is why we therefore consider inhalation the most effective method of employing propolis.

Its phytoncides are then taken up by the vapour from the water and on entering the lungs are instantly absorbed into the bloodstream. As worker bees normally eat pollen and nectar, Prof. B. Tokin writes that 'the bee in a manner of speaking, is itself a concentrate or "preserve" of flowers. Consequently honey should possess phytoncidal properties.'

That applies equally, in our opinion, to propolis. We believe that in the near future the arsenal of medicines will be enriched by an effective new remedy in the form of a phytoncidal preparation, propolis, one of the most valuable products of apiculture, which has not yet being taken into the armoury of medicine.

POLLEN

When bees visit flowers they transport pollen on their bodies from the anthers to the stigma, thereby promoting fertilization. The pollen grains are not only extremely important for the plants but also for the bees themselves, and a foraging bee will spend up to four hours on a flight collecting its two pellets of pollen.

Only bee colonies that have plenty of pollen from early spring onward can develop and reach their full strength, as it is an irreplaceable source of the protein the bees need for their daily activity.

Having filled the 'baskets' on its hind legs with pollen, a bee flies back to the hive, skilfully keeping its balance in the air. If. you watch the alighting hoard of a hive on a fine summer's day, you will observe an interesting picture as the bees return with their loads, for from the colour of their legs you can deduce what flowers they have been visiting.

If a bee's legs are blue then it has been on the flowers of wild mallow or Viper's bugloss. If the pollen is red it has been collected from pear, peach, or horse chestnut trees. A green load means the bee has been working on lindens, maples, or rowans, or on flax.

Golden yellow pollen means they have been to the flowers of rose hazel or gooseberry bushes, buckwheat, or angelica. Bees with purple loads have obviously been visiting campanula or phacelia, and those with white or grey loads apple trees or raspberry canes.

Brown loads mean that the bees have been to the flowers of sainfoin, white or red clover, or meadow cornflower. Bees with the orange pollen of sunflowers or dandelions look very handsome.

Each microscopic grain of pollen is a complex concentration of invaluable nutritive and curative substances (peptones, globulins, amino acids, carbohydrates, fatty substances, enzymes, minerals) and vitamins (B_1, B_2, B_6, B_{12}, A, P, E, K). Thus this tiny grain is a treasure chest of substances invaluable to the organism.

Bees make beebread from pollen. When foraging bees enter the bee space between the frames in the hive they unload their cargo of pollen into cells of the comb. Other bees ram the pollen into the cells while others still immediately pour honey on to the top layer, so that air cannot get at it and turn it bad.

Under the action of enzymes, significant changes take place in the pollen. Some of the sugar of the honey is transformed into lactic acid which acts as a preservative for the highly perishable components of the pollen.

Beebread differs from both pollen and honey in that it is the

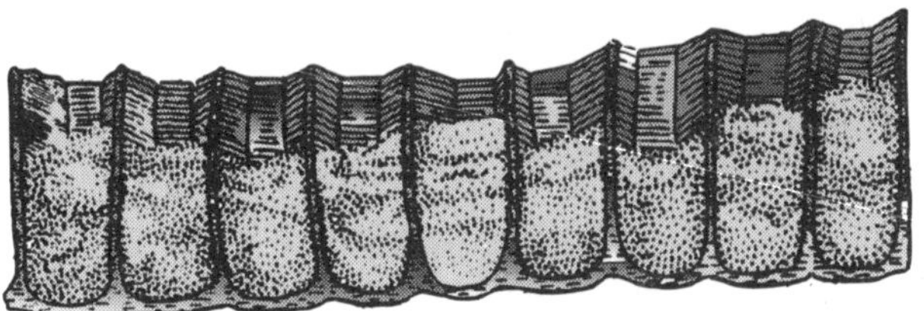

Figure 8.1: Cross-section of cells of pollen, showing layered contents (double magnification).

result of complex enzymatic processes taking place in them. It contains sugar, proteins, fat, minerals, and other elements.

When there is no pollen in a hive the queen ceases to lay eggs and the house bees stop making wax and building the cells needed for raising offspring and storing honey and pollen.

During cold springs, when willow, dandelion, and other pollen.-bearing plants have finished flowering before the bees have been able to make use of them, and the previous year's stock of pollen has already run out, the further development of offspring may be threatened.

Observant beekeepers have noticed that then, when there is no pollen in the environs of the hive, the bees bring in flour from mills and barns. V.Vaganov reported in 1952 that at such times the bees began to bring back yellow 'pollen' that was, in fact, dust from rotting wood.

The pollen from various species not only differs in colour, shade, and size, but is also different in shape. Pollen grains from willow and birch are seven microns in diameter while those of the pumpkin family are as big as 150 microns.

Their chemical composition also differs in the relative amounts of protein, fat, carbohydrate, vitamins, minerals, and hormones. According to S.Lebedev (1949) pollen can be used to obtain large quantities of carotene. The pollen grains of the lily and yellow acacia contain 20 times as much carotene as carrots (its main source).

It would seem expedient to extract provitamin A from lily or acacia (which can be done quite easily without any preliminary processing). It has been estimated that ten grams of pollen can be collected from 100 lilies, and that a hectare would yield as much as 100 grams of carotene.

Pollen is also exceptionally rich in rutin; buckwheat pollen, in particular, contains 17 mg per cent of rutin. The fact that valuable vitamins and hormones are present in pollen makes it suitable for medical and prophylactic purposes.

In folk medicine pollen was considered an all-purpose remedy. We ourselves have tested it clinically in several illnesses, and found it particularly effective mixed with honey (1 : 1) for treating hyperte-nsion, and are convinced that a honey and pollen mixture can be used in several other conditions, particularly in complaints of the nervous and endocrine systems.

The experiments of Chauvin et al. in France in 1957 demonstrated that mice given minute amounts of pollen in their food developed and put on weight more quickly than the controls. It has a beneficial effect even when the vitamins have been removed from it.

In the excrements of the mice fed pollen, no micro-organisms were found, which indicates that it has an antibiotic effect. Pollen normalizes the activity of the intestine (especially in cases of colitis or chronic constipation), improves the appetite, and increases fitness for work.

Pollen has been found useful in pernicious anaemia, lowering blood pressure, and increasing the haemoglobin and erythrocyte content of the blood.

The Romanian workers M.Jalomicianu, K.Christa, K.Butuianu, and L.Onitiu reported in 1965 that a daily dose of 25 grams of pollen mixed with honey did not give rise to any allergy, and noted that the mixture was effective in diseases of the liver.

The work of the Swedish researchers E.A.Upmark (Upsala University) and G.Jonson (department of urology, Lund University), published in 1959, indicated that pollen had a beneficial effect on the prostate gland. A pollen preparation (Zernilton) is sold in Sweden as a prophylactic for complaints of the prostate and adenomas.

Alin Caillas recommends every man over 50 to take 15 grams of pollen daily to prevent prostatitis or adenoma of the prostate. Pollen is a biological stimulator. Prof. N. Tsitsin, Member of the USSR Academy of Sciences, believed that the rejuvenating properties attributed to honey were due to the presence of pollen in it.

Plants produce great quantities of pollen. A single apple blossom contains about 100 000 grains, a juniper flower 400 000, a hornbeam catkin 1.2 million, a peony bloom 8.6 million, a hazel catkin (or lamb's tail) four million, and a birch catkin six million grains. The oak, elm, pine, fir, and cedar also yield much pollen.

The air in a pine forest in summer is literally saturated with it. Most of the grains fall on the ground and remain there; some are lifted by air currents as high as 2500 metres and carried distances up to 4500 metres.

One tassel of Indian corn releases about 20 million grains, of which only 800, at most 1000, are needed to fertilize a spike or cob. In fact millions of times more pollen is produced than is actually needed by plants for fertilization.

We estimate that in the USSR alone bees collect more than 200 000 tons of pollen in a single summer, which is only an infinitesimal part of what is produced. So, every year, in our forests, fields, meadows and gardens, hundreds of thousands of tons of a product possessing great nutritive and curative properties go to waste.

Bees being the main collectors of pollen, F.Zubritsky (1940) suggested a trap to remove it from them. The apparatus was simple, consisting of a board with vertical pins placed in the bee-entrance; and any beekeeper could make it.

The trap allowed the bee to enter the hive but kept back the pollen in its hind legs. This method of collection seemed very promising, and it was thought that the pollen so gathered could be used as an invaluable foodstuff for humans. Enthusiastic beekeepers with large apiaries collected 100 to 200 grams a day, and between ten and twenty kilograms in a season. But the practice never caught on, may be because it caused a considerable drop in honey yield.

Apart from that, it was impossible to collect the large amounts needed by the vitamin industry and medical institutions in this way. And the pollen so obtained could not be used for research or for practical medical purposes since a single type of pollen was required, as the chemical and biological composition, and therefore the curative properties of the pollen from different species is not the same and varies considerably.

It is worth remarking, also, that bees frequently bring poisonous pollen back to the hive (from plants like false hellebore, wild rosemary, monkshood, larkspur, rhododendron, etc.). Karl Johannson (1955) reported that 46 per cent of the pollen collected by bees and stored in a box at -17.5° C retained its ability to germinate for nine months, whereas 71 per cent of pollen collected manually (and kept in the same conditions) did so.

P.Lebedev and N.Kireev (1959) established that the pollen collected by bees in their pollen sacs is dampened with nectar and saliva and so loses its ability to germinate. Pollen collected from the surface of a bee's body, however, has not been wetted and remains active.

Manual collection of pollen must therefore be resorted to. It could possibly be organized in the same way as the gathering of medicinal herbs is. Schoolchildren, for example, could collect large quantities during rambles and excursions.

The branches of bushes in bloom, or the tassels of maize, etc., can be shaken into a glass jar. Large quantities of pollen can also be obtained by shaking a branch in flower over a clean sheet of paper or a clean, dry newspaper.

We have contrived a device that gives good results, consisting of five long thin sticks (or canes), joined like a fishing rod, with an ordinary twig-cutting knife fastened to the end of the top rod.

This enables flowers ten or eleven metres high on a tree to be reached. To gather pollen a sheet is spread on the ground beneath the tree or shrub to catch any pollen from the flowers as they are cut from it.

The flowers are collected in a sack (preferably cotton) and dried indoors for two or three days so that the pollen can be shaken from them. In this way large quantities of pollen can be collected manually from one species of plant.

The Romanian doctor and beekeeper K.Rosenthal (1965) considers manual gathering of pollen a matter of some urgency, as pollen is of great value biologically, and could occupy an important place in beekeeping. Many other workers have noted that pollen gathered manually has definite advantages over pollen obtained from bees.

QUEEN OR ROYAL JELLY

Ever since Aristotle researchers have been trying to find out why it is that the queen bee, which emerges from an ordinary egg, just like any other bee, should be twice as big and twice as heavy as worker bees, why she is able to lay such a large number of eggs (over 2000 a day), and how she can live for six years when her daughters, the worker bees, die after 30 to 35 days.

Chemistry has helped us to solve this. mystery. The nurse bees place the egg from which a queen is destined to be hatched in a special cell or 'uterus', shaped like a peanut, and feed the larva a special food, royal jelly.

At this time the 'uterus' is like a little barrel of wax in which the larva literally floats in a jelly-like mass the consistency of cream and the colour of milk (with motherof-pearl tones). This mass is, in fact, royal jelly, or as it is called in some countries, queen jelly.

Natural royal jelly contains up to 18 per cent protein, between 10 and 17 per cent sugar, up to 5.5 per cent fat, and more than 1 per cent minerals. To give you an idea of how nutritious it is let us recall that cow's milk contains 3.3 per cent protein, 4 per cent fat, and 4.6 per cent sugar.

Royal jelly also contains vitamins B_1, B_2, B_3, B_8, B_c, B_{12}, PP, and H, but very little vitamin C, A (carotene), or D (according to some researchers, none at all).

Vitamin E, which stimulates fertility, is also found in royal jelly. The jelly with which the larvae of worker bees are fed obviously does not contain this vitamin for, when rats were fed with it, they proved infertile (as shown by Gille's experiments in 1939). The jelly used to feed worker bees and drones contains the same other substances as royal jelly, but in smaller quantities.

Experiments have shown that the life span of animals fed very small amounts of royal jelly is increased by a third. It causes pullets to lay more eggs and stimulates old fowls to begin laying again.

Henry Hale demonstrated in 1939 that royal jelly contains a gonadotropic hormone. Female rats given subcutaneous injections of an extract of the jelly put on weight and exhibited increased follicular activity of the ovaries within a few days.

There are certain difficulties in obtaining royal jelly in quantity, since bees only make many cells for queens in certain conditions, i.e. when the colony is left without a queen or when the queen is old. In order to obtain quantities, the queen has to be removed from the hive; the bees then prepare several queen cells (sometimes up to a hundred).

To collect the jelly in quantity easily we suggest using a portable case that contains the instruments necessary for extracting, preserving, and dispatching or delivering the jelly to the laboratory, and also serves as a work table.

After scrubbing their hands with soap and water and putting on a clean white overalls and caps or straw hats, the collector and the beekeeper should remove the frames containning queen cells from the hive and place them in the stand.

Then the queen cells can be excised with a scalpel and put into the appropriate vessel. When sufficient queen cells have been removed the frame should be returned to the hive. The cells obtained should then be cut lengthwise with a scalpel and the jelly transferred to a wide-mouthed bottle or jar by means of a glass spade or spatula.

When the jar is nine-tenths full it should be topped up with a stabilizer (40 per cent spirit), and corked. The corked jar should then be sealed with molten wax and labelled with the date of collection, and the name of the collector. Each bottle should be wrapped in a paper napkin and placed in a special container.

The larva in the cells should be removed with forceps and placed in a vessel with a stabilizer to remove the jelly from them. The jelly precipitated to the bottom of the vessel should be transferred to another jar, and the larvae crushed in a porcelain mortar and put into a special vessel with a stabilizer. They can then be used for making cosmetics.

To obtain all the queen jelly from a cell, the inside of the cell should be thoroughly cleansed with a brush, which should then be washed in a measuring glass with stabilizer. (In addition to the equipment named above, the portable case also contains an alcohol lamp, matches, and a notebook and pen.)

As an alternative to the procedure described, the cells containing royal jelly can be sent direct in a special package to the institution employing the jelly.

(During the first three days of their development drone larvae also literally float in drone jelly. The extract we have obtained from drone larvae is an active biostimulant and possesses certain curative properties. The virus-stable anti-influenzal properties of the extract are not less than those of royal jelly.)

Much research has been done to test royal jelly and use it to treat disorders of the cardiovascular system and gastrointestinal tract (in tuberculosis, brucellosis, arthritis, etc.). It used to be regarded as a panacea for almost all illnesses, and even today one can still come across articles attributing unusual and absolutely unfounded properties to royal jelly; but fortunately the enthusiasm of certain researchers who have been unable to distinguish between claims and reality is giving way to serious experimental and clinical work.

After research and experiments over a long period in the Department of Pharmacology and Microbiology of the Plovdiv Higher Medical Institute, under the supervision of Prof. Peiko Peichev, a fairly stable sterile aqueous solution of royal jelly was obtained in various concentrations. (The extract was not sterilized by boiling, as boiling destroys the antibacterial and other properties of the jelly.)

Royal jelly, and extracts of drone larvae and of propolis, have anti-influenzal properties. The anti-influenzal effect of an alcoholic extract of the jelly has been studied experimentally by the virusologists A. Derevich and A. Petrescu.

Their work (using influenza viruses of strains A and B) indicated that the virucidal effect of the extract was due to the natural royal jelly and not to the stabilizer (40 per cent alcohol).

They injected a dose of virus and 2 mg of an aqueous extract of royal jelly into the allantois of chicken embryos; not once in three passages of the virus was it detected. No harmful effect on the embryos was observed, and they hatched at the same time as the controls.

We ourselves have studied the prophylactic and therapeutic effect of alcohol extracts of the jelly in influenza. (As an emulsion of 2 g of jelly in 18 g of 40 per cent alcohol, royal jelly can be preserved for a long time.

The spirit not only stabilizes the labile components of the jelly, but also promotes its absorption by the mucous membranes when the extract is placed under the tongue, in the mouth, or in the nose.)

We have found that smearing the membrane of the nose with the emulsion, and taking 20 drops a day under the tongue (or as a mouth rinse), prevents influenza.

As treatment for the disease, the process should be carried out three times (morning, afternoon, and evening) for one or two days. The complex chemical composition of royal jelly has not yet been fully studied, but medicine has been enriched by its biostimulating properties.

It is known to contain acetylcholine, which dilates the blood vessels, and is therefore used to treat hypertension.

The French doctor Destrem (1956) reported the results of treating 134 patients aged 60 to 89. Intramuscular injections (20 ml) of royal jelly were effective in 60 per cent of the patients. Blood pressure was normalized, appetites improved, the patients gained weight and their mood became more cheerful and active.

In a personal communication to the writer, Dr. Roberto Jelin (Argentina) writes of an interesting case of a woman with endarteritis obliterans, constriction of the lumen, and blocking of the blood vessels, being cured with royal jelly. 'The doctors had given her up as a hopeless case .... Gangrene was expected to set in in her leg.

Her son, a chemist; asked me for some royal jelly as a last resort. This was at the end of last year. No gangrene formed and now she feels quite well.' The jelly apparently normalized the activity of the suprarenal glands, which secrete adrenaline during endarteritis.

Joseph Matuszewski (1965) considers that royal jelly normalizes metabolism, has a diuretic effect, can be used to prevent obesity and emaciation, builds up resistance to infections, regulates the functioning of the endocrine glands, and is good for arteriosclerosis and coronary deficiency.

Chauvin, Curioti, and others have affirmed that it is a to nic, restoring energy, getting rid of the feeling of indisposition, and improving appetite. In 1967 Prof. Peichev and co-workers carried out observations on 23 clinically healthy old men at the Kocho Svetar Home in Bulgaria of the following ages (ten between 60 and 69; six between 70 and 79, and seven between 80 and 89).

They established that the combined use of royal jelly, honey, and pollen had an invigorating effect, made the old people feel better, improved their appetites and sleep, lessened pain around the heart, improved diuresis, lowered cholesterol content and blood pressure, and eased respiratory and sexual functions.

In some countries royal jelly is given by subcutaneous or intramuscular injections, or is taken internally mixed with honey and pollen. We advise against taking small doses of honey and jelly, or honey, pollen, and jelly, internally, as the gastric juices inactivate the curative properties of royal jelly.

It can be taken internally, however, if half a glass of an alkaline solution is drunk 15 minutes beforehand (a dessertspoon of soda in half a glass of boiled water).

For some time now the jelly has been administered under the tongue with success. The patient places a glass spoon containing the required amount of jelly under the tongue (or a solution of emulsion can be given as drops on the tongue).

It is readily absorbed by the mucosa under the tongue and rapidly enters the blood stream without passing through the stomach. We have found that large doses (100 to 200 mg a day), taken in this way, have an invigorating effect. Small doses are apparently only psychologically effective.

It is clear that no single prescription or scheme of treatment is correct for all patients. A special schedule should be drawn up for each patient. In serious cases, particularly of rheumatism or arthritis, a mixture of bee venom and royal jelly can be prescribed as part of a special diet; taken together they have a beneficial effect on the organism, acting pharmacologically and improving resistance.

The effect is the greater when the proportions of the two substances are correct for the individual. N.Boshev's experiments in the physiology department of the Pavlov Higher Medical Institute in Plovdiv (Bulgaria) have indicated that royal jelly generally stimulates higher nervous activity in animals.

Conversely bee venom, in therapeutic doses, inhibits the activity of the cerebral cortex. Apitoxin and royal jelly should therefore be prescribed in strictly individual manner to each patient, taking into account their various pharmacological properties.

When a relapse has occurred in cases of chronic arthritis, apitoxin therapy, even when combined with royal jelly, has no effect whatsoever.

ALLERGY

In conclusion I must mention that beeswax, propolis,, pollen, and royal jelly cause allergies in some people. This applies in particular to pollen. It has long been known that the pollen of trees, shrubs and bushes, and grasses causes allergic colds and hay fever.

9

Chapter

BEE-UTOPIA

NATURAL HEALTH FARMS

Anyone who has been in a bee-farm on a fine sunny day will know how pleasant it is to fill one's lungs with fresh air, heavy with the scent of flowers, fragrant honey, beeswax, and -propolis. The air in a bee-garden is quite pure and fresh.

Before it reaches the lungs it has passed through the natural filter of foliage in Nature's complex, living laboratory and been purified. It is an old popular belief that green leaves and flowers make the air bracing, and this has been scientifically demonstrated. Prof. B.P.Tokin demonstrated that wherever there are plants, volatile substances (which he called phytoncides) that destroy microbes are constantly discharged into the atmosphere.

And Prof. N. Kholodny has even advanced the more daring opinion that the volatile organic substances discharged into the air by many plants are 'atmospheric vitamins'.

The beekeeper working in an apiary during the best months of the year therefore breathes air that is not only fresh and pure but is also enriched with the fragrance of honey and these phytoncides and 'atmospheric vitamins'.

The serenity of a well-ordered apiary impressed Tolstoy greatly. In his story A ***Landowner's Morning*** he depicted this feeling marvellously. 'It was so cosy, pleasant, and quiet in the sun-lit apiary; the grey-haired old man with the fine close wrinkles radiating from his eyes who, with large shoes on his bare feet, came waddling and smiling with good-natured self-satisfaction to welcome his master to his own private domain, was so simple-hearted and kind that Nekhlyudov immediately forgot the unpleasant impressions he had received that morning, and his cherished dream vividly recurred to him.

He saw all his peasants well off and kindly, as old Dutlov, and all smiling happily and affectionately at him because they were indebted to him alone for their wealth and happiness. Many people of various professions have found beekeeping an absorbing hobby.

The Russian opera singer, G. P. Kandratiev, suffered from a serious nervous ailment. His doctors advised him to rest for four months and to spend the summer in the open air.

One day, at a meeting of the Free Economic Society, Kandratiev was sitting next to Prof. A. M. Butlerov and in the course of the conversation mentioned his doctor's orders. `What better than to take up beekeeping?' Butlerov said to him. The words shaped Kandratiev's fate. He became a beekeeper, and afterwards said that from then on life without bees would have been 'life devoid of aim and interest'.

V. Loginov, a prominent figure in the annals of Russian beekeeping, wrote in 1925: 'It is no accident that when in the company of famous beemasters, who have been keeping bees for many years, one often hears them say: "Beekeeping completely fills my life, and without it life would not be worth living." And that is quite true.'

'Beekeepers,' he maintained, 'usually enjoy good health and long life through their habit of eating honey and their healthy work in the midst of nature.'

We have collected interesting information of the healthful effect of beekeeping. From a questionnaire we sent to beekeepers in the Ukraine, mainly through the apiculture departments of the agricultural services, who checked the accuracy of the returns, 278 of the 390 questioned stated that in all the time they had been -working in an apiary they had not suffered a single day's illness.

Another 22 noted that before they took up beekeeping they had suffered from rheumatism, but after working with bees and being stung by them they had quickly recovered.

It is an old popular idea that the inclusion of honey in the diet is of great importance for prolonging life, and that people who eat honey regularly live to a ripe old age. In his book *The Beneficial*

Effect of Honey on the Human Organism, the Polish scientist and apiarist Vitwicki wrote (a hundred years ago) that the poet Trembecki whom he met at the age of 80 had been living on simple food and honey the last thirty years.

When he met the poet, be was surprised at the appearance and unfeigned cheerfulness of the seemingly ageless scholar. Many of the famous centenarians of the Caucasus worked in apiaries or kept bees.

Safar Husein, a 138-year old collective farmer in Azerbaijan, attributed his long life to the fact that he ate honey and worked in an apiary; 150-year old Mahmud Eivazov worked in his own bee-garden and considered work in the open air the best elhtir of longevity.

Three weeks after celebrating his hundred birthday, another collective farm beemaster, Asad Abbasov, walked a score of kilometres to have his photo taken to send to us.

At our request Yunisilau Mahomed Kair-Magoma; People's Artist of Daghestan, collected information about many beekeepers and honey enthusiasts in his republic who have enjoyed long life. Here are the names of some of them: Aita Hadjieva 100; Alikhan Bortsov 101; D. Bakhmudova 101; Dalgat Hasanov 101; Yusup Hazamov 101; Marjanasiyat Ispagieva 101; Said Hasanov 102; Supyat Mahomedova 102; Mairon Shabanova 107; Ahmed Aliev 108; Omar Aliev Agur Alil 118; Aishat Altaeva 122; P. Halitov 124.

We could cite many other examples of the prominence of beekeepers and honey-eaters among the centenarians of Azerbaijan, Georgia, the Ukraine, and other parts of the Soviet Union. At the time of writing the 110-year-old Azerbaijani beekeeper Panakh Mamed Valiev was fit, cheerful, full of life, and still had all his teeth.

'It is funny to think that people with a lot of money look to preparations from foreign institutes to renew their energy and strength,' N.E.Vorobiev said in 1927. 'They should turn to the bee-farm instead: to a pot of honey, a bowl of milk, and a crust of bread; the sunshine and work in the open air will do the rest.'

BEETOWNS

A cherished dream of ours is to see the creation of beetowns, macrobioutopias, or you might say bee-utopias, as special settlements for the elderly where retired men and women, enjoying good health and free of chronic illnesses, could live an active, socially useful, and productive old age in picturesque surroundings out in the country.

A beetown would not be a health farm, or a sanatorium, or an old people's home, though it would have elements of all of them in its financing and organization, but it would be a highly developed health resort cum apiary, producing bee products of every kind.

It would be built in wooded country thirty or forty kilometres from any big industrial city, preferably (in the USSR) in the south of the country, and would have a small area of land where a modern community could be built, with a large number of small houses, a well-equipped restaurant and dining-room, a health centre, a club, a swimming bath, sports grounds, and various communal buildings and services.

It would have a general sanatorium regimen of meals and medical care, but the residents would be permanent and not transient, and would work for three or four hours a day.

The heart or centre of Bee-Utopia would be a huge beefarm of several thousand hives, which would be the focal point occupying a special place in the lives of the residents. For everyone in Bee-Utopia would tend bees, whatever they had been before they retired, whether tinker, tailor, soldier, sailor, doctor, lawyer, economist, agronomist, cook, baker, accountant, artist.

Though the retired'doctors would find an additional interest bringing their years' of experience and knowledge to bear on studying the influence of environmental conditions on the elderly.

Like all utopians, I am tempted to describe the minutiae of every aspect of the life and activity of Beetown; how small two-room flats would be provided for married couples, and single rooms for the single; how the communal catering facilities, would provide four tasty meals a day with a menu devised by cooks and dieticians to be as sensible and nutritious as possible, and so on.

But the medicinal beekeeping combine or bee-farm fascinates me most. It could become a major production unit supplying vitaminized and medicated honeys to the medical profession. As I envisage it, in addition to the residential areas, shops, and social amenities, Beetown would have auxiliary premises for technical departments, laboratories, storehouses, etc. Top quality and medicinal honeys bearing the combine's trade mark would be produced and packed and supplied to medical centres, health resorts, clinical institutions, and the pharmaceutical industry.

The combine would organize the collection of bee venom (apitoxin) in quantity in crystalline and liquid form (ready packaged fn ampoules) without endangering the life or health of the bees. And by feeding its bees on the proper preparations it would produce a great deal of beeswax for the pharmaceutical and perfumery industries.

By using special methods to create an optimal balance within bee families, which would be devised in the combine's experimental labor-atory facilities, and feeding the bees special foods containing albumin and other proteins and enriched with vitamins and stimulants, it would be possible to obtain large quantities of royal jelly. And the combine would have facilities for preparing and packaging the jelly in ampoules and in tablet form.

Beetown would also organize the collection of pollen on a mass scale (pressed with honey, it would provide new medicine), and propolis (for the manufacture of new drugs).

And the combine would supply medical institutions with live bees for therapeutic purposes.

An interesting development might be a mobile apiary (resembling a pavilion cum trailer) that could be moved for a few days to areas where nectariferous plants were flowering in order to collect honey and contribute to the cross-pollination of field crops and orchards.

Utopia? I think it quite practical. And of inestimable value for a happy old age for the retired.

10 Chapter THE MAGIC WELL

In the East there is a saying whose wisdom needs no explanation: In a man's work lies his reputation. The names of scholars, philosophers, and writers, for example, live on for years, centuries, even millenia in their immortal works.

We apidologists (Latin *apis,* bee, and Greek *logos,* science) hold the works of Aristotle, the poems of Virgil and Ovid, and the works of other classical writers and thinkers in high esteem and glean much of interest from them on the life, habits, and work of bees.

Aristotle (384-322 B.C.) was the first researcher into bees, and has rightly been dubbed 'the sun of ancient apiculture'. His *History of Animals,* his writings on the 'parts' and 'reproduction' of animals contain many references based on experiments with and observation of bees.

He considered honey a remarkable product, capable of prolonging human life. Virgil (7-19 B.C.), the great 'poet laureate' of the Augustan Age in Rome, wrote of bees with great tenderness, warmth and affection in his *Georgics,* revealing a penetrating knowledge of them.

According to Cicero and Pliny, Aristomachus drew economic conclusions from his study of bees, and Hiliscus withdrew in his old age into the depths of the forest far from his fellow-beings in order to devote himself entirely to the study of these insects.

In his story of Aristomachus, Pliny tells how the philosopher was so enchanted by the life and work of the bee colony that he spent 58 years studying them.

Today, too, people from a wide range of professions and social backgrounds regard work with bees as a true source of happiness. As the beekeeper Anatole Butkevich remarked, apiculture brings the beemaster face to face with one of the marvels of nature, while the life of these little toilers, as it unfolds before his eyes, confronts him with a striking model of purposeful organization.

Unfortunately lack of space prevents us from telling about the hundreds of scholars who have done research on bees, or the thousands, and hundreds of thousands, who have found a cure for their ailments and a profession or hobby in beekeeping.

Here, however, we can only give the reader some brief sketches of the work of a few of those who have contributed to the development of apiculture and understanding of bees in the world, and especially in Russia. Many rulers and law-givers of the past are reputed to have drawn inspiration from bees.

Lycurgus, the founder of Sparta (circa 880 B.C.), is said to have been so impressed on observing the bees of a bee colony and amazed by the order and organization that reigned there that he took it as his model when he thought to bless his people with a perfect system of government.

That other famous Greek law-giver, Solon (circa 638558 B.C.), concerned himself practically with regulating bee-farming, and ordained that any new apiaries should be, set up in Athens not closer than 275 metres from existing ones.

In mediaeval times Charlemagne, the king of the Fra,nks (A.D. 742-814), energetically fostered beekeeping thrdCighout his broad domains. He was very fond of bees himself and thought that if his subjects and officials took up beekeeping it would greatly benefit his realm.

Beehives were set up in the forests, meadows, and gardens-wherever there were nectariferous plants. He gave his advisers, commanders, and state officials swarms of bees instead of medals, and at every assembly demanded an account of the collection of honey, a report on how the bees were swarming, and so on.

In the Eastern Roman Empire, Byzantium, over a thousand years ago (about A.D. 950), the encyclopaedic *Peri georgia eclogai* or *Geoponica was* written on the orders of the Emperor Constantine VII. It contained several articles on bees and bee-farming.

In more recent times beekeeping flourished in the Austrian Empire during the reign of Maria Theresa (17171780). On her direct instructions the post of teacher of beekeeping was instituted in many Austrian towns, and the best experts on bees were invited to apply for them by competition.

The famous Slovenian beemaster Anton Jansa was summoned from Krajna and appointed to the Vienna School of Apiculture, receiving the title of Imperial Beemaster. The Vienna School set the pace in Beekeeping for all Europe at that time.

The Russian Czar, Peter I (the Great) was greatly interested in bees. In P. Svinin's *The Sights of St. Petersburg and Its Environs,* published in 1818, there is a description of the palaces and parks of that great beauty spot, Strelnya. 'A little further from this elm,' the author wrote, 'Peter I set up an apiary.

The first hives were brought from Dorpat and the bees were kept under the Czar's personal supervision. Peter did this in order to disprove the idea that bees cannot be kept so far north and so close to the sea.'

Catherine the Great, too, was very fond of bees and held beekeeping in high esteem. In 1740 she issued an ukaze declaring that lands where trees with hives grew were not to be allowed to become private property.

In 1771, on her instructions, the two ablest students of the Smolensk Seminary (Borodovsky and Kaverznev) were sent to study the theory and practice of beekeeping under the eminent beemaster Schirach in Upper Lusatia.

In 1772, an ukaze issued on the occasion of the peace treaty with the Ottoman Empire showed favour to beekeepers, who were henceforth freed of taxes and dues. The Empress was so fond of bees that she had a beehive represented in her coatof-arms. When founding the Free Economic Society in 1775 she gave it a coat-of-arms, too, that contained a beehive.

Napole n Bonaparte (1769-1821) saw elements of the state in the bee colony. In drawing up the Code Napoleon, he made use of the ideal order, collectivism, and total commitment to the queen of the bee 'empire'.

He adopted the bee as his emblem, and during his reign the curtain of the Grand Opera was decorated with a bee pattern. But, these anecdotes apart, we are more interested in the contribution made by the great beemasters and writers. *Jan Swammerdam* (1637-1680), the illustrious Dutch doctor, microscopist, naturalist. and beekeeper, the father of insect anatomy, was the son of an apothecary and collector of butterflies, moths, beetles, grasshoppers, and other insects.

After studying medicine at Leyden University, he became a pioneer of microscopy. From an early age he began studying insect life, and was one of the first to define the sex of the three members of the bee colony, to describe the sexual organs of the queen and drone, the bee's sting, the hatching of a bee from the egg, the special features of the anatomical structure of bee larvae, etc.

Swammerdam demonstrated that the queen bee was a female and that it was she that laid eggs; at the time many scientists regarded the queen as a 'king'.

Swammerdam's findings put paid to that mistaken idea once and for all. In 1669 he published his *General History of Insects,* and 'four years later a *Tractate on Bees.*

His most famous work *The Bible of Nature (Biblia Naturae)* was published only 57 years after his death.

Moses Rowsden, beemaster to Charles II of England, published his *Further Considerations on Bees* in 1679.

Rene Antoine Reamur (1683-1757), the famous French physicist, and inventor of the Reamur thermometer scale, was an outstanding entomologist. He was concerned primarily with the honey bee to which he devoted much space in his *Memoires pour servir a l'histoire des insectes.*

Reamur carried out experiments with bees in a glass hive and pointed out that the only fully developed female in a bee colony was the queen, and that she mated with a drone. He also ascertained that bees hatched queens from larvae of a female worker bee by supplying it with special food.

Thus she was not really the 'queen' of the colony but a female whose work was controlled by the bees themselves. Reamur also described the relations between bees and plants.

Peter Rychkov (1712-1777), a corresponding member of the Russian Academy, was an outstanding historian and an expert on the economics of agriculture (including beekeeping). He was the first man in Russia to make a study of beekeeping and publish original articles on bees.

Prior to him, the only material appearing in Russian had been translations of works published in other countries. Rychkov was also the first man in Russia to record observations of the life of a bee colony in an improvised transparent hive (a glass jar 'half the size of a bucket' in which 'two rows of windows had been cut').

Some 200 years ago he published an article 'On Beekeeping' in the *Proceedings of the Free Economic Society,* in which he set out his views on the advancement of beekeeping.

Anton Jansa (1734-1773), the Slovenian beemaster, established that new queens are bred from the brood of female workers after the death of the old queen, and that drones are males and mate with queens during a nuptial flight. He developed methods for forestalling swarming, made a study of foul brood, collected voluminous notes on the life of a bee colony, and was far in advance of contemporary beekeepers.

He wrote a *Tractate on Bee Swarms* and *A Complete Course in Beekeeping.* In an article on the bicentenary of his birth, 'Anton Jansa: His Life and Work' (1934), Prof. Slavko Raich wrote that Jansa played a role in Slovenia comparable to Prokopovich in the Ukraine, Dzierzon in Poland, and Major Hruschka in Moravia.

Francois Huber (1750-1831), the Swiss naturalist, was blind from the age of 15, but with the aid of his wife and a devoted servant, he carried out some extremely interesting experiments with bees and made a number of major discoveries.

In 1787, at the age of thirty-seven, he described the flight of an active queen bee and her return to the . hive with clear signs of having mated with a drone. Two years later he demonstrated the mating of queens with drones in flight.

In 1789 he invented the 'book hive' with twelve wooden honeycomb frames fixed on hinges like the pages of a book, which has since been called after him.

Huber proved that worker bees laid unfertilized eggs from which only drones emerged, that worker bees. came from fertilized eggs, that queens mated with drones in flight, and that bees' feelers were organs of smell and touch. He was the first to describe wax scales and the construetion of honeycomb, and to note how much honey a worker bee consumes in the process of building comb.

In his *Latest Observation of,Bees* Huber described his observations over many years. The book was translated into Russian in 1908 (in Kazan) and for many years was regarded as a most authoritative work. Huber was elected to the French Academy and to many others for his research in this field.

Nicholas Vitvitsky (Witwicki) (1764-1853) travelled widely in Europe after graduating from the philosophy faculty of Lvov University, studying the agricultural methods used there, and in particular those relating to beekeeping.

For five years he held the chair of philosophy at the Kremenets Lycee (Volhynia) but dreamed all the while of devoting his energies exclusively to beekeeping; training beekeepers at the Lisinski Forestry School gave him much more satisfaction than teaching philosophy.

In 1849, at the age of 84, Vitvitsky took over the enormous bee-garden with 4000 colonies belonging to L.V.Kochubei (in Dikanka, in the former Poltava Province). He also owned a bee-farm of his own with 2000 hives in the Kovel County of the Volhynia Province.

Vitvitsky was the author of a book entitled *The Glass Hive or a Selection of Curiosities from the Natural History of Bees,* designed for readers of all ages and estates, and of both sexes, published in St. Petersburg in 1845.

The book contained short notes on plants enabling bees to make honey. 'I do not wish to offend our playwrights of genius,' he wrote at the end of his book, 'but to be honest I must say that I have not yet seen, either in Russia or elsewhere, a tragedy, drama, melodrama, or comedy that gave me a tenth of the intellectual satisfaction that I derive from a simple glass hive, when I sit before it for half an hour.... Turn your gaze to the glass hive and you will be bound to agree with mel'

For many people an initial confrontation with bees leads to a genuine friendship that lasts for many years and often for a whole lifetime. Such was the case with *Peter Prokopovich* (1775-1850). who visited his brother's beegarden in 1799 and took a lively interest in the absorbing life of the bee colony.

Later, when he was a world authority on apiculture, he wrote: 'When I looked at the hive, at the alighting board, at the bees themselves, sitting and buzzing around it, I was suddenly overcome with a strong desire to acquire some myself. Throughout the summer of 1799 I watched my brother's bees and by 1800 had decided to buy a plot of ground where I could set up my own apiary.'

In 1800, at the age of 24, Prokopovich took up beekeeping. For fourteen years he bred bees in the traditional non-collapsible log-hives of the Ukraine, Russia, and neighbouring countries. But his ingenious mind was not satisfied with the primitive techniques used then in beekeeping.

In 1814 he invented a collapsible hive, an invention that was of great importance as it served to rationalize beekeeping and promoted increased productivity and profitability. Prokopovich soon transferred more than 3000 bee colonies from log-hives to his collapsible ones. At the time beekeeping was looked upon as a hobby in Europe and was only developing in the United States.

The basic principle of his hive was the accessibility of the honeycomb, which could be removed in a wooden frame. It was the starting point for all subsequent improvements in frame hives. Prokopovich's hive made life very convenient for both the beekeeper and the bees. His investigations led a good deal further than simply to a collapsible frame hive.

He also made a thorough study of the biology of the bee colony and the effect of a favourable environment on bees, and evolved new methods for looking after them. He brought his findings to the attention of colleagues in articles published in the *Agricultural Gazette* and the *Proceedings of the Free Economic Society-'On* Bees', 'On Foul Brood', 'On Queens', 'On the Laws of the Bee Colony', to name but a few. They helped promote improvements in beekeeping.

In 1828 Prokopovich founded the first school of apiculture in Russia, in his native village of Mitchenki. The course took two years, later extended to three, during which time the students were given theoretical and practical training in bees, hives, choice of sites, nectariferous plants, and everything relevant to practical beekeeping.

In the fifty years of its existence the school trained more than 600 beemasters, all first-rate experts with a deep sense of vocation.

Prokopovich knew how to instil his own love of bees in his pupils. Prokopovich's work attracted many admirers during his lifetime in Russia and in other countries. The eminent historians Alexander Lazarevsky and Nicholas Kostomarov, and the great Ukrainian poet Taras Shevchenko, visited his bee-farm.

A. I. Root noted with good reason that Prokopovich was a beekeeper of unusual gifts using methods far ahead of his own time. The first work to acquaint foreign readers with Prokopovich's collapsible hive was *A. I. Pokorsky-Zhoravko's Outline o f Beekeeping in Russia,* which appeared in Russian and German in 1841.

Pokorsky-Zhoravko had an estate near Chernigov, not far from Prokopovich's bee-farm, so the author was in a position to study and describe the ingenious hive in detail. In his *Biographical Portrait of P. I. Prokopovich* he established Prokopovich's pioneering role in this field.

He himself noted that his essay became widely known precisely because of the hive, being reprinted in many European agricultural journals, and prompting the French Polytechnical Society to organize a special workshop for the production of such hives.

Epiphanus Gusev (1802-1873), beekeeper and inventor, was one of the first to recommend artificial breeding of queens (32 years before the American Doolittle) and one of the first Russians to use frame hives. Gusev kept a large bee-farm with such hives of his own design.

At the Vyatka Agricultural Exhibition of 1858 he showed his queen cells, a special scoop for capturing swarms, an iron smoking device (forerunner of the bee-smoker), a spray for making swarms cluster, knives for cutting comb, and other equipment for beekeepers of his own design.

In 1860 he exhibited a frame hive opening at the top, made of boards and reminiscent of Prokopovich's collapsible hive, and a contrivance for making queen cells and transferring eggs to them for breeding.

Peter Korzhenevsky (1810-1898) was working in Kiev as a lawyer when at the age of 38 he learned about the bees' way of life from a friend. He began to take such an interest in them that he set up an apiary of his own in a picturesque spot not far from the city.

Within a few years his amateur apiary had grown to 250 hives. Enchanted by his new charges Korzhenevsky devoted the next fifty years of his life to them, publicizing rational methods of beekeeping using frame hives. He made his own bee-farm open to everyone anxious to study beekeeping or to observe the life of bee colonies, and did much to promote beekeeping in the Ukraine.

The Rev. L.L.Langstroth (1810-1895) invented and developed a frame hive widely used in America. He was for many years President of the American Beekeepers' Association. His book *Langstroth on the Hive and the Honeybee,* published in 1853, is one of the foremost books in the world literature on beekeeping.

A. I. Root wrote in his memoirs that he first met Langstroth and heard him speak on beekeeping at a congress in Cincinatti and that he was as good a speaker as he was a writer, and one of the most pleasant, kind, and friendly men he had ever met, poet, scientist, philosopher, and humanist all rolled into one.

Johann Dzierzon (1811-1906) was granted an honorary doctorate by Munich University, was a member of many scientific societies, and received many decorations for his outstanding services to apiculture.

Dzierzon perfected a hive with movable frames, was an active participant in many beekeepers' congresses, and published a journal *The Silesian Beekeeper;* his many works include *The Theory and Practice of Modern Apiculture* (1848), *Rational Beekeeping* (1861), *The Double Hive* (1890).

Karl Roulier (1814-1858), the inventor of the pavilion hive, was a doctor and professor of zoology. He gathered a group of young scientists around him to whom he imparted his enthusiasm for insects; many of them became prominent figures in the bee world.

Roulier was an active member of the Moscow Agricultural Society, one of the first evolutionists among Russian zoologists, and the author of an interesting work for the layman *Three Discoveries in the Natural History o f Bees.*

Jan Dolinowski (1814-date of death uncertain), a prominent Polish beemaster, invented the horizontal frame hive named after him, which was widely used in the last century in south-western Russia.

After inspecting hives of various design Leo Tolstoy chose Dolinowski's type for his own apiary at Yasnaya Polyana.

August Freiherr von Berlepsch (1816-1877) developed his love for bees while still a child, and caused his nurse much trouble and bother by repeatedly running away from her to a neighbour's apiary. When he was seven his father gave him a hive complete with bees.

The day was a great occasion in the *boy's* life; from that time he began studying the life of bees and they remained his central preoccupation for the rest of his life.

While at school in Gotha he put his hive in the garden of Herr Doering, the headmaster of his school; a deep friendship grew up between the boy beekeeper and old Doering, who read the fourth book of Virgil's *Georgics* with him in Latin.

Later, when a student at Munich University, von Berlepsch's rooms always contained a beehive, which amazed visitors and kept the students amused. Von Berlepsch graduated in law, philology, and theology In 1841 he set up 100 straw hives in the park at Zaissbach.

The natural golden colour of the hives sparkled in the sun and made an effective advertisement for beekeeping. From that time on von Berlepsch devoted himself to horticulture and beekeeping. In 1852 he invented a frame hive (independently of Prokopovich and Langstroth).

His numerous scientific papers on the natural history of the honeybee encouraged the transition from traditional methods to progressive beekeeping using frame hives. His book *The Bee and its Care in Hives with Moveable Frames in Countries without Late Autumn Honey-gathering* was translated into many languages, including Russian.

Johannes Mehring (1816-1878), a joiner, took up beekeeping in 1849 at the age of 33, and soon became passionately interested in the art. In 1867 he invented an artificial comb foundation and tried it out in his own apiary. This invention, along with the frame hive and the honey extractor, did much to promote the advancement of rational beekeeping.

Charles Dadant (1817-1902) designed with the Swiss Blatt the hive named after them, which became widely used in Western Europe, Russia, and the Soviet Union. Dadant. was for long editor-in-chief of the *American Bee Journal. His Short Course in Bee Culture* and *Description of the Dadant Hive* and his revision of Langstroth's *The Hive and the Honeybee* are still widely read far beyond the frontiers of France and the United States.

Franz Hruschka (1819-1888) was a major in the Austrian army, but his true vocation was apiculture. It was his son who first put him onto the idea of using centrifugal force to extract honey from the comb. One day he had given the boy a piece of honeycomb on a plate. For some reason the boy put the plate in a basket and began swinging it round and round like a sling.

His observant father noticed that the honey started flowing out of the comb as a result of being swung, which gave the idea for his honey extractor. Although his first model was very primitive, and differed greatly from all modern types (which have been radically modified from the original), his device was met with high enthusiasm by beekeepers all over the world. In 1865 Hruschka demonstrated his extractor to German and AustroHungarian beekeepers at the XIV Beekeepers' Congress.

Johan Gregor Mendel (1822-1884), the founder of genetics, was an important researcher into the bee family. He had early developed an interest in bees and found favourable conditions for their study in 1843 in the Monastery of St. Augustine in Brno where he built a pavilion for over 50 bee colonies at his own expense.

Between 1870 and 1878 he was an active member of the Moravian Beekeepers' Association, of which he was elected president, and an honorary life member. His apiary contained bees of various varieties (Cypriot, German, Italian, and Egyptian); he tried to produce new varieties by crossing.

Y.G.Chesnokova is almost certainly right in thinking that Mendel began his experiment in bee selection in the Seventies. He soon abandoned his efforts, however; success in this field only became possible after the discovery of polyandry by Tryasko and Vojke and the development of a technique for artificial insemination by Mackenzie and Roberts.

Andrew Zubarev (1823-1902) studied law but became a leading expert on beekeeping and active propagandist for it. He became a beekeeper quite by chance, but was soon carried away by it, never to look back. While travelling abroad, he made the acquaintance of such outstanding beekeepers as Bertrand and Cowan.

After the death of Prof. A.M.Butlerov, Zubarev became editor of *Russkii pchelovodnyi listok.* He also translated Dzierzon's *Beekeeping* into Russian (1860) and Cowan's *Manual for the English Beekeeper* (1887).

For his energetic and fruitful work, Zubarev was elected an honorary member of the Russian Beekeepers' Society, was awarded a silver medal at the Geneva Industrial Exhibition, and a Diploma (2nd Class) at the All-Russian Industrial Exhibition of 1896 in Nizhny Novgorod.

F.W.Vogel (1824-1897) was only six years old when he made his first acquaintance with a bee colony. He was soon a favourite pupil of a local beekeeper. Young Vogel had absolutely no fear of bees, and tried to help a neighbouring beekeeper to extract honey from his hives, used his smoker to observe the life of the colony, etc. The beekeeper rewarded him with pieces of honeycomb. Ecstatic, young Fritz ran to his mother to tell her all about his work.

At the age of nine, his father, noticing Frederick's passionate attachment to bees, made him a present of his first hive. Vogel later recalled the occasion as follows: 'A great day in my childhood was the day when I was made a present of a beehive.

I would not have exchanged it for a royal crown.' 'When I took my first honeycomb out, hanging from its bar, and brought it to my fiancee, in my ecstatic happiness I wanted to kiss not her, but Pastor Dzierzon,' he wrote, giving a vivid picture of himself as an ardent beekeeper. His early hobby became his life's work. He was for many years editor of the German *Beekeepers' Journal.*

Alexei Andriyashev (1825-1907) became acquainted with bees while a teacher and headmaster of a Kiev boys' school. His interest was so intense that he resolved to try and instil it into his fellow-teachers as well as his pupils.

In 1860 he set up a model experimental apiary with the help of fellow-teachers, and gave wide publicity to beekeeping. It was on his initiative that a school for beekeepers was opened in Kiev in 1902, which was transferred a little later (in 1907) to Boyarka, near Kiev.

The Boyarka Technical School for Beekeepers continued to

function for years after the 1917 Revolution. Andriyashev spent 20 000 roubles from his personal savings on setting up the school and bequeathed his own apiary of 80 hives to it.

Prof. A.M.Butlerov (1828-1886), apart from being an eminent chemist, was the father of rational beekeeping in Russia, and first editor of *Russkii pchelovodnyi listok.* (The Russian Beekeeping Newsheet). In 1874 he was elected to membership of the Russian Academy of Sciences.

In the 34 years that he held the chairs of chemistry at Kazan and St. Petersburg Universities Butlerov found, what all beekeepers know, that once you surrender to the enchantment of bees there is no parting with them. He used to spend his vacations in the village of Butlerovka (Kazan Province) where he had an apiary of 100 colonies, including Caucasian, Italian, and Russian varieties, laid out in a beautiful orchard and garden containing flowering and nectariferous plants of all kinds.

In 1867-8, during a visit to Prussia, Butlerov met Dzierzon and von Berlepsch and other German beekeepers. In 1871 he read a paper on measures for the dissemination of rational beekeeping at a meeting of the Free Economic Society.

One of the things he considered essential for beekeepers was to be linked together in a special organization. On his initiative and that of his pupils and disciples (Kandratiev, Izergin, Kablukov, Kulagin, and others) a beekeeping commission was set up affiliated to the Free Economic Society.

In 1886 he organized the publication of the journal mentioned above, becoming its first editor. Leo Tolstoy (1828-1910), the great novelist, was interested in bees all his life. As a child he often visited the apiary in Ovsyannikovo, six kilometres from the family estate, Yasnaya Polyana, and derived great pleasure from his conversations with the old beemaster, whom he called Robinson, since he had made everything with his own hands.

Young Tolstoy frequently announced that when he grew up he would organize his whole life exactly like the old beekeeper's. In 1863 he acquired some bees of his own and looked after them himself. In 1864 he wrote: 'I have become a keen beekeeper'.

In 1865 his wife Sophia Andreevna recorded in her diary: 'The apiary has become the centre of the world for him now, and everybody has to be interested exclusively in bees.' In his writings Tolstoy described the life of bees, and the healing influence of the beauty of an apiary.

In *Anna Karenina* Levin's beegarden is a marvellous panorama of nature and of the fascinating life of the bee family, where man comes face to face with nature. In his epic *War and Peace* Tolstoy drew a vivid parallel between Moscow when Kutuzov left it and a hive without a queen bee.

In *Resurrection* he wrote: 'One can no more approach people without love than one can approach bees without care. Such is the quality of bees. . . .'

Nicholas Wagner (1829-1907) gained his D.Sc. at 25, and was appointed to the chair of zoology at Kazan University at 31. Bees were a constant source of happiness, health, and inspiration to him.

Ivan Lyubarsky (1832-1901) was a pioneer in the use of bee venom taken from. bee stings. He devised a project for a 'bee-flower conveyor' that is still of practical value.

In 1885 he wrote in this connection: 'My vision is not a fantastic one, but merely a dream that could well come true in some little corner of the Ukraine.' Dr. Lyubarsky's dream came into its own after the October Revolution.

Anatole Bogdanov (1834-1896) succeed Roulier, under whom he had studied zoology and apidology, in 1858 as professor of zoology at Moscow University. He himself was a brilliant zoologist and was elected a corresponding member of the Russian Academy of Sciences.

He was one of the sponsors, 100 years ago, of the setting up of the Izmailovo Apiary and the founder of a school that produced such illustrious figures as Prof. N. Wagner, Prof. N. Nasonov, Prof. Kozhevnikov, and others.

Bogdanov was an honorary member of the Russian Beekeepers' Society, which instituted a Bogdanov medal in his honour after his death. The medal is awarded annually for services in the field of rational beekeeping.

Gennady Kandratiev (1834-1905) had a beautiful voice, and soon after going to Italy to study, was performing at the famous La

Scale Opera House in Milan. On returning to Russia he began to work as chief producer at the Maryinsky Theatre in St. Petersburg (now the Kirov Theatre of Opera and Ballet, Leningrad).

As related above he took up beekeeping on the advice of Prof. A. M. Butlerov, and soon had a large apiary of his own. Often, when on tour, Kandratiev would visit famous contemporary beekeepers, and was able to study their methods on the spot.

In 1892 he organized production of a bulletin of foreign literature on beekeeping *(Vestnik inostrannoi literatury pchelovodstva).* He also edited the Russian editions of Langstroth's *The Hive and the Honeybee,* Cook's *Beekeepers' Companion,* Bertrand's *Care of Bees,* Dr. A. Dubini's *Practical Notes on Beekeeping,* and Dadant's *Description of the Dadant Hive.*

Kandratiev conducted experiments and observations in his own apiary; his findings soon convinced him that a well-appointed bee-garden was an ideal natural clinic (while engrossed in this work he cured himself of a serious nervous disorder).

Georges Layance (1834-1897) received a technical education in Lille, and developed a lifelong interest in beekeeping. He was the inventor of the horizontal hive that bears his name.

The publication of his *Introduction to Beekeeping* in 1874 made him famous in France and Russia. From 1890 (after the First Beekeepers' Congress) to his death, Layance was president of the French Beekeepers' Association.

Alexander Uspensky (1835-1902) was a leading propagandist for rational beekeeping. For his popular and interesting tutor *Pchelovodstvo-samouchitel' dlya shkol i naroda, uproshchennoe i chisto prakticheskoe* (Tutor for Schools and the Public, Simplified and Purely Practical) (1879) he was awarded the Peter I prize.

He also received a gold medal at the Paris Exhibition for the segmented log hive that he exhibited there.

Amos Ives Root (1839-1923), whom we have mentioned more than once in this book, was an outstanding American popularizer of beekeeping. In the introduction to the first edition of his *ABC of Bee Culture* (1877) (which has been translated into many languages including Russian), he related how, in August 1865, a swarm of bees one day flew over his head.

A workmate, noticing his interest, asked him how much he would pay if he captured the swarm. Root offered a dollar, little thinking it could be done.

To his amazement his colleague returned with the bees, which he had put into a box. From that day on Root, far from confining himself to watching bees, began to question everybody who could tell him anything at all about them.

He also recalled the first book he read on the subject of bees. Having gone to Cleveland, Ohio, on quite other business, he found himself unable to do anything else than go round the bookshops in search of books on beekeeping.

He found only two, and his choice fell on Langstroth's, in which the reader was introduced to the amazing life of the bee family with great affection. When he began to read it on his way home Root felt it was a real treasure trove. Never had the unknown seemed so attractive. Even *Robinson Crusoe* was less enthralling.

What appealed to him most was that he could see and test the fascinating things he was reading about without leaving home. When, a few years later, Root had managed to increase his apiary to 35 hives, which at the time created a small sensation, only eleven survived the winter. Naturally, neighbours and friends were quick to say 'We told you so'.

But quite undeterred he continued to work enthusiastically, and in one summer increased his apiary from 11 hives to 48, which produced 2780 kilograms of honey a year later. Soon he launched a magazine *Gleanings in Bee Culture.*

Thus, by losing a bet, he won an interest that made him world famous. *His ABC and XYZ of Beekeeping* has been republished time and again and is still a leading book on the subject.

T.W.Cowan (1840-1926), an engineer, and leading British beekeeper, was born in Russia, son of an engineer. After a visit to the USA in 1860 he acquired a lively interest in bees, and helped organize the British Beekeepers' Association, of which he became President.

He designed the honey extractor that bears his name. In 1923 he was awarded the gold medal of the London Beekeepers' Club for his great services to British bee culture.

He published several books: *The English Beekeeper's Guide* (1887), *The Honey Bee* (1895), and *Wax* (1911).

Ivan Trubnikov (1844-1906) trained as an engineer but became a beekeeper by profession and vocation. He did a great deal to promote beekeeping in Russia, publishing more than 50 interesting articles in scientific journals.

Gilbert Doolittle (1846-1918) was an American beekeeper famous for his methods of breeding queen bees by transferring the larvae to specially constructed containers, for which he made the prototype. His *Scientific Breeding of Queen Bees* was published in 1889.

Theophile Tseselsky (1846-1916), inventor of the Slavonic hive, was a professor at Lvov University. It is to him that credit belongs for demonstrating that foul brood was due to bacteria and not to a fungus.

Tseselsky has gone down in the history of apiculture as a gifted researcher, skilled teacher, and remarkable beemaster. His two-volume work *Commercial Beekeeping or a Scientific Approach, Long Years of Experience or the Profitable Bee-garden* and his *Mead-making or the Art of Producing Beverages from Honey and Fruit* were published in Polish and Russian, and had several editions.

Sergei Glazenap (1847-1937) was a well-known astronomer, Honorary Member of the USSR Academy of Sciences, Corresponding Member of the Longitude Bureau of the Paris Academy, and held the titles of Merited Scientist and Hero of Labour.

He was also a leading Russian expert on beekeeping. On the advice of Prof. A.M.Butlerov he began working with bees in 1886, and for 24 years edited the journal *Vestnik Russhogo obshchestva pchelovodstva* (Herald of the Russian Beekeeping Society). Glazenap's slogan was 'No garden without an apiary and no fruit without bees' that stressed the importance of bees for horticulture.

When the Russian Beekeeping Society was founded in St. Petersburg in 1891 Glazenap was elected its first president. With tremendous enthusiasm he organized the monthly members' meetings, persuading the best beemasters in the country to join, and arranged a central depot providing equipment, honey, and wax on a co-operative basis.

He was also an active sponsor of the First Russian Congress of

Beekeepers, held in 1891, and of the Second Congress held in Ekaterinodar (now Krasnodar) seven years later. In 1900 he received a gold medal at the Paris Exhibition.

Glazenap devoted 30 years of tireless, single-minded work to beekeeping. In 1926 he published a small but interesting booklet *The Small Bee-Garden.*

Kazimir Lewicki (1847-1902), the Polish beekeeper, invented the hive that bears his name, which was widely used in Poland and Russia. He studied apiculture in Austria, France, Italy, Germany, and Switzerland. His book *Bee Culture* ran to five editions.

Vasily Vashchenko (1850-1918) first 'made friends with bees' in Pereyaslavl, near Poltava, while still a child. He organized many beekeeping exhibitions in Kiev and later the All-Russian Exhibition of 1913, as president of the beekeeping section, paying for the cost of the whole pavilion at his own expense.

Vashchenko devoted much energy to expanding the Boyarka Technical School for Beekeeping. In 1907 he was put in charge of the school and later became chairman of the board. He used his own savings to build a two-storey teaching block for the school.

Ivan Klingden (1851-1912) was an outstanding agronomist who devoted much energy to promoting the organization of pollination by means of bees. He made a detailed study of the increase in crop yields brought about by pollination, especially in relation to red clover, drawing apt and useful conclusions on the inter-relation of bees and the yield of clover seed.

Frank Benton (1852-1919) was an outstanding American beekeeper, a pioneer of the organization of the sending of bees by post, the inventor of a portable and transportable queen brood chamber.

Having made a thorough study of apiculture, he began studying the various species of bees and the problem of domesticating the large Indian bee, which produces honey of exceptional quality and can leave the hive at temperatures below 0° C.

In 1905 Benton sent bees and Caucasian queen bees from Baku to the USA and made them known throughout the world. He was famous for collecting and studying the various species (Caucasian, Italian, Persian, Cypriot, Egyptian, etc.).

He had the honour of being appointed the director of the first apiculture section of the U.S. Department of Agriculture, a post he held for some years. A.I. and E.R.Root reported a dispute in 1900 between two brothers of the name of Etter, who lived in Amity, N.Y.

One of the brothers was a beekeeper and the other a fruitgrower. The latter claimed that his brother's bees nibbled all his fruit so that he was being ruined, and took his brother to court. The case was heard on 17-19 December 1900.

The battle was fierce, for the bees were 'accused'; it was only thanks to the expert evidence of Frank Benton, the Government expert, that they were finally 'acquitted'. Two years later the horticulturalist called on his beekeeper brother and asked him to move his apiary back to his orchards since without bees the trees blossomed but did not bear fruit.

Evlampy Kamenev (1853-1922) became passionately interested in beekeeping while a young man. At 35 he invented embossed cylinders that made it possible to produce artificial comb foundation, and for two years spent much time and energy exhibiting his device at exhibitions in St. Petersburg, Kiev, Moscow, and other towns and cities.

He also did much educational work in connection with exhibitions and the beekeeping society. He set up a model apiary for research purposes on the outskirts of Ivanovo, which he later presented to the entomology department of the Ivanovo-Voznesensky Polytechnical Institute.

Paul Kuleshov (18.54-1936) was a professor at the Petrov (now Timiryazev) Agricultural Academy in Moscow, a Corresponding Member of the USSR Academy of Sciences, and held the title of Merited Scientist.

From 1887 to 1894 he was in charge of the Academy's apiary for students. He was the translator of Cowan's *The Honey Bee,* and de voted much effort to testing hives of various designs and investigating beekeeping methods. He organized a museum of apiculture that became famous.

Gaston Bonnier (1855-1922), professor of botany at the Sorbonne and Member of the French Academy of Sciences, was President, then an honorary member, of the French Beekeepers' Association.

His book, written in collaboration with George Layance, *Complete Course in Beekeeping* was published in Russia.

Ivan Michurin (1855-1935) was a great hybridizer and transformer of nature. 'We cannot expect Nature to expend her favours on us,' he used to say. 'Our job is to wrest them from her.' While still a child Michurin enjoyed helping in his father's bee-garden and watching the bees about their work.

His famous horticultural estate in Tambov always contained an apiary, for Michurin regarded bees as the finest pollinators for plants adapted to insect pollination.

Nicholas Nasonov (1855-1933) was professor of zoology at Moscow and Warsaw Universities, a member of the Academy of Sciences, and a leading figure among Russian apidologists. He began to take an interest in bees while a student, when Prof. Bogdanov took him to the Izmailovo Apiary to work as a zoologist.

Later he was put in charge of the bee-garden (1878-1885). Nasonov made his name when he discovered the bee's aromatic gland (situated between the last and the penultimate segments of its abdomen), called the Nasonov gland in his honour. He was also an active popularizer of beekeeping.

Ivan Kablukov (1857-1942) was an outstanding beemaster as well as an eminent chemist. After graduating with distinction from Moscow University he studied under Prof. A.M.Butlerov who succeeded in interesting him in beekeeping as well as chemistry.

In 1882 Kablukov organized a beekeeping section in the Society for the Acclimatization of Animals and Plants (of which he was later President). After Butlerov's death be became the leading expert in Russia on apiculture.

Thanks to him travelling exhibitions were organized, transported from place to place on barges and special railway wagons. These mobile exhibitions were visited by thousands of peasants, who began taking an interest in bees. This field of Kablukov's activity was not only his second profession but his main source of creative inspiration.

In 1933 Kablukov was elected an honorary member of the USSR Academy of Sciences. The Uzbek SSR named its special state bee-farm after him (he died in Tashkent in 1942).

Anatole Butkevich (1859-1942) entered the Petrov Agricultural

Academy, after finishing at the Orel Realschule. After his first year, however, he was exiled to the Tobolsk Province in Siberia for political activity.

On his return from exile he settled on a farm near Krapivka (Tula Province), where he began in 1894 to take an interest in bees. He used frequently to say that beekeeping was undoubtedly the most rewarding of rural occupations.

It was not only profitable for him, however, but also.one that he regarded as the most poetic of all outdoor occupations. And he firmly maintained that the use of frame hives, which increased the profitability of bee-farming, in no way deprived it of its traditional poetic beauty.

Vasily Izergin (1859-1910) first encountered beekeeping while helping as a child in his father's apiary. While a schoolboy he paid a visit, on his way home from school in Simbirsk (now Ulyanovsk), to Prof. Butlerov's beefarm, where he received a warm friendly welcome and was a guest for a week.

Butlerov told the boy all about his work and showed him how his bee-farm was maintained. Izergia always recalled this visit with a special sense of excitement.

After graduating from Moscow University (history and philosophy), Izergin began teaching Russian literature, at the same time translating foreign books on beekeeping into Russian: Langstroth's *The Hive and the Honeybee* (1892 and 1902), von Berlepseh's *Care of the Bee-garden* (1893), Layance's *Care o f Bees Using Modern Methods (1904),* to name but three.

In addition he edited the then popular *Bulletin of Foreign Literature on Apiculture.* Izergin was a member of the Council of the Russian Beekeepers' Society and in that capacity did much useful work to spread the use of frame hives and rational beekeeping methods in Russia.

Nicholas Kulagin (1859-1940) was a zoologist and member of the Academy of Agricultural 'Sciences, and a leading Russian apiculturist. In 1905 he was responsible for the holding of the All-Russian Congress of Beekeepers.

Five years later at the I All-Slav Congress of Beekeepers in Sofia he was elected President of the All-Slav Union. Kulagin sponsored the holding of the II All-Slav Congress in Belgrade in 1911, and of the III Congress in 1912 in Moscow.

Kulagin devoted much attention to the bee-farm of the Petrov (Timiryazev) Agricultural Academy, of which he was in charge for forty years. This apiary is now named after him.

Kulagin published a number of interesting works in the field of apiculture, including *On the Biology of Bees, Feeding Bees, Bee Swarming,* and *The Selection of Frame Hives.* The writer had the good fortune to correspond with Kulagin for several years and to meet him on a number of occasions.

This charming and eminent scientist was a great advocate of the express method of obtaining medicinal honeys. Prof. Kulagin was highly respected by his fellow scientists, and was made an honorary member of the Moscow Society of Naturalists, the Entomological Society, the Russian Society for the Acclimatization of Animals and Plants, the Bulgarian Entomological Society, and other institutions.

Porfiry Bakhmetiev (1860-1913), professor at Sofia University, was not only an outstanding experimental biologist and well-known physicist, but one of Bulgarian leading beekeepers. For 16 years, from 1897, he devoted endless energy to the study of the body temperature of insects (including bees), a preoccupation that was only interrupted by his death, and devised a special electric thermometer for the purpose.

In an article in *Izvestiya Akademii Nauk,* entitled 'Conclusions from My Research into the Anabiosis of Insects and a Plan for Its Investigation in Warm-blooded Animals', Bukhmetiev advanced the bold and promising idea that anabiosis could be used in beefarming (think of the millions of bee colonies that would be wintered without food!) but also in the economy and in medicine (in combating tuberculosis, etc.).

His dream is coming true since wide use is now made of cold in medicine as well as a conserving agent in industry. In 1910 Bakhmetiev was elected General Secretary of the All-Slav Congress of Beekeepers.

Paul Orlov (1861-1928) was the inventor of a frame hive with sectional extensions. He was a remarkable expert on hives, who spent 42 years working with bees in the Izmailovo Apiary. Models of his hives were exhibited at the Paris Exhibition in 1900, where he was awarded a Grand Prix.

Thanks to his wide experience and detailed knowledge of the Russian literature on beekeeping, Orlov was a welcome guest at expert committees, especially when hives were under discussion.

Vsevolod Shimanovsky (1864-1934) was the son of a surgeon in Kiev. His father dreamed of Vsevolod following in his footsteps, but his son had other ideas. After finishing at the Kiev Military and the Moscow Artillery School he was appointed to General Staff H.Q. and was quite content with his chosen career. But while a young officer he made the acquaintance of P.I.Korzhenevsky, and that meeting was a turning point in his life.

He immediately resigned his commission and retired from the army to take up beekeeping and to work as a village schoolteacher in Volhynia near Kiev. He never became disillusioned with what he regarded as his romantic vocation as keeper of a bee-farm and teacher of beekeeping to village children.

In 1899, at the age of 33, Shimanovsky went blind, but he did not give up his teaching or beekeeping, and continued to do useful work. From 1910 to 1925 he worked in his own bee-farm, assisted by his wife, and lectured on beekeeping at the Boyarka School during the winters.

John Renny (1865-1928), the entomologist and parasitologist, professor at Aberdeen University, was an expert on bee diseases and discovered a number of cures for them.

Gregory Kozhevnikov (1866-1938), professor at Moscow University, and director of the University Botanical Museum, was also a leading beekeeper. Between 1890 and 1910 he read lectures at beekeeping courses on the natural history of the honeybee. From 1910 to 1920 he was in charge of the Izmailovo bee-farm. Kozhevnikov discovered Indian bees in the Ussuri Territory on the Pacific Coast in 1926.

August Ludwig (1867-1953) came to know about bees quite by accident. One autumn day in 1891 he read in the paper that the Rev. Ferdinand Harnstugg was giving a course of lectures for those who wished to study beekeeping, and decided to go along.

He became interested, made friends with his teacher, and began actively to disseminate his view that the bee family formed a single bee organism. After Harnstugg's death in 1925 Ludwig became editor of the magazine *German Apiculture in Theory and Practice.*

In 1916 he became head of a research bee-farm that he had organized at Jena University. On his 80th birthday, on 19 July 1947, he was appointed honorary professor in the faculty of mathematics and natural science of the University.

His good work is now being carried on by his friend and pupil Dr. Hans Ochsman, who became director of the University bee-farm in 1950. An independent Institute of Apiculture has been founded on the basis of this beefarm.

Edmund Alphandery (1870-1941) was a pioneer of French apiculture and author of the important *Dictionnaire d"Apiculture* (2 vols.), *Practical Guide to Beekeeping,* and *Encyclopaedia o f Apiculture (5 vols.),* which he completed a few days before his death. The first film about bees was shot in the early days of cinema on his beefarm.

Ippolit Korablev (1871-1951) started working with bees at 20 while a village teacher. As a student at the Petrov Agricultural Academy in Moscow he worked enthusiastically at the Izmailovo Apiary under Prof. N.Kulagin.

After graduating in 1902 he worked as a professional beemaster in the Poltava, Kharkov, and Chernigov Provinces, and for 44 years ran the bee-farm at the Uman School of Horticulture and Agriculture (now the Uman Agricultural Institute).

In 1945, on the occasion of his 75th birthday, he was appointed an honorary professor of the Institute. He wrote many original articles, the most important being 'The Importance and Benefits of Beekeeping', 'On Selecting Bees', 'Bee Diseases and Their Treatment', 'Nectariferous Plants and Their Culture'. His manual on beekeeping was published after 1917, and was reprinted several times.

Leonid Potekhin (1871-1912) worked as a youth on the bee-farm of his parents' estate under the supervision of G.P.Kandratiev. From 1889 he worked as an expert adviser in the Agricultural Department, and in 1906 became the editor of the *Herald of Foreign and Russian Apiculture.*

Ivan Serbinov (1872-1925) worked on bee diseases and became a member of the Russian Beekeepers' Society after being appointed a professor of bacteriology. In his experimental work he sought to find a way of immunizing bees against foul brood by supplying hives with large supplementary feeds containing an extract made from foul brood larvae (for inoculation was naturally out of the question).

His papers at the Moscow and Petersburg Congresses of Beekeepers stressed the need to have special demonstration bee-farms to raise the productivity of Russian beekeeping.

Enoch Zander (1873-1952), founder of the Institute of Apiculture at Ferlangen in Bavaria, designed a frame hive, developed a method of bee-farming in pavilion hives, introduced an ether dope for bees, and discovered the causal agent of nosematosis.

His many books had had a most important influence on the development of beekeeping: *Guide to Apiculture, The Life o f the Bee, The Bee and Its Structure, Rot and How to Combat It* and *Bees and Beekeeping. His* five-volume *Practical Beekeeping* is a standard work in many countries.

Victor Loginov (1876-1931) lectured on apiculture while ,professor of histology at the Kazan Veterinary Institute and at the Agricultural and Forestry Institute, and was in charge of the beekeeping department and bee-farm of the Kazan District Experimental Station.

As a leading member of the Kazan Beekeepers' Society Loginov organized a travelling museum with exhibits from collections, models, and items of beekeeping equipment. 'I look back to those days with the travelling museum,' he wrote many years later, 'as one of the happiest times of my life.' In 1906 the Society began publishing its proceedings on his initiative; it was later renamed the *Journal of the Kazan Beekeepers' Society.*

Loginov devoted much of his professional time to study of the pathogenic organisms causing bee diseases, in measuring the length of the probosces of bees, in investigating the harmful effects of honey-dew honey on bees, and so on.

He was an honorary member of the Russian Society for the Acclimatization of Animals and Plants, and was honoured by the Government of the Tatar Autonomous Socialist Soviet Republic. 'It is not for nothing,' he wrote in 1925, 'that one hears famous beemasters, who have devoted many years of their lives to this work, say: Living is working with bees, to stop keeping bees would be to stop living. This is absolutely true.'

Kh. N.Abrikosov (1877-1957) studied apiculture in England from 1898 to 1902. On returning to Russia he became Leo Tolstoy's secretary for three years and married the niece of the writer N.L.Obolenskaya. After his marriage he set up a bee-farm of 100 swarms at Zatishye, which Tolstoy was fond of visiting (his last visit was less than two months before his death).

In his article 'Bees and Beekeeping in the Works of L.N.Tolstoy', Abrikosov wrote that Tolstoy 'greatly encouraged me to engage in apiculture and said that of all the branches of agriculture beekeeping was the most independent, that one could follow in without hiring any labour, and exist on it alone.'

In the same article he related how Tolstoy, after hearing a visitor tell of peasants in the Ussuri Territory in the Far East who had as many as 600 hives, and that bees swarmed seven times a year there, and yield up to 200 pounds of honey a hive, said: 'If I were young again, I'd go to a country where people don't talk about newspapers and politics but about bees and agriculture' (3 Nov. 1906).

Victor Lebrun (1883) was born in Russia of French nationality. From 1900 to 1910 he was Leo Tolstoy's secretary. He moved to France in 1926 and settled near Marseilles where he kept bees, selling the honey and beeswax exclusively to pharmaceutical establishments. He once told us that during his years in France he had relied more on bees than people, and they had never let him down.

Eugene Pavlovsky (1884-1965), Member of the USSR Academy of Sciences, and Academy of Medical Sciences, and of the Czechoslovakian and Iranian Academies, honorary doctor of the Sorbonne and of Delhi University, Hero of Socialist Labour, and recipient of many other honours, did important experimental work on the structure and function of the digestive tract of bees, on the effect of bee venom, and other related subjects.

Karl von Frisch (1886) is famous for his research into bees and his 'decoding' of the 'language of bees'. The story of his life and work can be read in his remarkable book *A Biologist Remembers.* 'Thanks to the immortal works of Frisch and his colleagues,' Prof. Remy

Chauvin writes, 'we know as much, if riot more, about the sight and smell of bees as we do about human sight and smell.

And this knowledge was achieved using methods admirable for their simplicity.' Prof. Chauvin holds that Karl von Frisch is 'perhaps the greatest experimenter of all those who have worked for the glory of biology since Pasteur'.

It would be hard to add anything to that appraisal. In 1959 Prof. von Frisch was awarded the Kalinga prize in Paris, awarded annually for a major contribution in the field of biology. His books *From the Life of Bees* and *Bees, Their Sight, Smelt, Taste and Language* have been published in many countries, including the USSR. *He is a Noble* Prize Winner.

Alain Caillas (b. 1887) was born in St. Petersburg, where his family kept a big fashion house, but lived in France from the time he was two years old. He became admired by beekeepers the world over. His father was a beemaster of repute, Vice-chairmen of the French Beekeepers' Association, and general secretary of several beekeeping congresses (1897, 1900, and 1902).

So Alain was surrounded by bees and bee talk from early childhood. While still at school he published an article on a new technique for analysing honey, which could not pass unnoticed. He won innumerable prizes as a student, and in 1907 Edmund Alphandery, editor of *La Gazette apicole* invited him to work on the journal. Ever since its pages have been open to his many contributions to apiculture.

Alexander Gubin (1897-1956) was one of the outstanding Russian beekeepers of Soviet times. As a child he worked in his father's bee-farm. In 1943 he was appointed to the chair of apiculture in the Timiryazev Agricultural Academy in Moscow, and in 1945 defended his dissertation for D.Sc. on Honeybees and the Pollination of Red Clover. He developed a useful device for 'training' bees to pollinate red clover.

Remy Chauvin (b. 1913) is in charge of the French National Institute of Agricultural Research, and was for several years the head of the Institute of Apiculture.

He has his own laboratory of experimental ethology (animal behaviour) and lectures at Strasbourg and the Sorbonne. His books *The Physiology o f Insects* (1951), *The Life and Behaviour of Insects*

(1958), and *From the Bee to the Gorilla* (1965) are well known. *Moses Quinby* was the inventor of the bee-smoker or smoke bellows (1870), an invention comparable in importance with that of the hive with removable frames and the honey extractor.

Quinby's device, consisting of a rigid tube and bellows, though simple in appearance, represented a great step forward in rationalizing the smoking of bees. The Roots called him one of the most experienced beemasters that ever was; his name is held in great esteem by American beekeepers.

He was also the inventor of the Quinby hive, and of a honey extractor (which can be seen in the Langstroth-Root Library at Cornell University).

THE SONGS THEY SING

The ability to make sounds is one of the attributes of many insects. We are all familiar with the angry buzz of bees and wasps or the happy songs of katydids and crickets on summer evenings. While it is true that the songs of male katydids and crickets are mating calls and, as such, help in bringing the sexes together, some of these calls or songs seem to go beyond such mundane, instinctive objectives and to be sung for the sheer joy of being alive.

The first animal sounds were probably made by insects. This is not mere conjecture; the fossil of a large, primitive orthopteran having soundmaking organs on its wings was found in Australia.

This grasshopper ancestor lived about 200 million years ago, many million of years before the first birds arrived on the world scene. There seems no doubt that the sounds made by insects are a form of communication, just as are our own voices. Insects make sounds by rubbing parts of their armorlike bodies together; only rarely are sounds produced by air or by drums.

Human voice, of course, produces sound when air is forced between the vocal cords and the resulting sound is then modified by the mouth and lips. The howler monkey has resonance chambers on the sides of the neck which increase the volume of sound and give the voice great carrying capacity.

Birds produce sounds or songs in still another manner. At the point where the trachea divides in the breast cavity there is an enlarged structure called the *syrinx*.

This is actually the "voice box," and within it is a bar of cartilage called the *pessulus*. Air passing through the syrinx, from the lungs, causes the pessulus to vibrate.

This is the origin of birds' voices. In some birds-swans, for example—the trachea is very long and coiled within the breast bone. This has the same function as the coiled tube of a trumpet. Thus, the voices of birds and mammals differ considerably from those of insects, which consist of squeaks, buzzes, hums, clicks and drumming sounds.

Most insects make sound by rubbing parts of their hard bodies or appendages against each other. This is called *stridulation*. Thus, insects should really be called "instrumentalists" rather than "singers." It is an interesting fact that we humans sometimes communicate with each other by similar means. We clap our hands to indicate approval, snap our fingers or whistle to gain attention, or stamp our feet in anger.

On the other hand, there are a few rare cases where insects make sounds by forcing air from body openings. For several centuries it has been known that the deaths-head moth (*Acherontia atropos*) of Europe makes a sound by sucking or blowing air through its proboscis.

The pharynx or "throat cavity" acts as a pump and the stream of air is rapidly interrupted in the epipharynx or "roof of the mouth" in such a way as to produce loud squeaks. Some insects also produce audible sounds by forcing air from the spiracles or breathing pores along the sides of their bodies.

For example, lubber grasshoppers (*Brachystola*) force air out through the thoracic spiracles, making hissing sounds. Inside the thorax there are large, lunglike sacs filled with air. By contracting the body muscles, air is forced out of these sacs much as air from our own lungs is forced out through our throats.

Under certain conditions queen honeybees make piping sounds, but whether these are made by air passing through spiracular valves or by a vibration of the wings is still uncertain. Most authorities seem to believe the sounds are produced by the wings.

Sound making is more widespread in the insect tribe than was once supposed, and it often occurs where least expected. For example, a number of aquatic insects have well-developed sound-making equipment. The water scorpion (*Ranatra*) has a scraping apparatus located at the base of the coxa of each foreleg.

This makes a squeaking sound that can be heard either in the air or in the water; it is louder when made under water. Just what the purpose of this sound is has not been determined since it is made by both adults and nymphs or immature forms. If it were purely a mating call, it would be expected to be found only in the adults.

The backswimmers and water boatmen are also "wired for sound" and the sounds they make are of very high intensity considering the sizes of the insects. It is probable that these sounds are used to attract the opposite sex.

Recently, observations were made by Dr. Richard D. Alexander of an unusual sound-producing technique of a grasshopper named *Paratylotropidia brunneri.* This is a large grasshopper, and Dr. Alexander heard it making soft clicks on a prairie along the Mississippi River near Valmeyer, Illinois.

After close observation, it was discovered that the sounds were made by the mandibles of the insect clicking together at the rate of six to seven times per second. The sound can be heard for some distance and is, apparently, a means of communication.

Dr. Alexander was able to imitate the sound, and obtain a response from a nearby male, by striking two metal objects together. It seems probable that this method of communication was evolved from feeding sounds.

Some of those ancient insects, the dragonflies, have sound-making equipment in their larval stages. These consist of toothed areas on the sides of the abdomen against which the hind legs are rubbed, resulting in shrill tones. The sound is produced when the larvae are disturbed and may thus serve a defensive function.

Sound making is quite common among members of the beetle tribe. As a matter of fact, one authority has stated that sound equipment is apt to be found in any insect where one part normally rubs against another. The beetles all have hard, ridged bodies, so it is not too surprising to find that many of them have roughened areas that are capable of producing sounds when scraped by legs or other movable body parts.

A number of long-horned beetles squeak loudly when held in the hand. Probably these may be interpreted as sounds of distress or alarm. Some beetle larvae, too, make sounds. For instance in the case of *Passalus* grubs, which are the larvae of betsy-beetles, the hind legs are greatly reduced in size and they function only as scrapers which rasp upon roughened areas near the bases of the middle legs.

These large insects are semisocial, that is, they live in rotten wood in small colonies consisting of both adults and larvae or grubs. Their sounds are probably a form of communication or identification.

Of even more interest are the sounds produced by death-watch beetles that tunnel through wood. The adults make tapping sounds that can often be heard in old log cabins.

In early days when most of our ancestors lived in such structures, the tapping or ticking of these insects was sometimes heard late at night when all was quiet. The superstitious believed that the sound was associated with impending death.

In her delightful book, *Insect Fact and Folklore,* Miss Lucy Clausen quotes a piece of medieval poetry as follows:

Then woe be to those in the house that are sick!
For, sure as a gun, they will give up the ghost,
If the maggot cries click when it scratches the post.

Actually, the clicking sound is made by the adult beetles and is believed to be a mating call.

To insects such as the death-watch beetles that dwell in dark burrows some means of communication is apparently desirable, so it is not too surprising to find that termites, too, use taps to telegraph information or to sound alarms.

If a piece of wood containing a termite colony is broken open so that the inmates are exposed, the large-headed soldiers can often be seen in the act of tapping their heads against the floors of the galleries. The sound can be heard a foot or so away and resembles the ticking of a watch.

These soldiers are probably sounding a rallying call to the others. In the case of some kinds of termites, *Leucotermes* and others, the insects hammer in unison, producing a faint drumming sound.

A number of species of ants, too, make sounds. Good examples are the leaf-cutters or *Atta* ants.

Authorities are not in agreement as to the purpose of these ant calls, but it seems likely that they are alarm sounds. If an *Atta* ant is held between the fingers, its squeak can be heard several feet away. A number of other ants also make squeaking sounds.

It has been found that these are produced by a stridulating organ consisting of a series of striations on the base of the -aster (abdomen) and a scraper on the petiole (waist).

It is believed that some ants make tapping sound, like termites. One ant, *Carnponotus mus,* a native of Brazil, nests in bamboo and when disturbed makes a metallic, whirring sound like a rattlesnake.

There are a number of insects that make humming sounds with their wings for example. flies, mosquitoes and bees. In some cases these sounds are merely incidental to flight, but in other cases they are actually a means of communication.

The male mosquito is attracted to the female by her high-pitched wing sounds. The wing rates of the *Aedes* mosquitoes range from 300 to 500 vibrations per second. There is some variation among different species and, in some cases, beat effects occur.

Thus, these female wing sounds probably are selective in attracting males of the same species. Male mosquitoes are attracted to tuning forks vibrating at the same pitch as the females' wings. The wings of the housefly vibrate 335 times per second or at the scale of F. A bee's wings match the sound of A while vibrating at the rate of 440 times per second.

The vibration rates of insects' wings can be precisely measured by anchoring them with cement and placing them so that the tips of their vibrating wings just brush against the surface of a smoked kymograph cylinder revolving at a known rate.

From this brief discussion it is apparent that many insects use sound as a means of communication. Many insects have well-developed organs for the perception of sound waves. Insects' "ears" are located on various parts of their bodies.

The sound receptors of the katydid are on the front legs and those of the grasshopper are on the sides of the thorax. So far we have said little about those insects that are the real choristers of the insect world, the crickets, katydids, grasshoppers and cicadas. We have saved the best until last.

Second only to the birds, these insects are the world's foremost singers. Their songs may not be as pleasing to most peoples' ears as those of birds, but they serve more or less the same purpose.

The katydids belong to the order Orthoptera, a large and important insect group which also includes the grasshoppers, cockroaches, crickets, mantids and walking-sticks.

All the katydids and their close relatives belong to the long-horned grasshopper family Tettigoniidae, whose members have very long antennae and long, green wings.

The group includes the bush katydids, which are normally green but are occasionally pin the cone-headed katydids, which have cone-shaped heads and power I jaws; and the meadow katydids, which are of small or medium size and dwell in grassy meadows.

The champion songster is the so-called true katydid (*Pterophylla camellifolia*) of the eastern United States, which usually inhabits trees. The green coloration of these insects makes them difficult to see when they are resting among leaves.

They are also accomplished ventriloquists and are usually quite difficult to locate by their song, they never seem to be where one expects to find them.

The sound-making apparatus of the katydids is on their front wings and consists of a scraper on one wing, which is rasped back and forth across a filelike row of teeth on the opposite wing. This sound-making equipment is found only in the males; the females are silent but have hearing organs or ears on their front legs.

While the songs of katydids may sound attractive to other katydids, to the human ear many of them sound like a pocket watch being wound. The true katydid sings only at night, though some related species are often heard during the daylight hours.

They are called katydids because of a fancied resemblance of their calls to the words "katydid-katydid-katydid." In preparation for singing, or stridulation, the male katydid raises its forewings and then begins moving them rapidly back and forth across each other like the blades of a pair of scissors.

Near the base of one wing -usually the right there is a bladelike *scraper* and, on the opposite wing, a row of teeth which constitute *the file.* The scraper is on the under side of the uppermost wing and the file is on the upper side of the other wing. Thus, the scraper saws across the file when the wings are moved back and forth.

This is done very rapidly, causing the wings to vibrate. This operation may be compared to drawing an ordinary file across the edge of a piece of tin. Adjacent to the file and scraper on each wing there are clear areas sometimes called "mirrors" that resemble somewhat the heads of drums.

These are the resonance areas, and it is here that the vibrations of the wings are transferred or communicated to the surrounding air. The speed with which the wings are moved, or the rate at which the file and scraper are moved against each other, determines the pitch of the sound.

The sound is also affected by the vibrations of the wings themselves. The rate of movement of the wings can easily be determined in the laboratory by means of a stroboscope, an instrument which emits a series of flashes. The rate of flashing can be speeded up or slowed down.

If a stroboscope is focused on a rapidly moving object such as the revolving blades of an electric fan, the rate of its flash can be adjusted to match that of the fan blades.

When this is done the fan appears to stop. The speed of the fan can then be read on the dial of the stroboscope. A similar procedure can be used to determine the rate at which a katydid vibrates its wings. Insect songs can also be recorded and analyzed by means of various electronic devices of special design.

By using such instruments and equipment, the songs of many katydids have been studied and analyzed with rather interesting results. The cone-headed katydid (*Neoconocephalus ensiger*) is common in many places. The front of its head is shaped like a cone and extends forward beyond the bases of the antennae.

The wings are very long, and the female has a slender, swordlike ovipositor at the tip of her abdomen. There are 108 teeth on the file of the male's wing, and when he is singing vibrations are emitted at the rate of 13,700 per second, but these are not continuous. About 500 to 800 teeth are struck per second, but the high vibration rate is due to wing resonance.

The song consists of a string of twenty pulses, each about three-hundredths of a second in duration. Between each pulse, or burst of vibrations, there is a rest period of onetwentieth of a second. To the human ear, however, this sounds like a continuous buzz. Another cone-head (*Neoconocephalus robustus*) has only 50 teeth in its file but its wings emit about 7,000 vibrations per second as a continuous buzz.

Another, smaller, katydid (*Conocephalus*) has but 35 teeth in its file but the vibratory rate of its song is between 16,000 and 40,000. These are given in pulses several seconds long, between which there is a series of clicks. To the human ear, the song of this insect sounds something like *tse tse tse tse-e-e-e.* It sounds somewhat different to different people.

The meadow grasshopper (*Orchelimum*) closely related to the katydids, has but six teeth in its file, and it, too, emits its song as a series of pulses separated by intervals of several seconds, during which there are no clicks. Some members of the katydid tribe have very high-pitched songs, some of which have been determined as reaching 100,000 cycles per second.

These examples of the characteristics of katydids' songs are sufficient to show that each species has its own special sound-making technique. This, of course, enables individuals in the various species to recognize each other. Just as the songs of birds are different, so are the songs or calls of katydids. We might also compare insect songs or calls to the diverse languages spoken by different human communities.

It is quite remarkable that with such simple instruments the various species of these insects can emit calls having precise, recognizable qualities. These differences are due to four factors: rate of vibration, intensity, wave form and phase.

These sound qualities, as we have said, are more or less peculiar to each species. (Stridulation calls are also affected by temperature; there is a direct relationship between chirp rate and temperature.)

Generally speaking, katydids' calls have high intensities or degrees of loudness and these insects usually mount high objects to sing.

This seems to be related to the fact that katydids are never very abundant and their calls, to reach the ears of prospective mates, must be heard for some distance. The crickets, in many cases, resemble katydids to which they are closely related. They have long antennae and many kinds are green, though black is the more common coloration.

There are anatomical details, however, which set them apart. For example, the katydids have flattened, swordlike ovipositors whereas those of the crickets are spearlike. Most of them are enthusiastic songsters.

There are many kinds of crickets, including the black field crickets. the pale-green tree crickets, the diminutive bush crickets and, last and lend the tiny ant-loving crickets found only in ant nests. In this clan we might also include the strange mole crickets which tunnel along just bent l the surface of the ground.

Although mole crickets are not true crickets they are closely related to them and are also instrumentalists. The tic](: and tree crickets are chiefly responsible for the reputation of this tribe a, sound-makers.

Black field crickets of the genus *Acheta* (*Gryllus*) are found almost everywhere and have been eulogized in prose and poetry, for example, in Charles Dickens' classic *The Cricket on the Hearth.* In rural England, the singing of crickets in the home was once considered to be a sign of good luck.

To many people, the singing of crickets in the dusk denotes peace and contentment. They are so much a part of the normal night sounds that we are not even conscious of them. Henry David Thoreau describes the night songs of crickets as "slumberous breathing."

I once spent some months in a part of the world where there were no crickets or katydids. The nights were silent except for the rustling of leaves in the wind. I realized that something was missing and it gradually dawned on me that it was the songs of insects.

In many lands, especially China and Japan, crickets, were once so esteemed for their singing that they were kept in cages and carefully cared for. Some of these cages were beautifully made and are now preserved in museums.

One type was made of gourds which were allowed to grow inside bottles from the inside surfaces of which they took their shapes. Others were fashioned of porcelain or ivory. The lids were often of carved jade. Less expensive cages were made of bamboo or coconut shells. Caged crickets were always kept in the royal palace during the days of the ancient Chinese empire.

Even now, crickets are sometimes kept in cages in Italy, Portugal, Spain and Japan. Crickets have been kept not only for their songs. Since A.D. 960 they have been kept in China for their fighting abilities. Cricket fighting was once a national pastime, and the records of individual crickets were recorded just as we keep records of thoroughbred race horses.

The fighting crickets were fed special diets consisting of rice, boiled chestnuts-and mosquitoes which had been fed on the trainers' arms. This was believed to enhance the little gladiator's abilities in the ring. Such combats ended with the death of the loser. Previous to entering the ring, the crickets were angered by being tickled with rat or hare whiskers set in bone handles.

Large sums were often bet on such matches just as in the case of American cock fights. In fact, there was once a famous fighting cricket in Canton, China, named Ghengis Khan that won $90.000 in one tournament! In these contests, the crickets were carefully weighed on small scales to assure that each one fought in its own weight class.

These classes were designated as heavyweight, middleweight and lightweight. The sound-making apparatus of the cricket clan is similar to that of the katydids, but, whereas the katydids have the file on one wing and the scraper on the other, the crickets have both a file and a scraper on each wing.

Thus, they can swap wings in their singing. The name "cricket" is an onomatopoetic word derived from the supposed sound of their songs. To many people these songs sound like *creeket, cree-ket,* but to others they sound like *treat-treat-treat, tree-tree-tree* or, even, *gru-gru-gru.* Their songs are influenced by temperature, which may account for some of the variation.

Different species, of course, have their own distinctive songs. The song of the common black field cricket (*Acheta assimilis*) sounds like a series of chirps to the human ear, but when the sound is analyzed by means of recording instruments, it is found that each chirp is made up of three or more pulses.

This series of three pulses is given in on, tenth of a second; after each series of three there is a pause of about one fifth second. There is some variation among individual crickets; a few mit trips. consisting of four or even five pulses each.

This pattern is the ordinary song which is often continued hour after hour in a monotonous fashion. Seemingly, it has little to do with courtship, except to proclaim ownership of breeding grounds. In the presence of the female, however the male cricket dances about, at the same time giving high-pitched calls.

These are given at the rate of about 17,000 vibrations per second, which is very near the upper limit of human hearing. It has been found that some of the songs of these insects are actually far beyond the range of human hearing.

In this respect they are like "silent" dog whistles. The snowy tree cricket (*Oecanthus*) *is* found in almost all sections of the United States. There are a number of different species, but they are all pale-green insects that lay their eggs in tree bark or stems.

The black-horned tree cricket has 46 teeth in its file and its call is given at the rate of 45 pulses per second. The song of the snowy tree cricket is made up of a series of chirps, each consisting of about eight pulses. To the human ear the call sounds like *churr-churr-churr.*

Generally, these crickets do their singing from the concealment of short vegetation such as that found around gardens or in waste places. Each species has its own characteristic call as do the katydids. From an evolutionary standpoint, this has probably aided in maintaining the purity of the species.

In addition to his song, the male tree cricket uses another lure to attract the female. Once she has been enticed close to him by his song, she is further attracted by a glandular secretion just behind the bases of his wings. She is induced to feed upon this, and, shortly, the actual mating takes place.

Many years ago it was noticed that the chirp rates of tree crickets were directly related to prevailing temperatures and that formulas could be worked out by which temperatures could be determined from them. This, of course, is a very roundabout way of determining temperature. but it is an interesting scientific curiosity and the results are fairly accurate.

As a matter of fact, the snowy tree cricket has been called the "temperature cricket" since its calls are so directly related to variations in air temperature. A number of formulae have been devised for telling temperature by listening to these insects.

One of these is as follows: Count the number of chirps in 15 seconds and add 40. This gives the temperature in degrees Fahrenheit. Cricket calls can be used for temperature determination only between about 55 F. and 100° F.; beyond these extremes in either direction the insects do not sing.

Another formula, one devised by Professor A. E. Dolbear for the snowy tree cricket, is as follows

$$\text{Temperature} = 50 + \frac{N-92}{4.7}$$

N = the number of chirps per minute.

Similar formulae have been worked out for other crickets and katydids. For the field cricket use the following:

$$\text{Temperature} = 50 + \frac{N-50}{4}$$

For the katydid try this formula:

$$\text{Temperature} = 60 + \frac{N-19}{3}$$

There is considerable variation in the formulae worked out by various students of the subject. Actually, stridulation rates are affected by humidity and there are also differences between individual insects.

Usually, however, temperatures can be calculated within a few degrees or with an accuracy of about six percent. The songs of crickets and katydids are quite complicated, and when we say that their notes are given at so many vibrations per second we have told only part of the story.

If we delve deeper into the subject, we quickly find ourselves involved with complex harmonics. The note of the field cricket starts out at 4,600 vibrations per second and rises to about 4,725. It then drops to about 4,275 vibrations per second. This constitutes one chirp. The vibration rate determines its pitch.

What the human ear hears as one chirp is actually made up of about three pulses of sound, each lasting about 0.023 seconds. Our ears arc not sensitive enough to detect the short pauses between sound pulses; it is only when the songs are recorded and analyzed on electronic devices that their nature becomes evident.

Even though the songs of crickets and katydids are very complex and difficult to describe, it may be of interest to attempt to catalog some of them. These have been gleaned from various writers and may not sound the same to your ears.

Small meadow grasshopper or cone-headed katydids (*Conocephalus*)

s-s-s-s-s-s-s, or tse-tse-tse-tse-tse, or *tse-e-e-e-e-e-e*

Large meadow grasshopper or cone-headed katydid (*Neoconocephalus*) *dzeet-dzeet-dzeet-dzeet*

Pine tree katydid (*Orchelimum minor*)

s-s-s-s----------s-s-s-s

Fork-tailed katydid (*Scudderia furcata*)

tzit tzit tzit-tzit

Angular-winged katydid (*Microcentrum rhombifolium*)

click-click-click-click

Texas bush katydid (*Phaneroptera*)

zeet-zeet-zeet-zeet

Oblong-winged katydid (*Amblycorypha oblongifolia*)

it-z-zrc---------it-z-zrc---------it-z-zrc

Uhler's katydid (*Amblycorypha uhleri*)

itsip-itsip-itsip---------sh-sh-sh-sh-sh-sh

True katydid (*Pterophylla camellifolia*)

katy-did-she-didn't-she-did (There are numerous interpretations.)

Meadow grasshopper (*Orchelimum*)

tsip-tsip-tsip-tsip, or *zrrrr-zrrrr---------jip-jip-jip-jip*

Shield-back grasshopper (*Atlanticus*)

p-zee---------p-zee---------p-zee

Tree cricket (*Oecanthus*)

churr-churr-churr-churr, or *ch-ch-ch-ch-urr---------ch-ch-ch-ch-urr*

Black field cricket (*Acheta assimilis*)

treat-treat-treat-treat, or *chee-chee-chee-chee,* or *cree-cree-cree-cree,* or *gru-gru-gru-gru* (*low* temperature call)

Small ground cricket (*Nemobius*)

ti-ti-ti-ti, or *trru-tmr-tiii -toll*

Mole cricket (*Gryllotalpa hexadactyla*)

grrr---------grrr---------grrr, or *churp-churp-churp* (deep toned)

Tiny bush cricket (*Anaxipha exigua*)

ti-ti-ti-ti

At present I am seated beside a river in the deep forest, my favorite place to write. The hot August sun penetrates down through the dense foliage of oaks and hickories, casting patches of light on the forest floor.

Filtering down from the sunlit world in the trees' upper story come the rasping sounds of the cicadas. Each songster begins its call in a rising crescendo that increases in tempo, then slowly fades away like an alarm clock running down. Soon the song begins again and is repeated over and over without change all during the daylight hours.

The forest seems to vibrate with the combined songs of the cicada multitudes. Dusk is the time when most katydids and crickets begin their serenades, but the cicadas love the heat and the sunshine. This, perhaps, is not surprising when one considers that these strange insects have lived for many years in dark tunnels beneath the surface of the ground.

The "year of the cicadas" is the year when the thirteen-year brood is emerging. Thirteen years previously the parent insects sang in the sun and mated. After mating, the females alighted upon twigs and inserted their spearlike ovipositors, or egg-laying tubes.

Clusters of eggs were deposited within the woody tissues, which often injured the twigs to such an extent that they died. Within a week or so the eggs hatched and the antlike young dropped to the ground and burrowed in.

For the first year or two the young cicadas remained near the surface, feeding upon sap from trees' roots, and then they began moving deeper and deeper into the ground, always near the life-giving roots. Eventually, they were located five or six feet down, each one enclosed in a small cell. For these hidden insects, time seemed almost to stand still. During summer they sucked sap from the nearby roots, but when the sap flow stopped in winter they became inactive and waited, each one alone in its dark, silent cell.

But there came a time during the thirteenth spring when some inner timing device told them that their hour was near. Each one tunneled upward to a point near the surface, excavated two connecting cells and waited. By this time they were slightly over an inch in length and brown in color. Their forelegs were shaped like a crab's claws, well suited to digging.

No one knows how the cicadas time their emergence from the ground, but all of them suddenly received the urge to return once again to the world of sunshine.

During the night they crawled from the ground and slowly and awkwardly crawled up the sides of trees and bushes. Having selected a spot, they anchored their legs and settled down to await the processes of transformation. Soon a rent appeared down the hack of each one; slowly this began to open and soon the adult, winged cicada crawled forth.

At first it was pale and helpless, its wings mere fluid-filled sacs. Gradually these expanded into cellophane-like wings and the adult insects were then ready to fly away and sing, filling the forest with a cacophony of sound. For thirteen years they lived silent lives, but now the males seem overcome with the urge to make up for lost time. The females do not sing.

The above is the story of the 13-year cicada that occurs in southeastern United States. The 17-year cicada is merely a different geographical race of the same insect and occurs farther north. There is some overlapping of the races, but their life histories are the same.

There are many different broods, and periodical cicadas emerge somewhere each summer. Besides the 13-year and 17-year cicadas, which should be called "periodical" cicadas, there are many other kinds. Some of these spend only two years in the ground in the nymphal stage.

The males of all these cicadas are songsters of renown and occur in several parts of the world. Cicadas are sometimes called locusts, but they are not even remotely related to those insects.

The locust tribe contains the grasshoppers, crickets and katydids, while the cicadas are more closely related to the plant lice and the leafhoppers. In many ways, they are unique insects, not only in their life histories, but in their mode of sound making.

The cicadas' sound-making mechanism consists not of a stridulating organ, but of a pair of drumming organs located on the underside of the body on the first abdominal segment.

These organs are quite elaborate and concealed beneath hard plates extending backward from the thorax. If one of these plates is lifted, the cavity containing the drumming mechanism can be seen. This consists of two structures, the *timbal* membrane and the *folded* membrane.

The timbal membrane is located along the outer portion of the cavity and is caused to vibrate by· muscles attached to its inner surface. The folded membrane located in the forward portion of the cavity acts as a resonator or sounding board, increasing the volume of sound. In the posterior portion of each cavity is a shiny, mica-like membrane called the *mirror.*

Actually, this latter membrane is a soundperceiving organ or "ear-drum" and plays no part in sound production. In operation, the "buckling muscle" attached to the inner surface of the timbal membrane contracts very rapidly. causing it to snap in and out at rates of from 184 to 360 times per second.

This muscle is not under direct control of the central nervous system, the impulses arise in the muscle itself. Large air spaces within the insect's body increase the volume of sound, but the insect controls the volume by raising and lowering the plates covering the cavities.

As a boy, I often imitated cicada calls by placing a tin aspirin box between my teeth and causing the lid to snap in and out. Actually, this is quite analogous to the cicadas' drumming organs. The loud buzzing song of the cicadas is difficult to describe.

Perhaps the New Zealand Maori word for these insects, *kihikihi,* best describes it. Interestingly, there is a cicada in California that has taken up sound-making by stridulation, which is actually a more primitive method of sound production.

This cicada strikes its wings together *beneath* its body, making a click-click-click sound. It has been called the "watchwinding" cicada. In a way, the sounds or noises made by insects constitute their languages; they are the means by which they communicate moods of love, anger, fright or warning.

Insects were the first creatures to raise their voices in a world that had known only the scream of the hurricane and the rumbling of ancient volcanoes.

12 Chapter

THE NECTAR GATHERERS

Manufacturing honey from flower nectar is an ancient profession practiced by several species of insects. The nectar produced by flowers is secreted especially to attract insects. Its production is one facet of many plants' methods of enticing insects for their aid in pollination.

Flower nectars contain varying amounts of several sugar types, chiefly sucrose (cane sugar), fructose (fruit sugar) and glucose (grape su(Tar). In addition to sugars, nectar contains organic acids, plant pigments, minerals, essential oils and enzymes. All these are dissolved in water, the amount of which varies considerably among the various plants.

The total solids in nectars vary from 4 to 65 percent. To show the wide variation in sugar content of nectars we might list a few examples as follows:

Willow—60 percent

Dandelion—51 percent

Sweet clover—35 to 60 percent

Sunflower—31 percent

Eucalyptus—13 percent

Apricot—5 to 25 percent

Pear—4 to 30 percent

These figures, obtained from California, illustrate very well the wide variation in sugar content of nectars, even within the same species of plant. The relative percentages of the various types of sugars is also subject to considerable variation. For example, it was found that honeysuckle nectar contained 6.9 percent sucrose while that of red clover contained 27.5 percent. It is obvious that flower nectars have high food value and it is little wonder that honeybees can subsist and work on it during their entire adult lives. During their immature stage worker bees are fed on other food.

Of all the world's nectar gatherers the domestic honeybee (*Apis mellifera*) is the best known. It has been kept under domestication for thousands of years and is now a common "domesticated" animal in almost every land. It was mentioned in Sanskrit writings as long ago as 3000 B.C. and was well known in ancient Greece and Rome.

Inscriptions on early Egyptian tombs prove that these industrious insects were kept for their honey at least 4,000 years ago. The Babylonians used honey for food and medicine, as well as for offerings to their gods.

Honeybees are semitropical insects that have adapted themselves in temperate climates where they survive cold weather by forming themselves into winter clusters or balls within the hive, hollow tree or wherever the colony has taken up residence.

These clusters are formed whenever the temperature within the hive falls to 57°F. or lower. Within the cluster, a temperature of about 90°F. is maintained by the bees fanning their wings, thereby creating heat by muscular activity.

This temperature is remarkably constant and is one of the rare instances among the cold-blooded insects where any effort is made to control temperature. To many people, the terms nectar and honey are more or less synonymous, but there is a great difference. Nectar is the raw material gathered from flowers; honey is the product manufactured from it by honeybees.

Nectar is gathered from flowers and carried into the hive in the honey stomachs of the worker bees. When a worker bee sucks up nectar from a flower, it passes through its esophagus and into the thin-walled honey stomach located in the bee's abdomen. A valve prevents the nectar from passing on into the posterior part of the digestive system. Upon returning to the hive, the worker delivers her load of nectar to younger workers or "house bees."

It is apparently passed back and forth between the bees several times, and it is believed that during this process certain enzymes are added that digest the natural sugars. After this ritual the nectar is placed in the cells where it is fanned and evaporated. The final result is honey. If comb containing honey that has not been properly evaporated is removed from the hive, it will ferment or sour.

There is no other food quite like it, and it was once considered to be a great luxury since other sources of sweets were scarce. In ancient Europe honey was made into a potent drink called "mead" by fermentation. The term "honeymoon" is said to have arisen because of an old German custom of drinking mead for thirty days after a wedding.

In addition to nectar, honeybees gather pollen from flowers and carry large quantities back to their hives where it is stored in the cells. Nectar, as we have seen, contains much sugar and is thus high in carbohydrates, but larval bees must also have protein in order to grow.

Pollen, which contains about twenty percent protein, in addition to oils and other foods, fills this need. It is estimated that one pound of pollen is needed in rearing 4,500 bees. During one summer an average hive will use about a hundred pounds of pollen.

In collecting pollen the bees must often visit many flowers, though usually not as many as for nectar. Some flowers produce pollen abundantly so that a bee can obtain a full load from one flower. On the average, however, a bee visits a hundred or more flowers. Some flowers, such as those of white sweet clover do not produce much pollen, so bees must collect from many.

In one case a bee was followed as it collected clover pollen and found to visit 585 blooms to obtain one load. The number of visits bees must ordinarily make range from 50 to 1,000 flowers on a trip.

Studies have also been made to determine how much pollen a bee can carry. On the average, this ranges from one-fifth to one-third of its own weight, or about twelve milligrams. Pollen from different flowers varies considerably in weight, but the weight of pollen is not what determines the amount carried by a bee, rather, it is the amount that its pollen baskets will hold.

These baskets are located on the outer surfaces of the hind legs, the pollen being held by the surrounding bristles. In the process of collecting pollen the bee uses her body as a brush to sweep up pollen from the anthers of flowers.

The front legs are then used to brush the pollen from the eyes, antennae and head while the middle legs are employed to brush it off the thorax. Pollen adhering to the abdomen is swept off by the hind legs. The pollen thus collected is transferred to the pollen baskets for transport back to the hive. The legs of a worker bee contain a whole set of "tools" especially designed to facilitate her work.

In the case of nectar, the maximum load is about seventy milligrams, but, here, too, it is not the weight of the nectar but the capacity of the honey stomach that determines how much is carried.

The weight of an "empty" worker is about 80 milligrams, and it has been determined, by attaching small weights to bees, that they can fly with loads of more than their own weight. From the standpoint of aerodynamics, this is remarkable wing-loading performance.

It has been found that bees can carry heavier weights in warm weather than in cold. I have often seen individual bumblebees that had imbibed so much nectar that they could not fly, but I have never seen an instance of this in honeybees.

Honeybees take on larger loads of nectar when it is being carried from a greater distance. Perhaps this is a case of a "lazy man's load." Just as an airplane uses large quantities of fuel in flight, so does a worker honeybee. A bee in flight consumes about 40 milligrams of sugar per hour.

When we recall that a bee weighs 80 milligrams, it is evident that it is burning up sugar equivalent to its own body weight every two hours. At this rate a man, if he could fly, would use about 80 pounds of sugar an hour!

Honeybees, like the ants, hornets and bumblebees, have three castesworkers, queens and drones or males. The workers and queens are both females, but only the queens are fully developed reproductively and capable of laying fertile eggs.

While workers do occasionally lay eggs, the resulting offspring are all males since workers are incapable of mating.

Drones arise from nonfertilized eggs. Thus, we find here an instance of parthenogenesis, which also occurs in some other insects. (In the case of white-fringed beetles, for example, no males have ever been found; the females reproduce continuously without mating.)

As the queen honeybee goes from cell to cell depositing an egg in each one, she apparently has control over the fertilization of her eggs. At certain seasons the bees construct enlarged cells and the eggs she deposits in these cells are nonfertilized and develop into drones.

On the other hand, the difference between queens and workers has another explanation. Young worker and queen larvae are exactly alike which caste they will eventually develop into depends upon the food they receive.

For the first day or so, both worker and queen larvae are fed royal jelly, a special substance secreted by glands in the workers' heads. In the case of larvae that are destined to develop into workers, their diet is changed after the first day or two to a mixture of pollen and honey.

Queen larvae, on the other hand, are fed continuously on royal jelly, and it is apparently this highly nutritious diet that enables them to develop into perfect females capable of mating and laying eggs.

The unique properties of royal jelly have led to its being used for human consumption in the supposition that it would do many things, such as increasing beauty and prolonging life. The idea that royal jelly has the ability to prolong life has arisen because queen bees live so much longer than the other castes. While royal jellycalled "bee milk" in England is high in proteins and B vitamins, it is doubtful if it is the miracle food it is sometimes alleged to be.

It has been used in all sorts of concoctions from face creams to quick cures for hangovers. Since it sells for about twenty dollars an ounce, it is a very expensive source of vitamins. Small jars of face creams have appeared on the market selling for as high as fifteen dollars.

Actually, such jars contain only minute amounts of royal jelly, amounts too small to do any good even if it had any value in external application, which seems doubtful.

Beekeepers, of course, are aware of the potential profit and increase the production of queen bees for the market. Day-old worker larvae are placed in special queen cells that have previously been stocked with small supplies of royal jelly. The bees continue to feed these larvae with royal jelly and they all develop into queens.

The queen was once called the "king bee" in the erroneous

belief that she was a male. It is now known, of course, that she is normally the only functional female in the colony and as such is attended at all times by a retinue of workers-her ladies-in-waiting that continually. groom and feed her.

Even though her duty is confined to that of laying eggs, this is an arduous task since she lays from 1.500 to 2,000 eggs a day during summer. The eggs laid by queen ant and termite are received by workers and carried away to nurseries, but the honeybee queen must insert her long abdomen deep into each separate cell and cement an egg to the bottom.

It is a tribute to the care she receives from the the nurse bees and to her own metabolism that the total weight of the eggs she lays each day may exceed her own weight. Like the workers, the queen has a welldeveloped sting, but she uses this only on rival queens.

As previously stated, the fertilized eggs laid by the queen may develop into either workers or queens depending on the food they receive. The unfertilized eggs laid by her develop only into drones. It has recently been found, however, that in rare cases unfertilized eggs laid by queen honeybees may also develop into workers.

How or why this occurs is, so far, a mystery. The queen has considerable control over her subjects. Recent research has revealed that the queen has a very definite governing influence over the colony through glandular secretions which are passed on to the workers by their mouths.

This secretion, often known as the "queen substance" is passed from worker to worker so that everyone receives a small but continuous supply. It is secreted by large salivary glands located beneath the queen's lower mandibles. It is, in effect, a chemical messenger that coordinates almost all the bees' activities.

Such substances, that regulate the lives of many social insects, are now called *pheromones.* The pheromones secreted and passed along by the queen honeybee control, in turn, the development of the workers' glands, causing the workers to do various things.

For example, as long as the queen is healthy and producing these pheromones, the growth of the workers' ovaries is inhibited, but when the queen becomes old and decrepit and her glands slow down, the workers' ovaries begin to develop and eventually they may even lay eggs.

These eggs, however, develop only into drones since these laying workers have not mated. If the queen dies or is killed, this, of course, cuts off the supply of pheromones and all the workers are at once aware of the fact. If a hive is opened a short time after a colony has become queenless, it will be noticed that the bees are not reacting normally.

They rest on the combs and buzz in a characteristic manner. They have received "word" that their queen is dead. If a queen's glands are removed, her power over her subjects quickly disappears.

While the queen governs her subjects by means of chemical secretions. she is herself a slave to her own glands and is devoid of any "mothering" instinct. She has no interest in her offspring; all her instincts center in laying eggs and eating.

She is tied to her workers by a tenuous chemical bond, and while she may not have the authority of a royal despot, her influence is felt throughout the hive at all times. The usual life span of a queen is about three years, but some have lived for as long as ten years.

Most beekeepers, however, requeen their hives each year to make sure of having young, vigorous queens. Bees of the worker caste constitute the teeming labor force of the hive; their number varies from a few thousand up to 60,000, depending on the strength of the colony.

Except for the laying of eggs, the busy workers do all the work of the hive, such as feeding young, secreting wax, building comb, gathering nectar and pollen and cleaning the hive. They also gather resin from trees, which is used as a cement or glue for various purposes, such as making the hive watertight.

This material, called *propolis,* is also used for encasing foreign objects, for example, a dead mouse, that cannot be removed. Propolis is sometimes known as "bee glue."

After emerging from the cells where they have passed their larval and Pup al al periods, worker bees pas') through distinct stages of apprenticeship governed by their ages and the development of their glands. During the first two days of their adult lives the workers spend their time cleaning the hive.

Bees are quite clean insects and no one need ever fear that honey has been produced under unsanitary conditions. On the third day the worker bees are promoted to the task of feeding the older larvae and they continue to do this until the fifth day when they begin feeding the younger larvae.

They continue in this duty for about two days. This work is very arduous since each larval bee must be fed about 1,300 times a day or about 10,000 times during its growth. Human mothers should, indeed, be grateful that their charges do not require such attention.

As a result of the constant feeding of the larvae, they increase in size 1,570 times in the first six days out of the egg. At about ten days of age the worker bees begin the task of receiving food from the field bees and placing it in the cells for storage.

They serve in this capacity until they are about 16 days old, at which time they are again promoted and begin other duties. One of these consists of standing at the hive entrance and fanning their wings to cause currents of air to flow through the hive. It is during this period of their lives, also, that they begin making little exploratory or orientation flights in the immediate vicinity of the hive.

On their seventeenth day they take up guard duty at the entrance and continue in this important capacity until their twenty-first day out of the cell. At this time their lives change and they graduate to the status of full-fledged field bees.

Scout bees are continually out seeking new nectar sources, and when these are located the scouts return to the hive and do charadelike dances on the combs. These dances tell the field bees the exact direction and location of nectar-bearing flowers.

The field bees then (YO out and harvest the crop. Rarely do the worker bees go out on nectar-gathering flights without first receiving information from the scouts, which are older field bees which have been collecting nectar for a long time.

Field bees also collect pollen when it is needed in the hive, but they much prefer to gather nectar. Some individuals gather pollen in the morning and nectar in the afternoon, but others appear to devote their entire lives to collecting either one or the other.

They do not collect both on the same trip afield. The field bees also collect propolis and, during periods of warm weather, they carry in water. The water is spread on the combs to cool them by evaporation—a simple system of air-conditioning.

During summer while the bees are working hard they live for only about five weeks. Usually.. they die afield, but those that die within the hive are tossed out without ceremony.

Worker bees begin their lives as janitors and end them as scouts and dancers. All the successive changes in their duties are the results of instinct and the secretions of internal glands. Workers are subject only to the chemical messages that filter down from the queen.

Few of us realize fully what an amazing little "machine" a worker bee really is. In a single day a worker may collect nectar from 250,000 blooms and, in order to obtain enough nectar to make a pound of honey, the workers must make a total of about 37,000 trips afield.

The life work of a worker is but a spoonful or two of honey. In the process of gathering the nectar for a pound of honey, bees may sometimes fly a combined distance of 300,000 miles-more than the distance from the earth to the moon.

Think of this the next time you buy a pound of honey in the super-market. The production and use of wax is one of the basic functions of honeybees. Without this remarkable material a colony of bees could not live. It is out of wax that they construct their comb just as the hornets use wood fiber. Honeybees begin their lives in wax cells and, if they die in the hive, end them in these same cells.

Chemically, beeswax is composed of a complex mixture of esters, fatty acids, higher alcohols and hydrocarbons. When wax for comb building is needed, young workers from 10 to 17 days old form groups which hang from the top of the nest site.

These workers have previously filled themselves with honey and, as they rest quietly, their wax glands begin secreting wax scales. These glands are located in the abdomen and open on the last four sternal or abdominal plates, which have shiny surfaces called "mirrors."

The wax is in liquid form when first secreted, but rapidly hardens. Usually, it is light yellow in color, but there is some variation. After the scales of wax have formed. the worker then removes them with her hind tarsi and they are then grasped by the "wax pinchers" located between the tibias and the first (largest) tarsal segments of the hind legs. The scales are then carried forward to the mandibles. In using the wax for comb construction, the scales are formed into shape by the mandibles and the cells are gradually "drawn out" by the addition of more and more wax. While the walls of the cells are thin their outer edges always bear a thickened rim or coping.

This strengthens the cells so that they are not injured when the bees walk about over them. The wax cells constructed by honeybees are extraordinary structures when one considers that they are built by an insect that depends only upon instinct and works in the total darkness of the hive.

They are hexagonal in form. In worker brood cells, which are also used for honey and pollen storage, there are 55 per square inch of comb. Mathematicians have determined that the shape of the cells is such as to hold the largest amount of honey with the smallest amount of structural material.

They are very accurately built, there being less than three or four degrees of variation in their angles. Reaumur, the well-known French naturalist of the eighteenth century, conceived the idea of using the diameter of these wax cells as an international unit of measurement.

It was never adopted, but this idea is an indication of their uniformity in size. The walls of the cells vary from about 1 230 to 1 500 of an inch. One pound of wax will build about 35,000 cells which will hold about 22 pounds of honey.

In order to secrete a pound of wax it is usually estimated that the bees will consume about eight pounds of honey the production of this necessary structural material is rather expensive to the hive's economy.

Beeswax also has many uses in human industry; it is used in making floor waxes, candles, cosmetics and many other things. As human food, beeswax has no value, but there is a bird in Africa that appears to subsist on a diet of wax and bee larvae.

There are 11 species of these birds, the honey-guides, all sharing similar habits. They are related to the woodpecker clan. Two species will unerringly guide both humans and honey badgers to wild bee nests. These unique birds are about the size of small starlings and rather demurely colored.

Another strange habit of the honey-guide is their practice of laying eggs in the nests of other birds as do cuckoos. When the eggs hatch, the young honey-guide attacks the other bird's young, kills them with its hooked beak and pushes their remains out of the nest.

When the honey-guide locates a nest of wild bees, it then finds either a honey badger or a human being and, alighting on a bush, begins to chatter. If the chosen party shows interest in following it, the honeyguide flies farther off and chatters again, always in the direction of the wild bee nest.

When the bird has lured its "guest" to the bee nest and the colony has been plundered of its store of honey, the bird then gorges itself on the comb containing both wax and larvae that has been exposed or scattered about. Honey-guides have no interest in the honey, but can apparently digest and assimilate the wax.

Probably the first person to become acquainted with the wax-eating propensities of the honey-guides was a Portuguese missionary in the sixteenth century, who was astonished to see one of the birds fly in through an open window in his chapel and begin devouring one of the beeswax candles.

Truly, this is one of the world's most remarkable instances of symbiosis, a cooperative arrangement between two animals whereby each is benefited. In addition to the common domestic honeybee, there are a number of other bees that also gather nectar and manufacture it into honey, though in much smaller quantities.

For this reason they are not of value as commercial sources. Probably the best known of these are the bumblebees (*Bombes*) of which there are many species found in almost all parts of the world, especially in the cooler zones. Like their cousins, the domestic honeybees, the bumblebees live upon nectar and pollen harvested from flowers, but their nesting habits have many differences. Whereas the entire honeybee colony survives the winter in the form of a warm cluster, all the bumblebee workers die in autumn.

Only the mated queens survive by retiring to small cells they excavate in the ground. When spring arrives these queens emerge from their winter quarters and begin feeding upon nectar and pollen. During cool spring nights they retire to sheltered places again. This continues for several weeks during which time their ovaries are developing.

They then seek places to found colonies, such as deserted mouse nests in the ground, which are formed of dried grass, or other nesting sites, including haystacks or even old bird nests. During early summer, queen bumblebees can often be observed as they buzz about among vegetation, alighting now and then to investigate cavities and holes in search of suitable places to nest.

Having at last found a situation that meets her needs the queen clears a small space inside and settles down to wait for her glands to develop. Occasionally, she leaves the site and gathers food. In time she begins secreting wax after the manner of honeybee workers and uses this to construct a cup-shaped cell.

This is often stocked with pollen which she gathers from flowers. This done, she then lays a number of eggs in itusually about eight-and seals it over with wax so that its final shape is that of a sphere. The queen next begins the construction of a honey pot consisting of an open receptacle about the size of a thimble, located just inside the nest entrance.

Some species build the honey pot first. In this receptacle she places a store of nectar which will be used to feed the larvae during periods of bad weather when she cannot harvest it from flowers. This, in effect, is her "money in the bank."

In three to five days the larvae hatch and the queen mother makes an opening in the wall of the spherical cell and feeds them nectar. In some species a store of pollen has already been placed in the cell. As the larvae grow, the queen enlarges the original cell so that eventually there are a number of cells, all connected together.

When not out collecting food, she spends her time "brooding" the larval cells keeping them warm with the heat of her own body. In about seven days the larvae transform to pupae and, in about twelve days, to adult worker bumblebees which emerge from their separate cells.

When the workers have emerged, the colony becomes a social unit somewhat like that of a honeybee colony. The first workers, which are smaller than normal, take over the field work while the queen now remains in the nest.

It is interesting, however, that, unlike the queen honeybee, she does not become merely an egg layer but continues to help feed the brood and to engage in other activities within the nest. Brood cells are not reused for brood rearing, but after the young emerge they are used for food storage.

Stored nectar thickens by evaporation and the cells are then capped. As the summer advances, more young are reared so that the colony eventually numbers from a few hundred to several thousand workers, depending on the species. As in the case of honeybee workers, they live for only a few weeks.

During late summer when the colony has become populous and food abundant, a number of queens and drones are produced. Unlike larval honeybee queens. those of bumblebees do not apparently receive glandular food comparable to royal jelly. although food for bumblebee queens does seem to differ in both quantity and quality.

Once the production of queens and males has begun in late summer no more worker brood is reared. In the economy of the bumblebee colony, this would be a waste of effort since, with the coming of autumn, they all die anyway.

In late summer the virgin queens and males mate, but only the queens survive the winter to found the colonies of another year. In this respect they resemble hornets. Bumblebees are often confused with carpenter bees (*Xylocopa*) which make tunnels in wood.

Carpenter bees, however, are not social insects and do not belong to the same tribe as the bumblebees. While the robust bodies of bumblebees are usually black marked with contrasting colors, especially yellow or orange. the bodies of carpenter bees are usually black.

Carpenter bees have no pollen baskets on their hind legs even though they collect pollen. While bumblebees, like honeybees, often impress us with their industry, some kinds have degenerated into the role of social parasite.

One of these is the parasitic bumblebee (*Psithyrrrs*) which resembles the ordinary bumblebee but has no worker caste. Somewhere along the evolutionary line the queen *Psithvrus* lost the ability to found her own colony.

She is now a chiseler and instead of going to the trouble of rearing young she seeks out a bumblebee nest and lays her eggs in it. The bumblebees rear these "cuckoo" young. which turn out to be only males and queens. They leave the bumblebee nest and, after mating, the females seek other bumblebee nests to parasitize.

When the female *Psithvrus* enters a bumblebee nest she may be killed at once, but often she is more or less accepted and may live in peace with the rightful queen for some time.

Most people are aware that both honeybees and bumblebees gather nectar, but it may come as a surprise to learn that some wasps, too, collect and store nectar. Most of the species of these honey wasps are native to tropical areas, where natives often rob them of their honey or nectar stores.

Whether the substance they produce should be designated as honey is questionable, but in places where these insects occur the sweet material they store is known as honey and the insects themselves are known as honey wasps.

They are apparently quite common in Mexico, but one species, *Brach ygastra* (*Nectarina*) *lecheguana,* is found in the vicinity of Brownsville, Texas, and is part of our native fauna. These wasps-perhaps they should be called hornets construct paper-enclosed nests resembling closely those of our native hornets.

However, their nests are about 20 inches high and elongate in shape. Usually, they are constructed on low shrubs, such as Mexican mahogany. and their interior architecture is not much different from that of nests built by our common hornets.

They are apparently quite docile and do not usually sting in defense of their nest, although they will sting severely if handled or sufficiently aroused. But, curiously, they may be robbed of their honey or have their nest cut down with impunity.

Honey is stored in the paper cells which, like those of other hornets, are in horizontal layers with the cells extending downward. In a typical colony there are about 50,000 cells. The cells in which honey is stored are not capped.

Not much seems to be known about the biology of these wasps, but the colonies apparently survive more than one year, as do most other tropical wasps.

Instead of the new colony being founded by a mated queen, those of the honey wasps are founded by small swarms consisting of several queens and a few workers.

In studying insects, we should always be prepared for the unusual. Just as certain tropical hornets store honey, several ants, too, store honeydew or "honey." One kind occurs in North America and another in Australia. Those occurring in Australia are named *Camponotus inflates* while those in our country all belong to the genus *Myrinecocystus* of which there are a number of species.

The curious aspect of these ants is that they all dwell in arid regions where they can harvest their sweets only during short periods of the year. Under such conditions some method of storing the liquid food becomes a necessity-a method in this case which is most unusual.

Ants cannot secrete wax to build combs like bees, so they have evolved another storage method. They use their own bodies as honey casks. Not all individuals serve in this capacity, but those that do so are called "repletes," and their abdomens become so greatly distended with contained "honey" that they resemble small grapes.

After becoming repletes they are comparatively helpless and spend their time clinging to the ceilings of the underground galleries by their feet. The *Myrmecocystus* ants of our Southwest are found over an area extending from southern Idaho to deep into Mexico, usually at altitudes of from 5,000 to 7,000 feet.

My own experience with these unusual ants consists of two trips to Colorado's Garden of the Gods to observe and photograph them first-hand. The red, sandy ridges contain their underground colonies. Since they are nocturnal in habit, the identification of their nests is somewhat difficult because there are many other ground-nesting ants in the area.

The entrances to honey ant colonies are nearly half an inch in diameter, larger than might be expected for ants of moderate size. In my first search for these ants I dug up several harvester ant colonies which I mistook for those of honey ants.

However, I at last recognized a honey ant nest when I glimpsed one of the slender, yellowish ants in the entrance. Excavating the nest down to the galleries where the repletes were housed constituted a major undertaking since the gravelly soil was very hard and the sun was hot. About three inches beneath the surface I encountered a gallery containing pupal ants in gray cocoons.

It was not until I had dug downward about a foot in the hardpan earth that my trowel at last encountered a gallery that proved to be one of those where the repletes were kept. Clearing away the earth revealed a startling sight.

As far as I could see back into the dark gallery, dozens of repletes were suspended from the ceiling, their distended abdomens glistening in the light. In color they were translucent amber and, when examined under a lens, it could be seen that, in the process of expansion, the original sclerites or abdominal plates existed as mere islands on the globular surfaces of stretched membrane.

They were almost completely helpless and when I dislodged them from their perches they lay on their backs waving their legs in the air. In the meantime the normal workers rushed about in vain efforts to defend their nest. However, they have no stings and they make no effort to bite.

The first gallery or chamber I excavated was about an inch high and about eight inches across. When other, lower, chambers were excavated a total of several dozen repletes were unearthed.

In former years the Indians often dug into honey ant nests for the repletes, which they ate for their sweet contents. The Australian honey ants are also eaten by natives. The swollen abdomens of honey ant repletes are very delicate and burst very easily.

As a matter of fact, I noticed that when some of them fell from their perches to the floor of the gallery-a distance of only about an inch-their abdomens ruptured and the liquid contents soaked into the gravelly soil. When this occurred the normal workers gathered around and attempted to salvage the sweet contents.

I tasted some of this ant honey, but found it rather sour, not nearly as palatable as that from honeybees. In order to observe their nocturnal activities, my wife and I returned to the Garden of the Gods after dark when a full moon hung over Pikes Peak. After locating a honey ant colony we waited until they began emerging and crawling away across the ground toward scrub oaks.

They climbed up these and began imbibing the droplets of honeydew exuded from galls on the twigs. This is the source of their honey and explains its relatively poor quality. These galls, each about the size of a small marble, are produced by the activities of cynipid gall wasps whose larvae develop within them.

The droplets of honeydew that form on the surfaces of the galls result, probably, from the excess sugar that accumulates within them. We noticed also that some of the ants were obtaining honeydew from aphids on nearby wild rose bushes.

The honeydew gathered from oak galls or aphids is carried back to the underground nest where it is "fed" to the repletes. Later, whenever a worker ant is hungry it approaches a replete which regurgitates a drop of honey. Thus there is always a readily available source of food in the honey ant nest.

Here in this relatively barren region, honeydew sources do not last long, only from late June through August. Thus, the ants must have a safe means of food storage for the remainder of the year. Theirs is a remarkable solution to the storage of food in an inhospitable region.

Chapter 13

THE POLLINATORS

Insects and plants existed in the world for many millions of years before the plants began to depend on the insects for help in pollinating their flowers. The primitive plants such as pines were, and still are, wind pollinated. When the ability to fly was evolved by insects, they became ideal agents for carrying pollen from plant to plant.

Wind pollination is very wasteful, since sufficient pollen must be produced to literally blanket the countryside if there is to be any assurance that all female flowers will be pollinated. Insect pollination, on the other hand, is economical since insects usually fly directly from flower to flower gathering pollen and nectar.

No one knows which was the first insect-pollinated flower, but it was apparently a generalized flower, such as the ancestor of the buttercup and magnolia. From this were evolved all the great host of blooms that solicit the aid of insects by color, scent and nectar.

Today there are more than 150,000 species of flowers found growing in almost every climate from the Arctic to the Antarctic. Insects, especially honeybees, are very important to the farmer and fruit grower.

Many kinds of clover and fruit trees will not set seed or produce fruit abundantly unless sufficient bees are present. Bee hives are often placed in orchards and in clover fields for this purpose.

In the Utah area various wild bees are depended upon for the pollination of alfalfa, since the flowers of this plant must be tripped-the pistils must be forced out of the flower keel to bring about pollination.

However, there is often a scarcity of wild bees in alfalfa fields so hives of honeybees must be placed in such fields. Usually five or six hives per acre are used. Bumblebees are the most efficient pollinators of red clover, and when this crop was first introduced into New Zealand, it was found that no seed was produced.

It was only after bumblebees had been introduced from England that this clover began producing seed in commercial quantities. Long after the habit of insect assistance in pollination had become well established many plants reversed their evolution and turned again to the wind for pollen transport.

For example, the ancestors of the grasses, walnuts, maples and ragweeds were insect pollinated. Seemingly there are advantages in each method. There are not enough bees to pollinate all the grass on a prairie or to pollinate each flower in a walnut forest.

Flowers are, of course, the reproductive structures of plants and they may contain both male and female organs or only those of one sex. In the process of pollination the male cells or pollen grains are transferred from their containers (*anthers*) to the female organs (*stigmas*).

If the pollen is transferred from the male organs of one plant to the female organ of another plant, the process is called *cross-pollination.* If, on the other hand, the pollen is transferred from male to female organs on the same plant, or in the same flower, it is called *self-pollination.*

Pollination. like animal fertilization, is necessary to the perpetuation of the species. While self-pollination of flowers will usually result in viable seeds, crosspollination has a number of advantages. More seeds and better fruit are produced and the offspring are usually more vigorous and variable, which, from an evolutionary standpoint, affords a much greater degree of adaptability.

Nowhere are the relationships between plants and insects as complex as in the processes of pollination. There is probably no method of enticing insects for their aid that some plant has not adopted-and some of these methods are truly amazing in their invention.

Flowers seem to specialize not only in their techniques of attracting insects but in the types of insects they solicit. Many flowers depend on bees, which they lure by means of nectar and pollen, which are the insects' rewards for services rendered.

Such flowers are known as "bee flowers" and include such common examples as mint, snapdragon, clover, columbine, pea and numerous others. All these have colorful blooms and abundant nectar to attract various species of bees.

Most of these flowers are either yellow or lue, since bees are colorblind to the red end of the spectrum. Bees, of course, are day-loving insects, and the flowers they pollinate open during the daylight hours.

Flowers of another type specialize in butterflies and these often have rather deep throats where their nectar can only be reached by the long tongues of these insects. Butterflies, like bees, are day-loving and their flowers open during the hours of sunshine, but whereas the bee flowers are shades of yellow or blue, those that cater to butterflies are often tinted in shades of orange and red, since these colors are visible to many butterflies.

Among the common butterfly-pollinated flowers are the carnation, red catchfly, daylily and butterfly weed. In contrast to the flowers that seek the aid of butterflies, there are the night-blooming flowers that attract moths. Most of these flowers are pale or white, since these are most easily seen in the dusk.

A brightly colored flower may be very conspicuous in the sun but invisible in dim light. A red flower, for example, disappears as the dusk deepens. Common examples of moth flowers are datura, morning glory, tobacco, yucca and most orchids. Most of the moths that visit such flowers do not alight on the blooms, but hover before them, probing into them for nectar with their long tongues.

This is especially true of the hummingbird moths (family Sphingidae). Night-blooming flowers attract moths not only by their pale coloration but also by heavy perfume.

There are a number of flowers that are especially adapted to attract flies. In contrast to the brightly colored flowers that attract bees and butterflies, the fly flowers are not very colorful and their "perfumes" resemble decaying flesh or dung.

While these flowers are not colorful, some of them have interesting markings and shapes and so are often grown in gardens or greenhouses. One of these is the starfish "cactus" (*Stapelia*), which, as the name suggests, has a bloom shaped like a starfish. It smells like carrion.

Among the fly flowers is found the world's largest bloom, the Rafflesia of Malaysia, which attracts flies by its odorous "perfume." Included in this group of flowers also are the Dutchman's pipes, which have strangely shaped flowers within which flies are trapped, dusted with pollen and then released.

Still other flowers avail themselves of beetles for pollination. Most of these flowers are white or greenish and depend on perfumes to attract their beetle visitors. Among these flowers are the magnolia, water lily, California poppy, elder, dogwood and arum. Flowers which specialize in beetles often have unique adaptations.

For example, many of them hide their seeds and other flower parts inside protective coverings, since beetles are prone to gnaw away at any edible plant structure. Most of the beetle flowers occur in the tropics. One giant arum (*Amorphophallus titanum*) found in Sumatra generates heat at the time of blooming, presumably to volatilize its carrionlike odor.

Here in our own country are found several plants of this same family. One of these is the common little jack-in-thepulpit (*Arisaema triphvllum*), which attracts small flies into its vaselike spathe for the purpose of pollination. Most of the large, tropical arums, however, are beetle pollinated.

The so-called dragon lily or black calla (*Dracunculus vulgaris*) is a large exotic arum from the Nile region that is often grown in American gardens and greenhouses. It is very large, often being 2 feet tall. The inside of the spathe is tinted deep purple and an odor reminiscent of dead fish is generated within it. Dr. J. D. Meeuse once collected 162 beetles that had entered one such flower, which testifies to the effectiveness of its "perfume."

These beetles belonged to many different families. The voodoo lily (*Sauromatum guttatum*) from India and Pakistan is another showy arum grown in greenhouses and homes. Like other tropical arums it generates heat at the time of blooming to volatilize its odor. The heat is apparently produced by *calorigen,* a hormone secreted in the male flower parts. This arum, like most others, attracts beetles.

It is believed that beetle-pollinated flowers were the first ones to use insects for carrying their pollen, and later colorful, nectarbearing blooms developed to attract other flying insects.

Plants also protect their flowers from certain crawling insects that steal nectar and pollen but are of no value in pollination. Common examples of such insects are ants which feed upon pollen and nectar but are of little help in pollination, since they crawl about on one plant and do not fly from flower to flower.

To protect their wares from such plunderers, plants have evolved a number of techniques. For example, the fire pink and a number of other plants have their stems covered with sticky hairs that make it almost impossible for ants to reach the blooms.

Other plants, such as the common toadflax, have their nectar hidden in deep nectaries where only long-tongued insects can reach it. Of special interest is the technique used by the snapdragon bloom.

Its lower lip is pressed tightly against the upper lip and only a heavy-bodied insect, such as a bumblebee, can open the bloom and enter it. A flower advertises its wares in ways parallel to those used by man. Just as we erect signs advertising commercial products, so do flowers appeal to insects through colorful blooms with contrasting markings.

In many cases the flowers go to great extremes to make it easy for their visitors to find their store of nectar. Flowers such as the foxglove and some orchids have their throats marked with lines leading into the deep flower tube where the nectar is to be found.

These markings guide the insects. Many flowers have their lower petals formed into enlarged landing platforms for the convenience of flying insects. There are also many "target" flowers that are shaped and marked in ways to guide insects to a landing.

If you will examine a number of pansy blooms, you will see that they are designed to attract the eye to their centers where the pool of nectar is to be found. Note also in the case of narcissus that the margin of the central corolla tube is tinted in a contrasting color to guide insects to it.

We may appreciate the beauty of flowers, but their forms and colorations must, first and last, attract insects. It was for that purpose alone that flowers were evolved.

There are a number of instances where a very close working arrangement prevails between plants and insects to secure pollination and the production of seed. Probably the most remarkable of these involves the yucca and the yucca moth (*Pronuba yuccasella*).

Yucca are common on the southern portions of the Great Plains, where they are conspicuous features of the landscape. Some kinds are also grown in gardens. They belong to the lily family and their blooms are large and white but are not attractive to most insects.

Only the small white *Pronuba* moth is adapted to their pollination, and this moth shows no interest in any other bloom. The female moth has special appendages on her mouthparts with which she collects a ball of pollen and places it upon the stigma.

This assures her that the flower is properly pollinated and that seed will be produced. The *Pronuba* moth also plunges her ovipositor into the yucca ovary and deposits several eggs. As the seeds develop, the *Pronuba* larvae feed upon them and grow.

By the time that the larvae are mature most of the seeds will have been consumed. Only rarely, however, are all the seeds destroyed, and the plant is able to produce enough seeds to feed the *Pronuba* larvae and to perpetuate the yucca species.

Here is a classic example of symbiosis, a case where two organisms cooperate to their mutual benefit. Without the moth the yucca would not be pollinated, and the yucca is the sole host plant of the moth larvae.

One could not exist without the other. In the case of the yucca and the *Pronuba* moth, the moth is a voluntary cooperator in the ritual of pollination, but there are many other instances where insects must be tricked into aiding in pollination.

There are so many cases that space will permit the discussion of only a few outstanding examples. One such example is that of the epiphytic orchid (*Epidendrum tampensis*) that grows upon trees in the Everglades. The attractive little blooms of these orchids have their pollen enclosed in small containers (*pollinia*).

In the act of probing into the flower for nectar a moth's eyes come in contact with the pollinia which adhere to them. When the moth flies away the attached pollinia are carried along and are rubbed off upon the stigmatic surface of the next orchid visited.

The moth is thus the unwilling vehicle by which the pollen is carried from one orchid to another to bring about cross-pollination. A number of other orchids employ this same trick, including the coral-root orchids (*Corallorrhiza* and *Habenaria*) which are found in many places in the more northern parts of the United States.

There is another orchid (*Ophrvs*) found growing along the Mediterranean and in various European countries that employs an underhanded trick. The blooms of this orchid resemble rather closely the females of *Scolia* wasps.

When an amorous male wasp sees one of these orchids and attempts to copulate with it, a pollinium is attached to it and this is later rubbed off on another orchid. Thus is the male wasp tricked into pollinating the orchid. A somewhat similar trick is used by an Australian orchid which emits an odor resembling that of a female ichneumon wasp (*Lissopimpla semipunctata*).

The male wasp is attracted and attempts to mate with it. In South America there is an orchid (*Catasetum*) that shoots its adhesive pollinia like bullets so that they become attached to the thorax of a visiting moth.

Here in our own country, the grass pink orchid (*Calopogon pulchellue*) employs another trick. The upper lip of this attractive little orchid is held erect and is colored to attract bees. When a bee alights upon it, however, its weight causes the lip to flop down so that the bee's back comes in contact with the lower lip where pollinia are cemented to the bee's back.

This orchid contains no nectar but the bees seem not to learn by experience, so a bee that has been tricked by one orchid and has pollinia cemented to its back soon alights upon another orchid where its pollinia become detached.

These orchids achieve pollination without the use of nectar or any other reward for the bees. Another native orchid, the lady's slipper (*Cypripedium*), employs yet another trick. The lower lip or "petal" of this pretty orchid is greatly enlarged and formed into a bulbous structure having an opening in the top.

Within this hollow cavity are found the orchid's sex organs. Bees are attracted into the bulbous cavity where escape is somewhat difficult. As the bee crawls about it eventually finds that it can force its way out of a slit at the back of the flower. In escaping, however, it is smeared with pollen. When another lady's slipper is visited, the pollen is rubbed off on the stigma within the bulbous "petal." Of all the techniques employed by flowers to secure cross-pollination, that used by the common milkweed is probably the most remarkable.

Since milkweed is common almost everywhere, its pollination can be easily observed. If you will examine one of the small individual blooms, you will find that there is a central column surrounded by live nectaries. When a bee or other insect visits such a bloom and imbibes the nectar, its legs come to rest at the bottoms of U-shaped slits surrounding the central column.

When the bee is ready to leave the flower, its legs are pulled up through the slits where tiny wishbone-shaped structures are attached to them. There is a bag of pollen attached to each prong of the wishbone. When the bee visits another milkweed bloom one or more of the wishbones and their attached pollinia are apt to be rubbed off onto the central column, which is actually the stigma.

If a number of bees, wasps or butterflies are collected in a field of milkweeds, the legs of almost every one will be found to have attached pollinia. Sometimes the insects are loaded down with them. If many of the blooms are examined it will be found that many small flies have been trapped with their feet anchored in the slits. Such insects are not strong enough to extricate their legs and so they die, victims of the flowers' pollinating mechanism.

The Dutchman's pipe (*Aristolochia*) also traps insects for their aid in pollination, but the technique used is different from that of the orchids and milkweeds. These are mostly flowers of the tropics, but some kinds are grown here in our own country.

The largest and most unusual kinds are called "pelican flowers" because of the shapes of their blooms. These blooms are deep-throated and beyond the expanded front part of the bloom there is a narrow, curved neck opening into a bulbous expansion.

Small flies are attracted into the bloom by odors which often resemble decaying flesh. Within the narrow neck of the flower tube there are backward-directed hairs that prevent the escape of the flies once they have entered the expanded portion at the back of the flower. Here the small flies buzz about.

In 'Lime, which may be several days, the flower releases pollen and the flies become well dusted with it. Then, as if by a miracle, the hairs which have so far prevented the escape of the flies, now wither and the flies are able to leave their prison. The foolish flies. however, have not learned by their experience, so they enter other pelican flowers carrying the adhering pollen.

Within the flower they are again trapped but the pollen they carry is dusted off upon the stigma, bringing about pollination. This certainly seems to be a roundabout means of achieving the desired result, but it seems to work.

Sometimes so many flies are trapped by large *Aristolochia* blooms that their unhappy buzzing can be heard several yards away. A number of flowers have evolved mechanical devices as aids to pollination. One of the more interesting of these is that used by salvia or sage (*Salvia*).

This common garden flower has a deep throat with its nectar glands located at the far end. The lower lip of the flower tube is formed into a convenient landing platform for flying insects such as bees. When a bee alights upon this platform and pushes into the bloom, its head comes in contact with the lower ends of two levers.

The upper extensions of these levers are long and curved and have pollen-filled anthers attached to their ends. As the bee pushes into the bloom, its head presses against the lower extensions of these two levers, causing the anthers to swing downward and smear pollen on its back. When the bee visits another salvia bloom, this pollen is trapped upon the stigma which extends outward above the flower tube.

In order to prevent self-pollination flowers have evolved a number of interesting devices. One of these is illustrated by the common iris. When a visiting bee alights she crawls into the flower over a path covered with hairlike papillae.

These were apparently evolved to aid the insects in forcing their way into the bloom. As the bee pushes into the flower to reach the nectar deep within, her back rubs against a membranous flap and any pollen adhering to her back from previously visited blooms is rubbed off onto the sensitive outer surface.

After the bee pushes on into the flower to sip her fill of nectar, her back comes in contact with the pollen-covered stamens. Now, as she withdraws, the membranous flap swings outward preventing the newly acquired pollen from being rubbed off upon the sensitive outer surface.

Thus, it is only when the bee is in the act of entering the iris bloom that the sensitive surface of the stigma can be dusted with pollen. In this manner the flower is assured that it will only be pollinated by pollen from other flowers.

Catalpa blooms and some others use a somewhat different technique. In this case the stigma is forked with one lip curving upward and the other downward. When a bee enters the bloom any pollen on its back is rubbed off upon the open lips of the stigma.

While the bee is in the flower imbibing nectar, the lips of the stigma rapidly close, pressing tightly together. When the bee withdraws there is no way that the new pollen dusted on its back within the flower can come in contact with the sensitive surface of the forked stigma.

Pollination of flowers is often an intricate and ingenious process-one that required many millions of years of evolution to develop. Perhaps nowhere in nature are the ways of evolution better exemplified.

HONEY AND BEESWAX

Honey was one of man's first foodas and the first available sweet. It has been highly valued by Indians from time immemorial. It has been defined as 'an aromatic, viscid sweet material derived from the nectars of plants through the collection of honey-bees and modified and stored by them as a denser liquid.'

It consists chiefly of two simple sugars, dextrose and levulose, the latter more predominant, and occasionally contains more complex carbohydrates, moisture, ash (mineral matter) and some plant colouring matter, acids, enzymes, vitamins and pollen grains.

Honey is a natural, unrefined food and is the only unmanufactured sweet available in commercial quantities. It has as many tastes and colours as the flavours and colours of plant nectars from which it is derived. Honey-bees 'visit only one source at a time and keep on visiting it until it dries up.

In a locality where several minor honeyflows occur in a certain period, a colony may gather nectar from several sources and the beekeeper may produce a natural blend of several distinct flavours. Since at one time blossoms of a particular source predominate, it is generally possible to produce honeys by far the major portion of which is derived from the nectar from a single source like mustard, soapnut or barberry.

CHEMICAL COMPOSITION

As stated above, the bulk of honey is simple sugars and moisture. Some sucrose (table sugar), dextrins and gums also occur. In its ash are found the compound.s'of silica, iron, copper, manganese, chlorine, calcium, potassium, sodium, phosphorus, sulphur, aluminium and magnesium. Acids like formic, acetic, malic, critic, and succinic; plant colouring matter like carotin, xanthophyll, anthocyanin and tannin; and pollen grains and beeswax particles are found in honey.

Enzymes like invertase, diastase, catalase, inulase and vitamins A, B complex (B_1, B_2, B_6, H, Folic, nicotinic and pantothenic acids) and C occur in it in varying quantities. The composition of representative honeys from different regions are given in Table elsewhere in this chapter. For a wider comparison, figures for American and English products are also given.

It may be mentioned that honey is prized for its delicate flavour and fragrance which can better be enjoyed than described. But its real value lies in simple sugars found in large amounts in it. They do not tax the digestive system, are directly assimilable and are a ready source of bodily energy.

The quantities of aminoacids, mineral matter, enzymes and vitamins present in an ounce or two of honey, the quantity taken by a person in a day, are too small to become a regular supply of these substances to the human system. Their presence is not the major consideration for which honey is valued. They are of some use.

Its colour and taste are no guides to the purity and quality of honey. Honey from *Plectranthus,* soapnutt and white clover is light (almost water-white) in colour and mild in flavour; that from mustard looks yellow and has a little pronounced flavour and that from Shishm (*Dalbergia*) is dark amber and strong in flavour.

Barberry and buckwheat honeys are very dark in colour and have a strong taste. The flavour of barberry honey is suggestive of molasses. It is said that a person likes that honey best which he took in his childhood. As honey available in the market varies from time to time, *connoisseurs* should ensure a regular supply of their favourite brand from a particular beekeeper season after season.

In cold weather, honey usually solidifies, that is, forms into grains. Such granulation is the best evidence of its purity. If liquid honey is preferred, it can be melted by keeping the container in hot (60°C to 71°C) water for some time.

In the West, honey in the comb either as section or chunk honey is used on the table but a similar use has not become poular in this country where liquid, ungranulated honey is relished.

Description of honey	*Moisture* %	*Glucose* %		*Levulose* %	*Sucrose* %	*Ash* %	*Acidity as formic acid*
Indian—average of 61 samples	19.19	32.82		37.95	1.66	0.29	0.10
Coorg—average of 12 samples	18.16	35.68		39.3	o.68	0.17	...
Punjab—average of 44 pure samples	16.43	34·71		38.74	3.18	0.362	0.13
Punjab—average of 36 market samples	19.25	33.67		37.42	4.16	0.264	0.11
Mahableshwar	19.62	30.08		41.37	1.60	0.21	0.13
Jeolikote (U.P.)	19.10		76.91		0.85	1.06	0.23
Cotton (Coimbatore, Tamil Nadu)	14.89		73.96		5·84	0·47	...
Cotton (1952) (Coimbatore, Tamil Nadu)	21.99		69.68		6.96	0.22	0.07
Gliricidia (1952) (Coimbatore, Tamil Nadu)	23·57		63·95		7.91	0.15	0.09
Neem (1952) (Coimbatore, Tamil Nadu)	22.88		69.16		7.46	0.06	0.10
Barberry (1944) (Katrain, Himachal Pradesh)	19.00		75.60		2.90	0.128	...
Plectranthus (Oct. 1940, Katrain, Himachal Pradesh)	15.00	38.40		40.0	3.30	0.31	...
Plectranthus (average of 8 samples Oct. 1948 Katrain, Himachal Pradesh)	14.87	35.35		41.21	2.15	...	0.15
Soapnut (May 1939 crop, Nagrota, Himachal Pradesh)	20.95	35.40		41.80	5.39	0·30	...

(Table 14.1 contd.)

escription of honey	Moisture %	Glucose %		Levulose %	Sucrose %	Ash %	Acidity as formic acid
Soapnut (May 1945 crop, Nagrota, Himachal Pradesh)	17.0			78.1	4.94	0.14	0.18
Mustard (Feb. 1943 crop, Punjab Lyallpur, Pakistan	20.95	33.9		38.7	nil	0.18	...
Dalbergta (April 1943 crop, Lyallpur, Punjab, Pakistan)	18,75	34.6		39.1	1.04	0.18	...
Clover (May 1943 crop, Lylipur, Punjab, Pakistan)	20.0	32.a		37.3	4·75	0.09	...
U.S.A. (average of 92 samples)	17.7	34.02		40.50	1.9	0.18	...
California (average of 106 samples)	16.5.	34.54		40.41	2.53	0.21	...
English	18.48		74.43		1.52	0.15	...
Belgaum	22.94	27.15		39.77	3.22	0.83	0.25
Maximum permissible under U.S.A. Pure Food Law	25.00				800	0.25	...
Tentative standards suggested for India by the Central Agril. Marketing Directorate	22.00				500 0·75	0-5	...
Honeydew Honey (Madras)	15.58	66.53			6.51	1.2	...

HONEY AS FOOD

It is estimated that 200 g of honey is as nourishing as 1.135 kg of milk or 1.658 kg of cream cheese, or 340 g of meat, or 425 g of boneless codfish or 8 oranges or 10 eggs.

It is a rich energy-giving food and with milk forms a perfect food. This fact was given a practical test by Dr Haydak of the University of Minnesota. He lived on honey and milk with an occasional glass of orange juice for 12 weeks doing normal work without any ill effects.

It is highly appreciated as food for infants, the aged and invalids both in this country and abroad. It has been shown that it helps to build haemoglobin of the blood. As it provides energy in a readily available form, honey is largely taken by athletes after hard exercise or long races to regain lost energy.

The tired or overworked can recover by drinking 29 g (i oz) of honey in a glass of water, warm in winter, cold in summer. In an average Indian home, honey may be used in tea, coffee, milk or buttermilk in place of sugar. The drink to which honey is added acquires an attractive and delicate flavour. Honey and curds, and honey and butter on a chapati, toast or biscuit has a delicious taste.

A honey-lemon *sherbet* can be prepared by adding 2g g (i oz) of honey and a piece of lemon in a tumbler of iced water in summer or warm water in winter. Honey-lemon tea is made by adding two teaspoonfuls of honey in a cup of hot tea, flavoured with lemon instead of milk. Iced tea can be used in summer in place of hot tea.

Honey when used in baking bread, cakes and biscuits improves their flavour and enhances their keeping quality by retarding their drying up because it is hygroscopic and absorbs and retains moisture.

Thus it enables a housewife to do her baking well in advance of her parties. It can be used on fruits, cereals, in salad dressings, canning and preserving and for flavouring meats and vegetables.

Honey as Medicine

Just as lactose is used as the '*carrier*' of almost all homoeopathic medicines, similarly honey is put to the same use in the Ayurvedic and Unani systems of mtdicine. It is a measure of the housewife's belief in its efficacy that countless home remedies and nostrums have honey in them. Some of the tested uses of honey are as: a laxative, a blood purifier, a preventive against cold, coughs and fever and a curative for sores, eyes, for ulcers of the tongue, sore throat and burns.

Its regular use is recommended in severe cases of malnutrition with 'heart attack, impaired digestion and stomach and intestinal ulcers.

Under certain circumstances it has proved useful to diabetic and allergic patients. Honey is potentially alkaline in the same way as fruits and does not produce acidosis or flatulence.

The germs of typhoid fever, dysentery, etc. die when introduced into honey. In fact, it is considered to be about the safest food from the sanitary point of view in marked contrast to milk which is an 'ideal' medium for the propagation of disease germs.

At Religious Ceremonies

Honey has an honoured place in various religions of the world. It is necessary at *pujas* by Hindus and is also given as the first feed to the new-born for its purification. Jews use it in preparing special cakes during certain religious festivals. Catholics prepare mead from honey 'foi a similar purpose. The *Quran* has a special chapter on honey and its uses.

ODD USES

In India which does not produce enough honey even for religious and medicinal purposes the varied uses to which honey is put in the West seem a little odd. Large quantities of honey go into the making of alcoholic drinks, mead and wine; skin and beauty lotions; for stimulating milk yield of dairy cows; for increasing the stamina of race horses; for fattening steers, poultry and fish; for curing smoking-pipe bowls and as an ingredient of cigarette and chewing tobacco to improve its flavour and texture and keep it moist.

Chewing-gum owes its sweet taste to honey. It is also good for curing ham. It has been used in the shock absorbers of the cars and as the centre of golf balls. In the laboratory, honey has been found to stimulate plant growth and helps the rooting of cuttings. It prevents eggs put in cold storage from becoming gummy. Honey also plays an important part in the preparation of bacterial cultures and in the inoculation of seeds of clovers, etc. and is used with good results in poison baits for fruit flies, etc.

Storage Suggestions

Honey darkens in colour, granulates and ferments in storage. To check discolouration it should be placed in a cool (21.1 °C) dry place because heat tends to darken it due to chemical reaction between the break-down products of the unstable levulose, and the amino-acids of the proteins and tannates with iron salts.

Besides, acidic honey acts on the metallic covers of the containers and produces dark substances. The glucose in honey crystallises at low temperatures and initially gives a cloudy appearance to the fluid which eventually solidifies into one mass.

Crystallisation is accelerated by the presence of minute air bubbles, colloids, seed crystals, pollen and dust particles. If honey is heated at 7i.1°C for 30 minutes, the air bubbles disappear and the crystals are dissolved. Then fine straining will remove large particles.

Heated honey does not normally crystallise, but in long storage and under severe cold conditions rather big crystals are formed at the bottom of the container and the rest of the honey remains fluid.

Hence storage in a cool and dry place is suggested. Certain sugar-tolerant yeasts are present in the air, hives, flowers and soil with which the bees come in contact and, therefore, honey gets contaminated with them. In ripe honey, these yeasts are not able to grow because of the high sugar concentration.

Unripe honey (with more than 20 per cent moisture), however, provides favourable mdium for such yeasts and their action on glucose and levulose results in the formation of alcohol, carbon dioxide and eventually acetic acid and water. Such fermentation results in acidity and honey becomes sour and has a foamy layer on top.

On granulation even ripe honey also is liable to ferment as glucose can have 9 per cent moisture only and the excess moisture yielded by it during crystallisation thins down the remaining levulose in which it becomes possible for the sugar-tolerant yeasts to grow.

To prevent fermentation, only ripe honey with less than 2o per cent moisture and heated to 71.1°C for 30 minutes should be bottled in airtight containers while still warm.

Purity Standards

There is no rough-and-ready method to test the purity of honey by a customer. The best thing to do is to obtain supplies from a good beekeeper or a reputable concern. The popular notions that honey is not eaten by dogs and that it does not burn readily have no scientific basis.

Much reliance can also not be placed on the pieces of combs dipped in honey at the bottom of the container, a device too often emplpyed by nomads to make thick sugar syrup pass for honey. However, honey combs *with capped cells* cannot be manufactured and should be trusted. Homogeneous granulation is another sign of purity.

About 4.5 litres of honey should weigh 6.350 kg or over. Liquid honey should be clean and free from cloudiness, foreign matter such as wax, propolis, parts of bees, or dirt (strained through a cloth with 86 meshes per inch at 54.4°C).

All blossom honeys are levo-rotatory* that is, they deflect a beam of polarised light to the left in the polarimeter. The presence of commercial invert sugar in honey can be detected by the resorcinol or' aniline chloride tests in a laboratory. The Indian Standards Institution's Standard on Honey may be consulted.

Refining Process

At the present stage when beekeeping in India cannot meet fully the demand for honey, recourse has to be taken to refine honey from the combs of *Apis ind ca, Apis dorsata* or *Apis florea* bees. Crude honey available in the bazar which contains such impurities as wax, pollen, parts of the bees, cocoons, dirt, etc. has also to be made more presentable.

Only wellcapped white combs should be taken, cut into pieces with a knife and placed in the wire gauze basket of the strainer which is placed in a warm room 32.2°C. The honey strains through the wire gauze, cheese cloth anu voil by sheer gravitation and collects at the bottom.

Pieces of comb should be stirred occasionally. Straining is a slow process (three to six hours) and should be done either in a bee-proof room or at night. The strained honey should be allowed to settle so

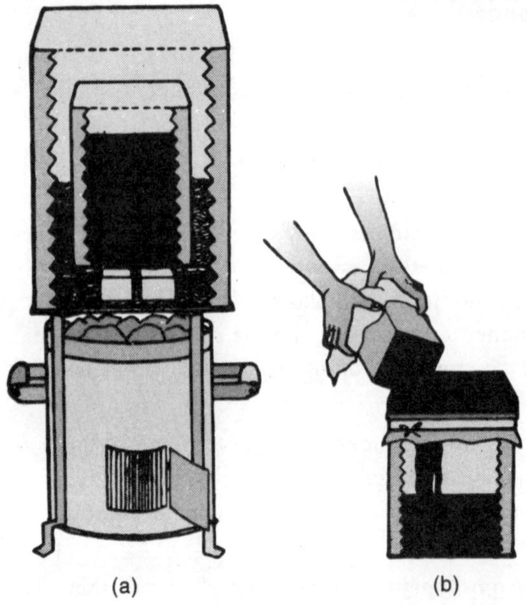

Figure 14.1: Refining crude honey; (a) heating honey in a water bath, (b) straining honey through wire gauze and double thickness of cheese cloth

that air bubbles which get entrapped while the honey falls to the bottom of the container may rise to the surface.

This scum should be removed with a knife before the honey is bottled. The left-over pieces of comb should be heated in the manner described below to extract the last drops of honey.

A simple outfit for heating honey can be improvised by cutting the tops of a one-gallon and a four-gallon hydrogenated oil empties. The smaller tin which contains the honey to be heated is placed in the bigger tin with water so that their bottoms do not touch.

The water is heated on a stove. Honey is stirred continuously and its temperature not allowed to rise above 4o.g°C. If no thermometer is available, heating should be stopped when the honey becomes thin and it is uncomfortably hot.

Overheating even in the water damages the aroma, flavour and colour of honey. Besides, beeswax in the honey melts at 6o°C to 62.8°C and clogs the strainer. The heated honey should he passed through the strainer, allowed to settle and bottled.

MARKETING METHODS

The beekeeper should try to develop a local market for his goods. A road-side stand on a well-travelled road near the apiary would sell a major share of its output. House-to-house peddling by the beekeeper himself during the slack season builds up personal contacts and increases sales.

Ripened, properly strained and bottled honey should be offered in tall narrow glass jars if it is dark and in short squat ones if it is light-coloured. One-and-half-pound jars should be packed and suitably labelled.

Five-pound lever lid tin containers are also very convenient and cut the cost per pound in addition to the advantage of safely carrying them over long distances. One-gallon and four-gallon tins with wide openings and lever lids may also be packed. It is urged that standard brand new containers should always be used and the label should indicate (a) contents, (b) net weight, (c) colour grade (when in opaque containers), (d) floral source (if possible), and (e) name and address of the producer or the packer, as the case may be.

Only liquid honey should be packed in glass containers, tin containers being preferred for granulated product. Indian beekeepers have a great opportunity of developing mail-order trade. Only well-sealed tin containers packed in wooden boxes should be sent by post or rail. One broken or leaking tin is liable to ruin one's reputation built over a long time.

Standard eight-gallon dairy cans suitably locked can also be used for transit by rail with an arrangement for return of empties. A lucrative local market in cut comb (chunk) honey can also be developed.

Co-operative marketing has proved a great success in Coorg and the Coorg Honey and Wax Producers' Society, Virajpet, should serve as a model for those who want to trv this method of marketing.

About 8,ooo producers from i3o villages have combined to put up a honey and beeswax processing plant at Virajpet and market over 16,344 kg of honey annually through out India in attractive, properly labelled containers. The Society supplies beehives, comb foundation etc. and lends the services of its bee instructors to members.

BEESWAX

It is an important byproduct of the beekeeping industry. It is produced from honey combs,old combs, cappings collected during the extraction of honey and odd bits of burr and brace combs.

The output of beeswax in a modern apiary is not much as honey combs are not crushed but are used again and again.

In India the main sources are the combs of wild bees, particularly of *Apis dorsata,* from which several lakh pounds are produced annually. Beeswax is a yellowish to grey brown solid and has an agreeable honey-like odour. It is somewhat brittle when cold and when broken presents a dull, granular, non-crystalline fracture.

It becomes plastic by the heat of hand. It is insoluble in water but completely soluble in ether, chloroform and in fixed and volatile oils. Its melting point varies from 63° to 65°C and is higher than all paraffin waxes.

Vegetable waxes (Carnauba and Chinese) have much higher melting points. Chemically beeswax consists of a mixture of cerotic acid and myrican (myricyle palmitate).

Properties of different varieties of Indian beeswax as worked out by Hooper and the Agricultural Chemist, Punjab (unpublished) are given in Table elsewhere in this chapter.

Varied Uses

Beeswax is used in the manufacture of more than 300 items. The largest consumer is the cosmetics industry closely followed by the Catholic Church which needs it for candles, and beekeepers for comb foundation.

Beeswax goes into the making of face creams (cold, cleansing, actors', camouflage, etc.), ointments, lotions, lipsticks, pomades, rouges. polishes for boots, furniture and floor, harness oils, lubricants, electric insulating apparatus, dentist's accessories, pharmaceutical preparations, modelling and plastic works, waterproofing compounds, protcetive coatings, different kinds of inks and waxes (ski, sealing, grafting, etc.), paints and varnishes, etc.

The total quantity used in any year depends upon its availability and cost. Carnauba and Chinese waxes, and resins offer continuous competition.

Rendering Process

Every apiary should have a solar wax extractor. An improvised one is shown in Figure elsewhere in this chapter. It consists of an empty tin whose one side has been replaced by a glass pane. In it a piece of wire gauze is held over supports.

Odd pieces of comb (old combs, burr and brace combs), wax-moth infested combs, dead brood combs from a transferred colony etc. are placed on the wire gauze. The extractor is kept in the sun and the heat melts the wax, which is strained to the bottom of the tin.

The extractor should be bee-proof and cleaned every few days. Such an extractor is a very handy tool, and saves considerable quantity of beeswax in addition to checking wax-moth infestation and robbing among bees.

Larger quantities of combs, however, should be boiled in sufficient water in a suitable container. When all the wax has melted, the mixture should be passed through a wire gauze strainer.

To recover the last quantities of beeswax boiling water should be added and the mass again stirred A jet of steam played upon this mass gives better results. The vessel containing the strained mixture of beeswax, water and finer impurities should be kept in a comparatively warm place to cool slowly.

The lighter impurities will rise to the surface and the heavier will settle to the bottom. Dirt, etc. will be found at the bottom of the container.

In due course, the cake of beeswax can be removed and the impurities below and above it scraped off with a sharp knife. This cake may be re-melted in water for further refining. Wax presses, using hot water or steam designed according to special requirements of beekeepers may be locally manufactured.

Direct heating darkens the colour of beeswax and should be resorted to sparingly. Light coloured beeswax is extracted from cappings. Yellow beeswax may be bleached by breaking it into small pieces and exposing them to the sun's rays for several days. Water should be sprayed over it during the hot period of the day so that it does not melt into one mass.

A POLLINATING AGENT

Reproduction in the vegetation world may be asexual, by the formation of buds, bulbs and tubers or sexual that is through seeds. Flowers are specialised organs responsible for the production of seeds. A flower is a composite structure.

Its outermost whorl is formed by the usually green sepals which protect its inner components in the early stages. Next come the petals, the brightly coloured parts specially of the ornamental flowers. They are followeo by stamens (containing male cells-pollen) and carpels (containing female cells ovules).

The nectaries, glands which secrete sweet fluids, are generally located at the base of the petals. Collectively the sepals are called calyx; the petals, corolla; the stamens, androecium; the carpels, gynaecium; several fused ovaries, pistil; and the flowers, inflorescence.

Various parts of a typical flower are illustrated in Figure elsewhere in this chapter and apple flowers in Figure elsewhere in this chapter.

So that an ovule may develop into a seed, it is necessary that the contents of pollen should unite with it. The deposition of pollen on the stigma (receptive part of the carpel) of the same species is termed pollination and the union of the pollen with the ovule is termed fertilization.

Flowers of some plants contain both the essential organs, namely, stamens and carpels and are called perfect, bisexual or hermaphrodite. If the flowers are unisexual and contain only stamens or carpels they are termed staminate or carpellate (pistillate) flowers respectively.

If both types of unisexual flowers are borne on the same plant, it is called monoecious and if on different plants dioecious.

When a flower uses its own pollen grains to pollinate its own stigma, it is called self-pollination. Cross-pollination, on the other hand, is the conveyance of pollen to the stigma of another flower on the same plant or different plant.

In fruit culture, however, self-pollination refers to the transfer of pollen from the anthers of a flower of one variety to the stigma of a flower of the same variety and cross-pollination to the transfer of pollen from a flower of one variety to a flower of a different variety of the same fruit species.

Self-pollination is met with in such plants as wheat. In many species it is, however, avoided in various ways so that crossfertilization is the rule n the plant kingdom Most commonly the stamens and carpels ripen at different times when present in bisexual flowers or are present in unisexual flowers on monoecious or dioecious plants.

When pollen from a flower may be physiologically incapable of effecting self-pollination it is called self-unfruitful (self-sterile or self-

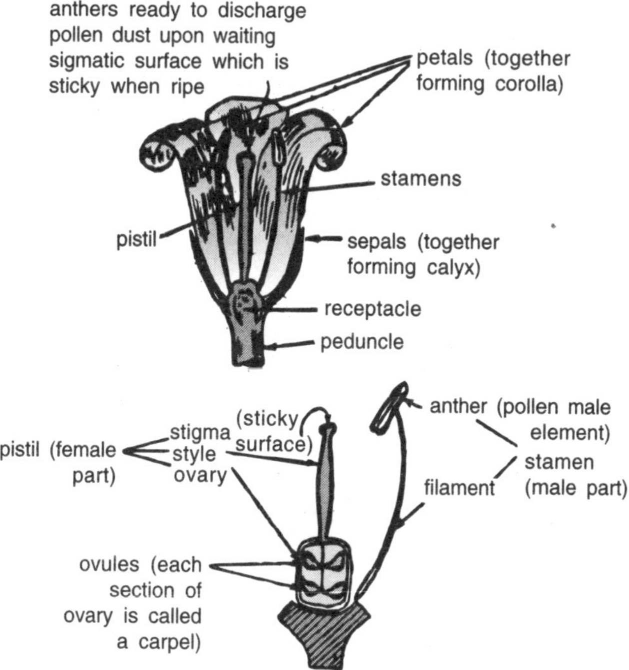

Figure 15.1: Parts of a typical flower (Diagrammatic).

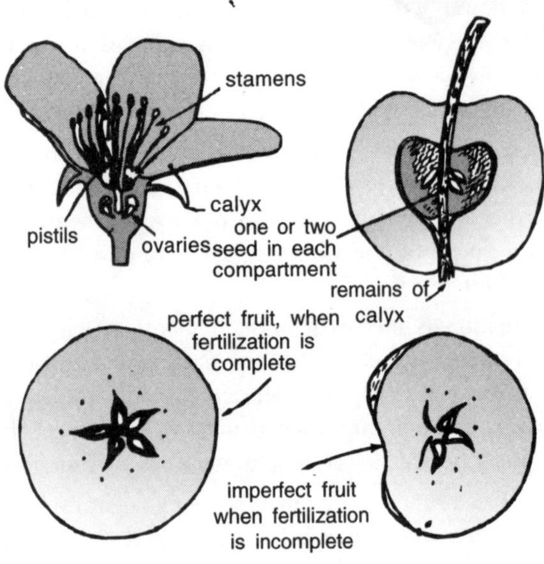

Figure 15.2: Parts of an apple flower and fruit.

incompatible). The self-fertile or self-compatible pollen is also called self-fruitful.

A pollen-yielding plant (pollinizer) that can produce a commercial crop of another variety is termed cross-fruitful, cross-compatible or cross-fertile and if it is unable to do so, it is called cross-unfruitful, inter-sterile or cross-incompatible. Cross-pollinated flowers may either be wind pollinated (anemophilous), insect pollinated (entomophilous), animal pollinated, water pollinated or they may he pollinated by gravity.

The first two forms are more common. Anemophilous flowers which produce an abundance of pollen to allow for the enormous wastage, are relatively simple, inconspicuous, dull in colour and their pollen is readily liberated. Maize is a common example. On the other hand, entomophilous flowers are brightly coloured, showy, large, odoriferous and produce nectar.

Generally, pollen grains liberated by them are sticky and cannot he carried away by wind. Insects visit such flowers for food-sweet nectar and proteinaceous pollen. Nature made them showy and gave them characteristic odours to enable them to attract pollinating agents.

They are so constructed that while insects are collecting nectar, pollen grains get entangled in the numerous plumose hair on their bodies or the flowers bring into play a certain phenomena for the liberation of pollen on to their bodies or on the stigma.

The insects, during their visits to other blossoms, drop pollen grains on their stigmas and thus help cross-fertilization. Some insects-solitary and social bees, take the pollen home to serve as proteinaceous (likemeat) food for their young.

It has been shown that the bodies of pollinating insects have been evolved for the special purpose of visiting certain flowers and the flowers are correlated with the shape and habits of insects that visit them, their beautiful colours and pleasant odours serving as attractions.

Well over a thousand blossom-visiting species of insects are known. Though most of these go to blossoms for nectar and pollen, quite a number are there either to suck the juices of the plant, eat its tissue, lay eggs in the blossoms or prey upon foraging insects.

The former group is really important from the pollinating point of view. The latter's contribution is not big. To this class belong such insects as earwigs, grasshoppers, mantids, bugs, aphids, aphid-lions, ant-lions, thrips, beetles and various kinds of wasps, etc. Butterflies, moths, two-winged flies and social and solitary bees belong to the former class.

Butterflies and moths have admirably adapted themselves to flowers. Biological literature is replete with the details of various arrangements made by nature in wild and ornamental blossoms to make them suitable for pollination by various species of butterflies and moths.

Unfortunately, moths and butterflies are not fond of fruit blossoms or flowers of commercial crops. Flower flies, flesh flies and bee flies are better in this respect. *lilastophaga* wasps are essential for the caprification (cross-fertilization) of figs.

Among the solitary bees, the mining bees (*Andrena* and *Halictus*), the carpenter bees and the leaf-cutting bees are good pollinators. *Andrena* and *Halictus* rival honey-bees in efficiency and steadfastness and are responsible for the pollination of blossoms in certain localities. Bumblebees, stingless bees and honey-bees are the three kinds of social bees available in India. Bumblebees live in the Himalayas at 1,525 m or more above sea level and stingless bees in south India.

Only preliminary work has been undertaken to study the pollinating habits of the three species of honey-bees in India, but it is surmised, that they are similar to their European relations in this respect. The latter have been studied in detail in many parts of the world.

POLLINATOR'S QUALIFICATIONS

Constancy

The insect should show 'flower fidelity', that is, it must restrict itself to the blossoms of plants of one species at a time so that pollen grains left by it during its visits on the stigmas of the flowers may fertilize the ovules. Insects which flit from flowers of one plant species to those of another will cause little fertilization. However, too much specialisation may limit the usefulness of the insect.

Thoroughness

The visitors should work their way into the flowers so that they conic into touch with the essential organs, namely, anthers of stamens and stigmas of carpels. Otherwise they will not be able to transfer pollen from one flower to the other.

If they take both nectar and pollen for food, they will be more effective as compared to those who visit the blossoms for nectar only. The contact of the latter class of insects with pollen grains is accidental and no sure results can be expected.

Working Hours

Those visitors which start their work early in the day and continue late in the evening naturally put in more work quantitatively. Further, those visitors which work for comparatively long periods during inclement weather such as cloudy and cold days will be beneficial to those crops which put forth blossoms under such conditions.

Total Population

It would be highly desirable to have big population of pollinating insects at the blossoming time of a crop so that a maximum yield of the crop is jbtained and the number of insects available at the

Table 15.1: Characteristics of some important insect pollinator groups.

Insect Group	Charateristics			
	Constancy	*Throughness of Work*	*Working Hours*	*Population*
I. Two-winged flies				
(*i*) Flower flies	If they continue to obtain food, they work blossoms of one species and also restrict their activities small areas, otherwise haphazard work.	Flit about quickly; pollen distribution accidental to their visits for nectar; do not collect pollen.	Inactive at cold ternperatures, high wind velocity and dim light; they have no nest to go to, stay in the field and start work when conditions permit; working hours longer than those of solitary bees.	Distribution very much localised as population depends upon availability of breeding materials to such as polluted waters, insect and plant hosts, etc.
(*ii*) Flesh flies	Haphazard work,	do	do	Breed in decaying flesh and parasitise on animals: hence high population under unhygienic conditions. Maggots parasitic on various stages of other insects.

(Table 15.1 Contd.)

(Table 15.1 Contd.)

Insect Group	Charateristics			
	Constancy	Throughness of Work	Working Hours	Population
(*iii*) Bees flies	do	do	do	Maggots parasitic on various stages of other insects.
II. Solitary wasps				
(*i*) *Blastophaga*	Breed in caprifigs but female wasps visit other kinds of figs also. Visit figs only and are highly specific.	They are the only insects which can pollinate figs.	Not known	They can be bred artificially in laboratories and the population can be controlled.
III. Solitary bees				
(*i*) Mining bees	Rival the honey-bees in constancy.	Rival the honey-bees efficiency-	Working hours short, they are warm weather visitors, do not stir out on cold, cloudy and windy gettdays	Nests found in waste lands but with the spread of agriculture and clean cultivation, their population is inq reduced in various localities; cannot be artificially bred.
(*ti*) Carpenter bees	Flower fidelity lower	Flit about quickly;	do	Build holes in timber

(Table 15.1 Contd.)

(Table 15.1 Contd.)

Insect Group	*Charateristics*			
	Constancy	*Throughness of Work*	*Working Hours*	*Population*
	than social bees and mining bees.	collect pollen in scopa; considered good cross-pollinators.		to serve as nests, hence considered pests; population very variable, cannot be bred artificially.
(*iii*) Leaf-cutting bees	Flower fidelity lower than social bees and mining bees.	Flit about quickly; collect pollen in scopa; considered good cross-pollinators.	Working hours short, they are warm weather visitors, do not stir out on cold, cloudy and windy days.	Build cells in soil or specially formed mud cells in various types of cavities, population very variable and cannot be bred artificially; a nuisance in residences.
IV. Social bees				
(*i*) *Bumblebees*	One out of three pollen loads are mixed in their case as compared to 3% mixed loads in honeybees *(A. mellifera)*	Quick workers and their haphazard work is an advantage in cross-pollination; some times nectar-robbers cut holes, do not come into contact with anthers; such visits	Work longer hours and under severer climatic conditions.	Distribution in India restricted to higher hills; population in spring restricted to queens only, hence their utility as pollinators of blossoms of deciduous fruit trees

(Table 15.1 Contd.)

(Table 15.1 Contd.)

Insect Group	*Charateristics*			
	Constancy	*Throughness of Work*	*Working Hours*	*Population*
		are useless from the point of view of pollination.		limited: cannot be bred artificially.
(*ii*) *Stingless bees*	Little information available about tneir pollination qualities but habits, in general, assumed to be comparable to honey-bees.			Not domesticated in India; population in nature variable and cannot be depended upon.
(*iii*) *True hones-bees* (a) *Apis dorsata*	Assumed to be as constant as the European bees.	Assumed to be as thorough as the Furopearl bees.	These bees are known to have longer working flours than the *Apis indica* bees.	Population variable; cannot be domesticated;
(b) Aj;is florva	do	do	During winter have shorter working hours than *Apis dorsata* and *Apis Indira.*	Ditto
(c) Apis indica	do	do	They start work each in the morning and slap work late at dusk if light temperature and wind conditions	Population vari: hle in various localities but can be increased at will by man with modern beekeeping

(Table 15.1 Contd.)

Table 15.1 Contd.)

Insect Group	*Charateristics*			
	Constancy	*Throughness of Work*	*Working Hours*	*Population*
			are favourable. Do not work during the: noon hours in summer.	methods.
(d) *Apis incllifera*	Very faithf.il to a crop and an area; get Iota-lined to small areas and continue to work on the sar.e plant and field throughout life as long as the blossoms continue.	Thorough workers and pollinators.	Have long working hours (depending up-on the crop they are working on at the time).	This spec:ies has been successfully introduced in India.

time does not act as a limiting factor. If the pollinators and their placement is under the control of man, it would be an added advantage.

'Though certain species of insects have adapted to pollination of certain crops on a commercial scale, namely, *Blastophaga spp. to* figs or flesh *flies-Phorima* and *Lucilia* to onions in breeding cages, most insects are general pollinators.

Table elsewhere in this chapter lists the qualities of these insects in the light of the above observations. It should be clear that honey-bees are the most constant and faithful friends of flowers rivalled by mining bees and followed by bumblebees and flower flies. 'They are thorough workers though bumblebees and flies may bring about more cross-pollination with their haphazard methods. Honey-bees are surpassed by bumlebees and flies in hours of work but are better than solitary bees in the daily amount of work in all kinds of weather.

The populations of insects vary from locality to locality but honey-bees number more than others. Moreover, hive bees (*Apis indica* or *Apis mellifera*) can be moved into any desired area and their population adjusted to the needs of a particular crop.

COMMERCIAL CROPS

The following is the list of major fruits, vegetables, oilseeds and fodder crops that require cross-pollination and are greatly benefitted by insect visits.

Fruits

Almond, apple, apricot, avocado, black and raspberries, blue and huckleberries, cherry, citrus, cocoanut, cranberry, figs, gooseberry, grapes, mango, peach, and nectrines, pear, persimmon, plum and prune, strawberry, etc.

Vegetables

Asparagus, broccoli, brussel's sprout, cabbage, cauliflower, carrots, collards, coriander, cucumber, fennel, kale, kohl rabi, lotus, melon, onion, pepper, pumpkin, radish, rape, rutabaga, squash, turnip, watermelon, etc.

Oilseeds

Mustard, rape, *raya* (*Brassica juncea*) *toria* (*Brassica napus* var. *toria*), sesamum, etc.

Fodders

Clovers (alsike, crimson, Egyptian,ladino, Persian, red, strawberry, white), lucerne, *raya,* sunflower, trefoil, vetch, etc.

Special pollination needs of temperate-zone fruits require special treatment. Though all these plants require cross-pollination for the proper formation (size and shape), development of colour and proper yield, there are some fruits like apples, sweet cherries, pears and some varieties of peaches, plums and prunes, strawberries and grapes which are self-unfruitful. In their case cross-pollination (in the horticultural sense) is required with cross-fruitful varieties.

Almond

All common varieties, namely, Texas, Drake, I.X.L., Ne Plus Ultra, Non-Pareil, etc., are self-unfruitful and provision of cross-fruitful varieties is essential.

Apple

Of the common varieties grown in India, Cox's Orange Pippen, Beauty of Bath, Fameuse, Gravenstein, McIntosh, Yellow Bellflower, R.I. Greening, Wine-sap, Northern Spy and Delicious varieties are self-unfruitful and Jonathan, Yellow Newtown, Black Ben Davis, Rome Beauty, Brameleys' seedling and Worcester's Pearman are very slightly self-fruitful and may be considered as practically self-unfruitful. Cross-fruitful varieties will be necessary in the plantings of the above varieties of apple.

Sweet Cherries

Napolean, Black Tartarian, Roundel, Elton, Bing, Early Richmond, Morello and Black Biggarean are commonly grown in India and are self-unfruitful and it is necessary to grow cross-fruitful varieties in their blocks.

Peaches

Only J. H. Hale, Red bird cling, Salway and St. John varieties grown in India are self-unfruitful and require cross-fruitful varieties.

Pears

Most of the pear varieties are self-unfruitful and require to be intermingled with other varieties. Of the common pears grown in India, William Bartlet, Clapps Favourite, Beaurre d' Anjou,

Conference, Beaurre Bose, Beaurre Hardy, Winter Nelis, Flemish Beauty and Seckel are self-unfruitful.

Information regarding other common varieties, namely, Doycnne Dette, Doyenne Decomice, Burnum, Jeiasui, Napolean, Josephine, Eastern Beaurre, Ded Melinis, Windsor and Duchess is not available. However, it may be stated that all varieties of the European pear (*Pyrus communis*) and those of hybrid origin such as Keiffer (*P. communis x P. serotina*) have been found to be self-unfruitful. Moreover, varieties which are closely related are cross-incompatible.

Strawberries

The perfect (hermaphrodite) flowered varieties are self-fruitful but often they produce only pistillate flowers or environmental conditions reduce the viability of their pollen. Other varieties are imperfect (pistillate flowers only) and require pollinizing variety plants in their fields.

Grapes

There are hermaphrodite, pistillate and staminate as well as self-unfruitful varieties among grapes. Except the seedless varieties, which belong to the staminate group provision of staminate variety plants in every third row is recommended for adoption.

It has been noticed that plants grown from crosspollinated seeds generally 'have greater vigour, weight and height and produce flowers earlier than those that result from selfpollination.

HONEY-BEES IN ORCHARDS

As pointed out already, honey-bees in hives (*Apis indica* or *Apis mellifera*) are the only insects whose population can be increased in an area by bringing in colonies from another area at the blooming time of a particular fruit. vegetable, oilseed or *fodder crop.*

In localities where there are no large areas of wasteland around orchards and fields and where clean cultivation is practised with consequent low population of ,yvild pollinating insects, fruit growers and farmers will be well advised to bring in colonies of honey-bees.

As a general rule, a strong colony of *Apis mellifera* bees and two colonies of *Apis indica* bees to the acre will suffice. For crops like

Lucerne with difficult pollination problems, the number of colonies per acre should be twice the normal.

Colonies should be brought into the orchard or fields, just before the flowers are to open, otherwise a major portion of the field force of the bee colonies may get localized to other crops or other areas. It is better to spread the colonies around the orchard or fields in groups of two or three instead of locating several dozens at one place.

In this case such of the foraging bees of strong colonies as are localized to nearby areas will take advantage of short spells of bright weather during inclement weather and will visit the blossoms. The spraying of trees or crops with inorganic or modern synthetic pesticides during the blooming period should be avoided.

If, however, there is no other way to control harmful insetcs, application of insecticides etc. should be resorted to between 7 P.M. and 7 A.M. and restricted to materials which are comparatively safe for bees when used in proper strengths. Some of the newer materials which are relatively safe for bees are toxaphene and methoxychlor.

The renting of bee colonies by fruit growers and farmers from beekeepers at the blossoming time of crops is a common practice in Western countries particuarly in the U.S.A. where rentals go as high as $ 5.00 to S 10.00 (Rs 25 to 5o) per colony per crop.

At the present stage of development of beekeeping in India renting of bee colonies in most localities may not be possible and horticulturists and farmers themselves will have to undertake beekeeping, not so much for honey as for pollination.

In most localities which are deficient in insect populations, the placing of bee colonies in orchards, fields of vegetables, oilseeds and fodders grown for seed has increased the yields. An increase of io to 25 per cent is a very common experience. Money spent on renting bees or establishing a modern apiary will be fully repaid in the form of bigger and better crops.

THE LIFE HISTORY OF HONEY BEE

EXTERNAL MORPHOLOGY

Worker Bee

Worker bee is the smallest member of colony and makes up the largest number of colony individuals. It is black or brownish in colour with body densely covered with hairs.

Like all other insects, the body of worker bee is divisible into three regions : *head*, *thorax* and *abdomen*.

Head

It is a wide triangular structure with the apex pointed below. It bears dorso-laterally a pair of large *compound eyes* and three *ocelli* on the middle of its top. A pair of short and 13-jointed *antennae* (12-jointed in male) are borne on the middle of face and probably serve as tactile and gustatory organs. From the bottom of head project the specialized mouthparts.

Mouthparts

Mouthparts of honey bee are of *chewing* and *lapping type*, adapted for sucking nectar from flowers and moulding the wax. A broad and short *labrum* lies below clypeus and a fleshy *epipharynx* projects beneath it. The spoonshaped and smooth-edged *mandibles* are situated below and one on either side of labrum.

They work sideways and are used for moulding wax and manipulating pollen. In each *first maxilla*, lacinia is absent, maxillary palp is reduced and galea forms an elongated blade. Glossae of *second maxillae* or *labium* form a tongue-like process or *ligula* with a spoon-like depression at its tip, called *labellum* or *honey spoon*.

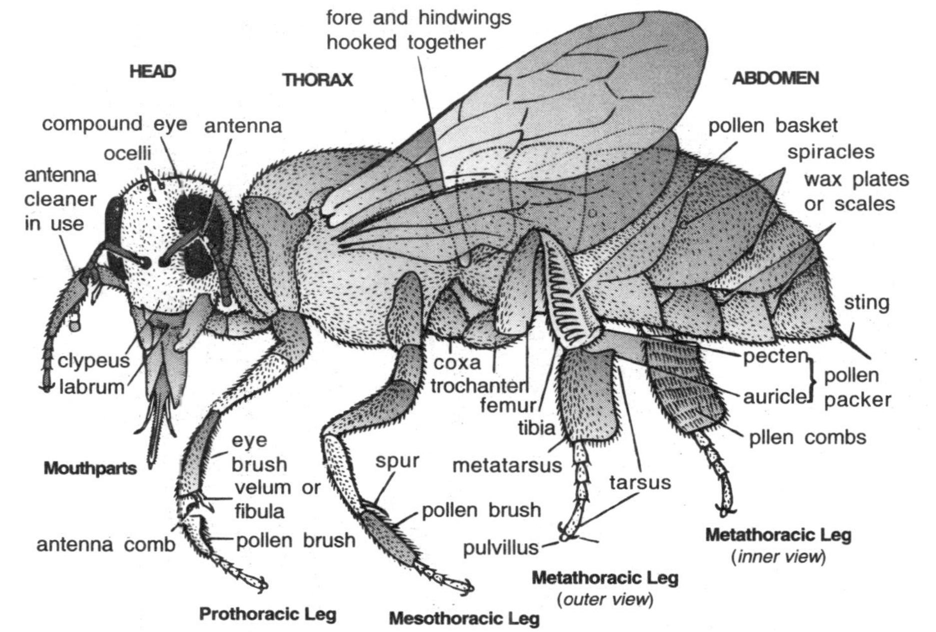

Figure 16.1: Worker honey bee in a lateral view.

It has a mid-ventral groove (food channel) and constitutes a tube or proboscis for sucking up the nectar. *Labial palps* are well developed and elongated. Paraglossae are very much reduced.

Feeding

When the bee sucks nectar, it extends its ligula or tongue into the nectary of flower. The nectar rises up through its ventral groove or food channel by capillary action. Moreover, the shortening of ligula and the sucking action of pharynx helps in sucking up the necthr.

Thorax

Thorax is divided into the usual 3 segments : an anterior *prothorax*, a middle *mesothorax* and a posterior *metathorax*. Each of these segments bears a pair of *legs* and a pair of *wings* is borne by each of the mesothorax as well as metathorax.

Legs

Three pairs of legs are densely covered with hair and are variously adapted. Because of their complexity and differences, each leg will be considered separately.

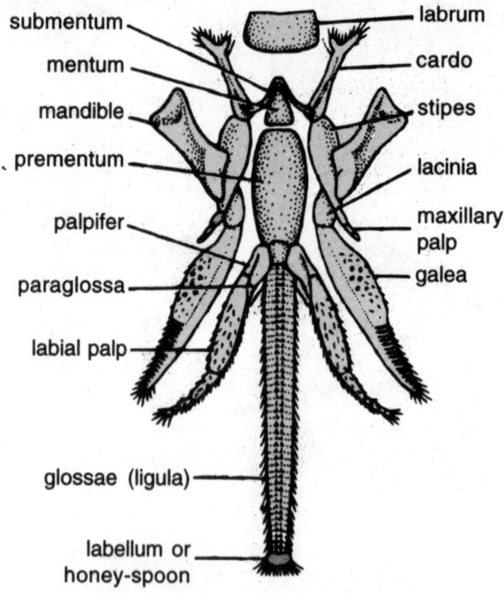

Figure 16.2: Honey bee. Mouthparts.

(*i*) *Prothoracic legs.* The segments of a prothoracic or foreleg are:

(1) an oblong *coxa*;

(2) a-short *traohanter*;

(3) a long *femur* provided with pollen-carrying hairs;

(4) *a tibia* with a fringe of stiff hairs, or *eye brush*, along its medial edge for cleaning the compound eye, and a movable spine-like *velum* and *a pollen brush* on opposite margin at the distal end, and

(5) a 5-segmented *tarsus* terminating in a pad-like *pulvillus*, which secretes a sticky substance for adherence, and a pair of *claws*. Its proximal segment or *metatarsus* bears a semicircular notch, called *antennal comb*. This comb, along with tibial velum, forms the *antenna cleaner* that serves to clean the antenna drawn in between them.

(*ii*) *Mesothoracic legs.* A mesothoracic or mid-leg has all the segments as seen in the foreleg. It has a spike-like *pollen spur* at the distal end of tibia and *a pollen brush* on the inner surface of metatarsus.

Spurs of both the mid-legs are used to remove pollen from *pollen baskets* of hindlegs, and to dislodge wax from wax pockets on the ventral surface of abdomen.

(*iii*) *Metathoracic legs.* Segments of a metahoracic or hind-leg too -are the same. The expanded tibia bears *a pollen basket* on its outer concave surface which is partially covered by rows of long curved bristles along both its margins.

Lower end of tibia bears a row of stout bristles forming the *pecten.* Proximal end of metatarsus bears a smooth, concave, lip-like plate, the *auricle.* Pecten and auricle together form *a pollen packer* to convey and pack pollen into the pollen basket.

Inner surface of metatarsus bears many transverse rows of stiff bristles, forming the *pollen combs.* These brush off pollen from the body parts and handle wax.

(*b*) *Wings. Two* pairs of wings are double-layered, small, narrow, membranous and tranparent. They have a much modified and reduced venation. Front margin of each hindwing bears d row of minute hooks, called *hamuli,* that fasten to the grooves along rear margin of forewing forming a single flight blade.

Wings may vibrate over 400 times per second during flight. Workers may travel as far as 15 km to gather nectar and pollen.

Abdomen

It consists of 6 visible segments and bears the *wax glands* and the *sting.*

Wax glands

The glandular area secreting wax lies on the ventral surface of the last 4 visible segments of abdomen. Wax is secreted through minute pores in the form *of* flat scales. It is masticated by the mandibles before its use for building the "cells" of the honeycomb.

Sting

Sting is the modified ovipositor, of the insect and is used for injecting poison for protection. It is composed of two straight grooved *stylets* or *lancets.*

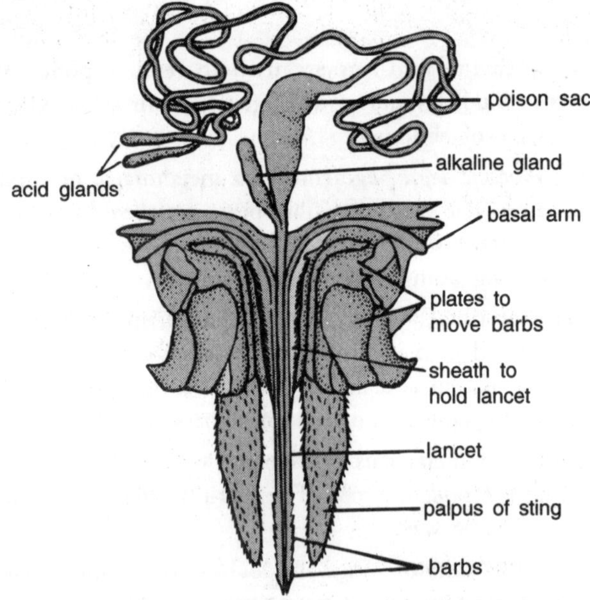

Figure 16.3: Honey bee. Sting.

Their distal free ends are provided with many anteriorly-pointed spines or *barbs* which prevent the removal of sting. The muscles associated with the sting help in the operation of lancets. A set of 3 chitinous plates on either side act as levers to move the barbs.

A pair of filiform *poison glands* secrete the acidic material that is stored in a sac-like storage *poison sac* located at the base of the sting. Associated with it is an elongated *alkaline gland* that secretes an alkaline material.

The two materials mix to form the poison or *bee venom* that flows down the sting into the wound *of* the victim. After stinging, the worker bee leaves the sting apparatus and dies.

Sting of queen bee is longer but less barbed and can be withdrawn without injury to her own body. Males do not have a sting because they have a copulatory apparatus instead of an ovipositor.

Queen

Queen is the only fertile female in a beehive, having immensely developed ovaries. She is elongated, 15-20 mm long and is easily distinguished by her long tapering abdomen, short legs and wings.

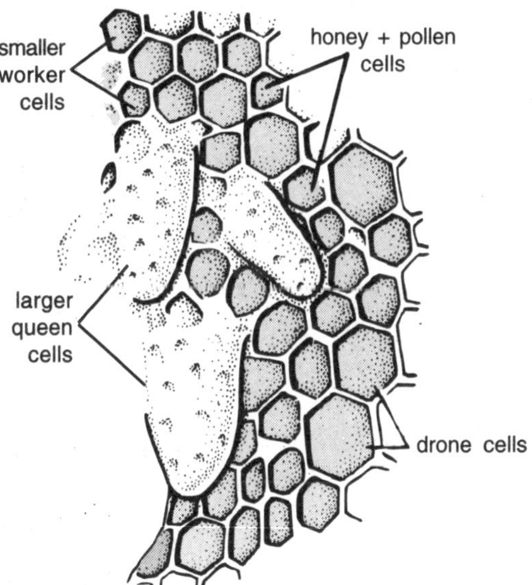

Figure 16.4: A portion of the honeycomb showing various types of cells.

She has pointed mandibles and shorter mouthparts. She can sting repeatedly as there are no barbs on her sting.

She is unable to produce wax and honey or gather pollen or nectar. She is a specialized and degenerate individual with a small brain and without salivary glands.

The queen arises from a fertilized egg and larva especially fed on *royal jelly.* She alone lays eggs and is the mother of almost all the members of the hive. She lives for several successive years laying about 2,000 or more eggs a day and up to about 1,500,000 eggs during her lifetime.

Drones

Flying idly near the hive in the sunshine can be seen the male bees or drones. There are usually 100 drones in a typical colony, depending upon the season of the year. They are intermediate in size 15-17 mm long, but considerably stouter and broader.

They possess very large eyes, small pointed mandibles and lack' wax- producing glands, pollen-collecting apparatus and a sting. Drones do not work and may be seen begging for honey from workers.

If not fed by workers, they will die. They live for about 5 weeks only. They develop parthenogenetically from unfertilized eggs laid by the queen and exist only to mate with the queen of their own or some other colony.

BEEHIVE OR HONEYCOMB

The honeycomb or nest is commonly built *hanging d*own vertically from a rock, building or branch of a tree. It consists of two layers of hexagonal chambers of cells made by the beeswax secreted from the abdominal glands of worker bees.

Their walls are extremely thin and fragile. *Storage cells,* containing honey and pollen, are usually built near the top and margins of the comb. *Broad cells,* generally occupying the lower and central positions, contain the young stages. In *A. dorsata,* brood cells are similar in shape and size but in other species they may be of three types.

Worker cells, in which workers are reared, are small like honey cells. *Drone cells* are slightly larger, while *queen cells* are enormous, irregular, cylindrical or vase-shaped structures hanging down from the bottom. Queen cells cannot be used again like other cells.

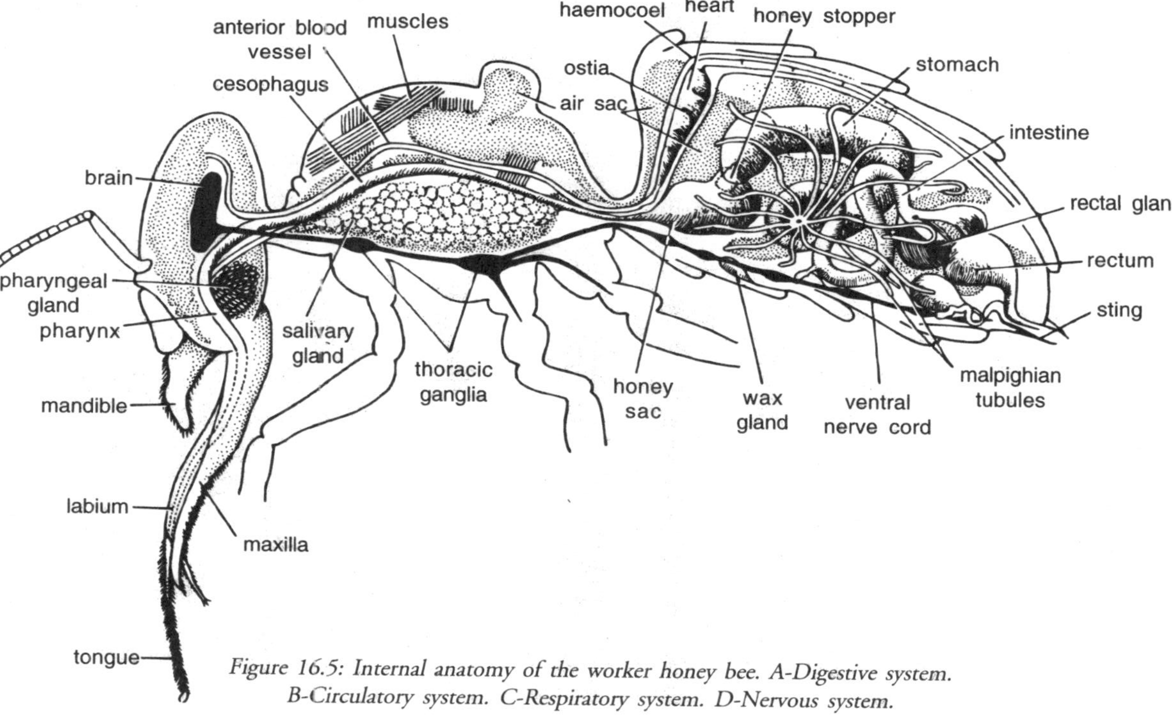

Figure 16.5: Internal anatomy of the worker honey bee. A-Digestive system. B-Circulatory system. C-Respiratory system. D-Nervous system.

Internal Anatomy

Body cavity

Body cavity is a haemocoeL True coelom is greatly reduced.

Digestive system

Mouth parts of honey bee are fitted for both chewing and sucking pollen and fluids which *are* sucked through *mouth* into a small *pharynx.*

An elongated thin *oesophagus* joins a globular *crop* or *honey sac* in the anterior part of abdomen, where nectar of flowers is chemically changed into honey.

Honey sac emptities into a large cylindrical *stomach,* followed by a narrow *intestine* and an expanded *rectum,* which opens at the *anus.*

Circulatory system

A long, tubular, muscular and 5-chambered *heart* lies mid-dorsally in *a pericardial sinus,* receiving blood through 5 pairs *of ostia,* with valves to prevent backflow.

Blood is pumped into head region through an anterior *aorta,* and it diffuses through haemocoel back into pericardial sinus. Blood is colourless, with *white blood corpuscles* in its plasma.

Respiratory system

7 pairs of very small lateral *spiracles* (2 thoracic and 5 abdominal) admit air into a branched system of *tracheae* which convey 02 to all body parts. Certain tracheae enlarge to become *air sacs* which are larger than those of grasshopper.

Excrgtory system

Numerous hollow, glandular and thread-like *Malpighian tubules* excrete wastes from haemocoel into the anterior end of intestine, much in the same manner as in grasshopper.

Nervous system

It is similar but *brain* is proportionately larger than that of grasshopper. *Ventral* nerve cord is double containing *2 thoracic* and *5 abdominal ganglia.*

Sensory system

Sense organs are more highly developed than in grasshopper. The *antennae* bear end organs of smell (*olfactory*), hearing (*auditory*) and touch (*tactile*). Bristle-like taste setae (*gustatory*) are located near mouth and on the so-called "tongue". There are two large *compound eyes* (*visual*) and *3 ocelli* on top of head.

Reproductive system

The sterile worker honey bee contains only vestigial reproductive organs. The *female reproductive system* of queen bee includes a pair of large *ovaries* almost filling the long abdomen, a pair of *oviducts* that unite to form the *vagina*, and a large *spermatheca* for storing spermatozoa and arising from the dorsal wall of vagina.

The *sting* is a modified *ovipositor* formed by the external genitalia. The *male reproductive system* of male or drone consists of one pair each of *testes, vasa deferentia, seminal vesicles* and *accessory glands*, and an *ejaculatory duct* that leads to the *copulatory apparatus.*

During *spermatogenesis*, there is no reduction division or *meiosis* because drones develop parthenogenetically from unfertilized eggs so that their cells are haploid containing 16 chromosomes.

Whereas in *oogenesis*, meiosis occurs because the cells of female are diploid containing 32 chromosomes.

Habit and Habitat

Honey bees are highly organised social insects reported from all over the world. Although they are active throughout the year but in winter season they do little work and do not rear the brood. In spring seasons i.e., at the time of flowering they prepare a strong colony with honey rich combs.

They exhibit polymorphism and good division of labour. The bee hives with thousands of individuals are observed hanging down from the branches of the trees and ceilings of houses.

The workers communicate informations for the location of the food sources through the 'Waggle Dance', a phenomenon called as 'Language of the bees', by the eminent biologist Karl Von Frish.

He has mentioned that the rate of dance is directly proportional to the distance of the food.

SPECIES OF HONEY BEES

Four species of honey bees are reported.

Apis dorsata F. (Rock bee)

This the largest bee, about 20 mm. in length, so named as GIANT HONEY BEE. SARANG and BOMBARA are other names of this bee which yields maximum amount of honey in comparison to other species. A single comb may yield 60 pounds of honey which is the maximum amount for a comb.

The workers are very smart and active which may pollinate 12,000 flowers daily. But due to its ferocious and irritable nature, specific hive and migratory habit it is very difficult rather practically impossible to domesticate them for the bee keeping industry.

Apis indica F. (Indian bee)

Commonly found in forest and plain regions of India. This is slightly smaller than A. *dorsata.* They prefer to live in dark places and construct several parallel combs about one foot across the protected places like cavities of tree trunks, mud walls, earthen pots, thick bushes, wells and. walls of the buildings. This species is very gentle in nature, so can be domesticated easily. The production of honey is much less i.e., 6 to 7 pound per comb.

Apis florea F. (Little bee)

This is smaller than A. *indica* and yields very small amount of honey. The bees are not of gregarious nature and form a single

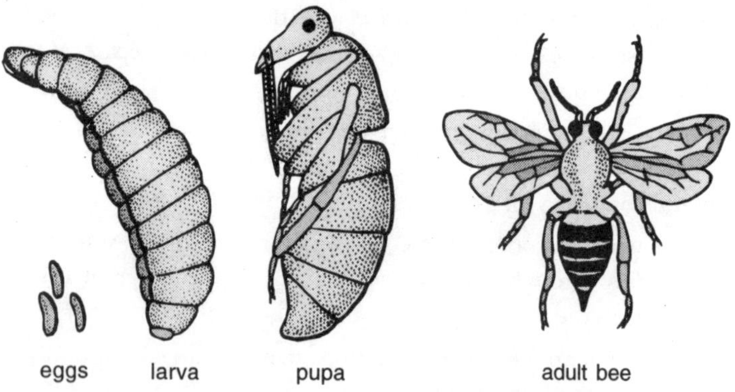

Figure 16.6: Life history of Apis indica.

comb. Due to its docile nature and rare stinging behaviour the combs can be removed easily for the honey extraction.

Apis mellifera F. (European bee)

Although this bee produces less honey yet it is found to be the best species from the commercial point of view. Due to their docile nature they can be domesticated easily and can be improved by breeding for several hundred years. Out of its several varieties, the Italian variety is reared every where in Europe and America in artificial hives for honey.

LIFE HISTORY

After mating the queen generally lays one egg in one brood cell. The eggs are pinkish coloured, elongated with cylindrical body generally attached to the bottom of the cell. Larvae emerge out from both the fertilized as well as unfertilized eggs.

Thus, the larvae from the unfertilized eggs form the drones while the workers are developed from the larvae of the fertilized eggs. Amongst the larvae of the workers one is fed on the royal jelly, a special. diet secreted by the young workers in the colony, and becomes the queen of the colon.

The royal jelly consists of digested honey and pollen, mixed with a glandular secretion into the mouth of the workers. After 5 days of feeding the cell is sealed and the larvae undergo pupation. It spins a thin silken cocoon and pupates completely.

Emergence of the young ones takes place after three weeks and they get busy in the indoor duties for about 2 to 3 weeks. Later on they are sent for the outdoor duties. All the bees pass through a complete metamorphosis with the various changes in the life-cycle taking place within the comb.

Swarming

The process of leaving off the colony by the queen termed as swarming. It happens towards the end of spring or early summer but the real cause of swarming is still not well known.

In summers when plenty of food is available and hive is overcrowded by the bees, the queen leaves the hive on a fine fore-noon with some old drones and workers and establishes a new

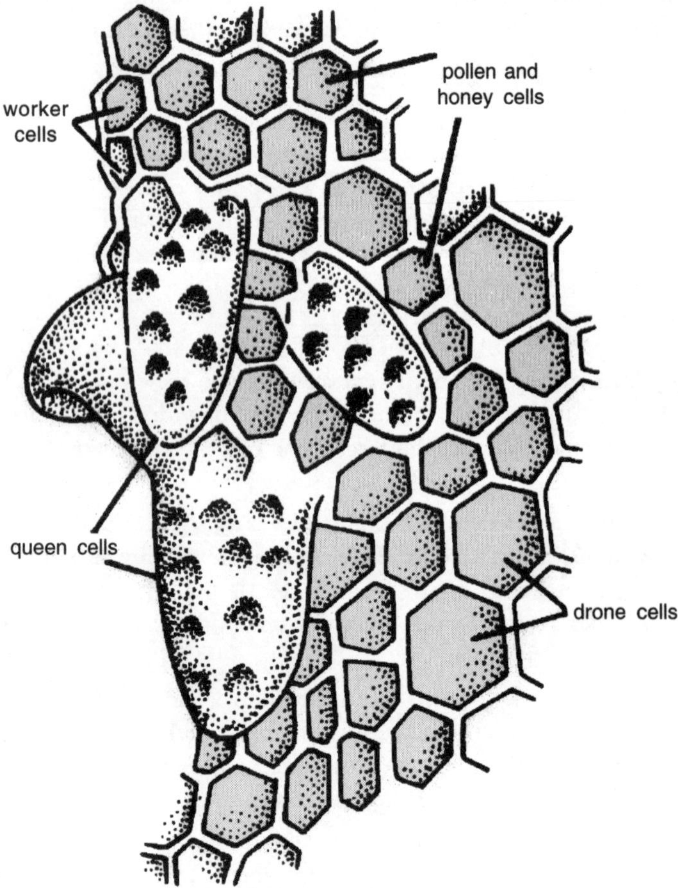

Figure 16.7: Hive of Apis indica showing various cells.

colony at some other place. Now in the old hive a worker is given Royal Jelly and is converted into a new queen of the colony.

This new empress of the colony never tolerates her successor, as a natural law in the hive, so she orders to kill the other sisters, if any, in the hive.

Supersedure

When the egg laying capacity of the old queen is lost or it suddenly dies, a new young and vigorous queen takes the position of the old queen and is called as supersedure.

Absconding

The migration of the complete colony from one place to another takes place due to some unfavourable conditions of life, such as destruction of the comb by termites or wax-moths and scarcity of nectar producing flowers around the hive. This phenomenon is quite different from that of swarming.

Nuptial or Marriage Fight

The first swarm is led by the old queen but the second swarm is led by the 7 days old virgin queen which is followed by the drones and is called marriage flight.

One of the drones starts copulating with the queen in the sky and fertilizes the queen and dies during the course of copulation.

The queen receives spermatophores and stores in the spermatheca. Along with the queen, died drone falls on the ground and the queen reaches -the hive.

Hive

The house of honey bees is termed as hive or comb. It consists of hexagonal cells made up of wax secreted by the worker's abdomen. These hives are hanging vertically from rock, building or branches of trees.

Each hive has thousands of hexagonal thin walled fragile cells arranged in two opposite rows on a common base.

The resins and gums secreted from the plants are used for the repairing of the hives. The young stages are generally occupying the lower and central cells in the hive which are the 'BROOD CELLS'.

In *A. dorsata* broad cells are similar in shape and size but in other species brood cells are of 3 types viz., WORKER CELL for workers, DRONE CELL for drones and QUEEN CELL for the queen. The queen cell can not be used again while the rest are used a number of times.

There are no special cells for lodging the adults which generally keep clustering or moving about on the surface of the comb. The cells are mainly intended for the storage of honey and pollen specially in the upper portion of the comb while those in lower part are for brood rearing.

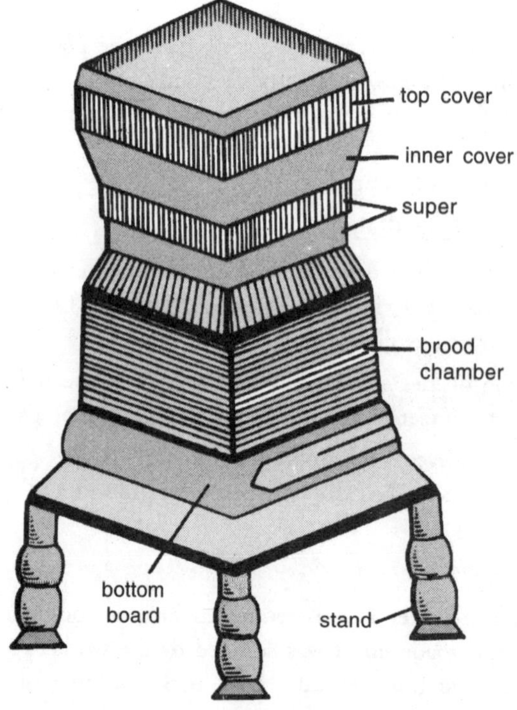

Figure 16.8: Typical movable hive.

APPLIANCES FOR MODERN METHOD

(1) Typical movable hive.
(2) Queen excluder.
(3) Honey extractor.
(4) Uncapping knife.
(5) Other equipments.

Typical Movable Hive

An artificial movable hive is constructed by wooden box based on bee space theory. The size and number of frames are variable from hive to hive according to the need. A small space is enough to permit the entrance and exit of workers and drones but queen once placed in hive never comes outside the hive.

The perforation size on zinc sheet is only of 0.375 cm but the thorax of the queen is 0.43 cm to 0.45 cm, so the queen can never pass through this pore. This typical hive consists of 6 parts as given below

Stand

It is the basal part of the hive on which the whole hive is constructed. The stands are adjusted to make slope for the hive. Due to this slope rain water comes down quickly.

Bottom board

It is situated above the stand and forms the proper base for the hive having two gates in the front position. One gate functions as an enterance while the other as exit.

Brood chamber

The bottom board carries the brood chamber which is the most important part of the bee hive. It is large in size provided with 5 to 10 frames. In each frame a wax sheet bearing haxagonal frames is held up by a couple of wires in a vertical position.

Along with the margin of every hexagonal mark, the bees start making wall and ultimately the cells. Here every sheet of the wax is known as COMB FOUNDATION which attracts the bees and provides the base for the comb preparation on both the sides.

The frames are kept vertically in brood chamber which is covered over by other frames having a wire meshing through which the workers can easily pass. The comb foundation helps in obtaining a regular strong worker brood cell comb which can be used repeatedly.

The Central Bee Research Station at Pune arranged the manufacture of a comb foundation mill which manufactures, different cell sizes required in several regions of the country. The brood chamber is covered by another chamber known as super.

Super

It is also without cover and the base. Super is provided with many frames containing comb foundation to provide additional space for expansion of the hive.

Inner cover

It is a wooden piece used for the covering of the super. It has many holes for proper ventilation.

Top cover

It is meant for protecting the colony from rains. It is fitted with zinc sheet which is plain and sloping.

Queen excluder

It consists of a wire-gauze, extrans guards and drone traps with individual wires placed 0.375 cm apart. It readily permits the workers to pass through it but keeps back the queen in the brood chamber.

Honey extractor

It is used for the extraction of the honey from the comb and functions on principle of centrifugal force. When combs are centrifuged by this device the pure honey is thrown out without any damage to the comb.

Uncapping knife

When all of the combs are filled with honey they are sealed by capping with the wax. So, before such capped combs are placed in the honey extractor, the wax sealing has to be removed with the help of an uncapping knife heated by steam before use.

Other equipments

Most of the useful equipments for the successful management of the bee are locally manufactured which are very cheap. As they are made locally, they may not be exactly similar to those made at other places.

Thus, Indian Standard Institute has standardized some very common equipments for the production of uniform and interchangeable articles. Some materials like protective garments, gum cages, gloves, net veil, bee net, brush etc. are required for easy and well planned handling of the bees.

ADVANCES OF MODERN METHOD

In the modern method of bee keeping there-are several advantages which encourage the well planned bee keeping.

(1) A proper watch on the activities of the bees can be had.

(2) A strong colony can be developed by providing sugar, syrup, pollen substances to honey bees.

(3) Swarming of bees is checked by modern hive.

(4) The same hive is used again and again so the workers pay their attention more for the honey and not for the hive formation.

(5) Under adverse climatic conditions the hive can be transferred from one place to the other for the protection of the bees.

(6) Comb can be protected from the enemies.

(7) Pure honey in large quantity can be obtained.

COLONIAL ORGANISATION AND DIVISION OF LABOUR

The honey bee presents an example of social and organised living. The member are well defined into various castes with their special works. They are divided into (1) Queen, (2) Drone and (3) Worker. Numbers of insects in a colony varies according to species of the bee and ranges from 40—80,000 per colony in extreme i cases whereas in case of Melipona or other it may be only few thousands only.

Queen

Largest of all the bees with small legs and weak wings. Queen bee is the real ruler of the hive. She has an extended abdomen, full of eggs and the last segment is modified as an oviposter: She has no work except eating and laying eggs.

She lives for 3-3½ years and lays about 14-15,00,000 eggs during her life span. The rate of egg laying under favourable conditions may be 2,000 eggs per day.

Generally only one queen is found in a comb but in case when her egg laying capacity is reduced she can be changed and -replaced by another queen. In extreme cases such a old queen comes out of the hive and establishes another hive.

In some of the cases a colony may have more than one queen but only one is allowed to live in the hive rest are pressed to leave the nest.

Queen is supposed to be the mother of all the drones and workers ' and queens (if they are) present in the comb. She lays both fertilized and unfertilized eggs which later on develop as male and workers.

Some of the workers which are in real sense the females are fed with a special substance called "Royal Jelly" and the larvae fed on Royal Jelly develops as a queen rest as workers.

By the time the egg laying capacity of the queen goes slow a new larvae is fed with Royal Jelly and is developed as future queen. A single fertilization is sufficient for the whole life. The queen moves from cell to cell of the comb and lays eggs.

She has no special cell to live in and is always surrounded by the workers. She is generally found in the lower border of the hive. A mated queen collects the sperms in a receptacle and it is on her will to decide which batch of the eggs should be fertilized and which should not the males or drones are generally unfertilized whereas the queen and the workers develop from the fertilized eggs.

There is no difference in the organs or morphology of the worker or queen but for the size of legs and wings. The queen bee is fed with a highly nitrogenous food mixed with pollen honey and a secretion from the lateral pharyngeal glands.

All these are mixed and make as Royal Jelly. An egg develops as a larva in days and grub into pupa in 5-7 days. The pupa emerges out after a week as an adult.

Worker

More than 90% of the total population present in the comb consists of workers. These workers are the atrophid female which are unable to lay eggs and they sacrifice their total life in the service of queen and the hive and its residents.

The longivity of a worker depends upon the type of work and activity, generally they live for about three months in a off season but in busy seasons this is reduced to half.

The newly developed worker has weak wings, so she is employed feed the grubs, help the queen in laying eggs, feeding the queen and cleaning the hive. The work is allotted to them according to their age and they are named after their work as nurse bee, cleaner bee or builder bee.

The *builder* bees are provided with a wax gland in their 4 to 7th abdominal segments on the ventral side and these are engaged in making the nest cells whereas some of the bees produce bee *glue* (propolis) which is used in repairing the cracks and crevices there are known as *repairers.*

The duties of a nurse bee is to produce Royal Jelly for the developing queen and *"bee breed"* for rest of the grubs. She looks after the development of the grub and before they pupate she seals the door of the cell. Cleaning of cell, maintenance of hygenic conditions removal of debris and dead bodies are done by the cleaners.

The workers have other important job to maintain the temperature of the hive. At the time of production of honey a fairly good amount of water is found which in later stage may spoil the honey.

So to avoid the loss the worker bees assamble near the newly filled cell and keep that cell worm. The water vaporises and level is lowered down. On reaching a certain point the bee seals the cell and protects the honey. On the other side the temperature may not damage the egg laying capacity of the female in hot summer she is always kept cool by the workers.

There are certain bees with long wings they always viberate their wings so the temperature is lowered down: In the month of June when the sun is too hot, some of the fanner bees go out and take a dip in water and again come near the queen. This gives an air conditioning to the queen.

In the same way they keep the queen worm during winter by assembling themselves near the queen. Collection of food, pollen and honey is again an important work of the workers. These workers are good flier and can cover a long distance in a shorter duration.

They have their own language and by dancing before other bee they tell the direction and distance of the food from the hive quantity of the food and its quality. Such bees are provided with long and powerful flight muscles and wings. Their legs are provided with pharyngeal legs.

These legs are armed with big structure above the tibia called pollen basket which helps in collecting the pollen grains.

Workers are the soldiers also they have a powerful sting in their last abdominal segment and protect the hive from outside attacks. They have a tendency to chase the enemies.

Drone

The males in the colony are called drone. They develop pathenogenitically and have no stings. They depend on workers for their own food and have the sole responsibility to fertilize the queen. They are of intermediate size and pupae period ranges, from 10-13 days. Total adult life span ranges from 7-8 weeks.

The reproductive organs are well developed and sometimes they die just after copulation. They are developed only at the time of breeding when a new queen is under process otherwise they are kicked out of the colony in days of scarcity. A hive generally keeps 200 drones at a time. Drone cells are little bigger than the workers cell and' smaller than the queen cells.

Honey Comb

Various types of bees make various types of honey combs but their lay out pattern is almost same in all the cases. They have a common partition wall having serially arranged cells on either sides. These cells are hexagonal, their walled anu fragile. The bee may have a separate comb as a brood chamber or may use the same hive as a brood chamber. In most of the cases the hive is divided into certain chambers the brood chamber having eggs larvae and pupae whereas storage is done in another chamber.

The size of the cell for larvae and pupae of the brood would be male and workers differs in size. The cell of a drone is large as compared with that of the worker whereas that of queen is the largest. The storage cells are sma„ and much more in number. These are built near the margin or on the top of the hive.

Life Cycle

The fertilized female lays eggs. Number of eggs laid daily vary according to the environmental condition but it may range from 1500-2000 eggs a day. The eggs are small, cylindrical, pale yellow or white. One egg per cell is laid by the female and eggs adhere with the cell wall. Generally three types of cells are found the Royal., brood cell, Drone brood cell and Ordinary brood cell which give rise to queen, drone and the workers.

The sex of the developing larva is decided by the quality and quantity of the food fed to the larvae. The eggs hatch in three days giving out of the grubs. Grubs are yellowish or white and curved structure and develop in pupal form in 5-7 days their development depends on the food.

Some of them are fed with Royal Jelly where others are fed with bee bread. Bee bread inhibits the growth of reproductive organs. So only workers come out of such larvae they pupate inside the cell and pupae come out as adult in 7-14 days. The queen, drone and workers have different life span:

	Egg	*Larva*	*Pupa*	*Adult*
[illegible]	[illegible]	[illegible]	[illegible]	[illegible]

Swarming

During spring season or in early summer sometimes the comb is over crowded by the natives so the queen along with some of the workers and drones leaves the colony and gets settled somewhere else in a more suitable and secured place. Such a swarming is done mostly in the afternoon hours.

In such a case when there is no queen in the comb one of the workers is developed as queen and she is fed a good amount of Royal Jelly. She develops and queen and other developing queens, if they are, are killed by the workers.

Swarming takes place by the virgin queen also. She swarms ;for nupital flight. It is done by a 7 days old queen followed by 10 'days old drones.

This swarm contains a large number of drones following the queen. Copulation and fertilization takes place in the air.

The sperms are stored in the spermetheca of the queen and some time the male dies during copulation. It rarely happens that copulation is not performed in nupital flight, but in case it happens. The queen again takes another flight after 3 days.

Swarming sometimes is followed by absconding. In such a case the complete colony is transferred from one place to another where there is safety security and plenty of food. It generally happens when enemies start attacking the colony.

Supersedure

It is a phenomenon when the egg laying capacity of the queen is minimised. She is killed immediately and a new queen is developed a fresh.

Honey

Honey is produced by the bee and is of an important medicinal value. It contains a variety of minerals e.g. Ca, Fe, Silica, Mg, Mn, K, Cl, S, Al, and phosphores whereas amino acids, citric, formic, succinic, malic and acetic acids are also present in traces, pigments like Carotine, Xanthonine and Anthocynin and vitamin A, B complex and C are also reported in it. Besides all these enzymes like invertase, distage are also found. The chemical composition of honey constitutes as follows:

Lavulose	38-41%
Dextrose	21-35%
Maltose and other sugars	8-10%
Enzymes and pigments	2- 3%
Ash	1%
Water	17%

Pure honey gets granulated after long storage. The granulation 1 becomes faster due to presence of air bubble pollen, and other colloid I substances. It has density 1.2.

Economic Value

It is of great economic importance and is widely used in medicine and as antiseptic. It has its own food value and gives high calorific value and energy. It is used in candies, cakes, breads and cold drinks.

Alcoholic drinks, livestock feeds and poison baits are also made from honey. It is the only substance which requires minimum energy for its digestion that is why it is given to new born infants.

Bees Wax

It is the most useful bi-product of the honey bee.

It is secreted by the dermal glands of the abdomen from 4th to 7th segment and is completely soluble in ether, chloroform and other organic solvents. Brown or yellowish brown in colour it does not dissolve in water. It melts easily.

It is used in manufacture of cosmetics creams, paints, ointments, plastic works, polish and a variety of lubricants.

Enemies of Bee

Honey being sweet, tasty it has a number of enemies also.

***Wax Moth** (**Galleria mollonella Linn.**)*

Wax Moth (Galleria mollonella Linn.) lesser wax moth (*Achroia grisella*) are the worst enemies of honey bee. Their catterpillars creep inside the comb and feed upon the brood comb. They spoil the complete colony. Quite often the bees undergo absconding swarm and leave the hive.

Sphinged moth (*Achorontia styx*) is a strong and powerful moth which enters the colony and feeds upon the honey, but the bees after sometime kill them.

Besides above mentioned insects black ants, termites, dragan flies are the powerful insects which destroy the bee hive.

Not only the invertebrates but some of the vertebrate pests like lizards, catoles, king crows, birds and bear cause serious damage to the bee hive and there is no escape for the bee.

The bees are subjected to bacterial diseases also like dysentry, fowl brood disease, caused by *Bacillus plutan* and *B. alvei.* Nosema and Bee paralysis. Certain mites like *Acarapis wood!* kill the bees and damage the hive.

INDEX

A

B

C

D

E

J

K

L

M

N

O

P

Q

R

S